THE LIMITS OF SOCIAL CHANGE

THE CASE OF A MEXICAN AMERICAN COMMUNITY

José Amaro Hernández, Ph.D.

Professor Emeritus of Chicana/o Studies, California State University, Northridge

Kendall Hunt
publishing company

DR. H PUBLISHING, INC
José Amaro Hernández, PH. D., President/Ceo

Cover image © Oscar Hernández

www.kendallhunt.com
Send all inquiries to:
4050 Westmark Drive
Dubuque, IA 52004-1840

Copyright © 2015 by Kendall Hunt Publishing Company

ISBN 9781465266675

Printed in the United States of America

The book is dedicated to my wife, Carol O'Brien Hernández, and to my grandchildren, Jonathan Casillas, Isabella Casillas, and Audrey Patrice Petlin.

CONTENTS

South Brand Boulevard, City of San Fernando. Courtesy of Richard Arroyo Collection.

PREFACE

This is a case study of the Mexican American community of San Fernando, a small city that has been the heart of Southern California's progressive forces changing the city's political landscape into a political base of Mexican Americans.[1] It is also the story of determined progressive men and women profoundly dedicated to positive change, and a mayor and city council bent on social and cultural issues who played a key role in transforming local politics. They were proud of the progress made during the progressive period of social engagement that began in the middle of the 1960s and ended with the successful special recall election of 2009.[2] Some aspects of social and economic life will be observed, however nonpolitical, to learn more about politics and about Mexican American perennial efforts to gain recognition as first-class citizens in San Fernando. In addition, this study will show that given the opportunity, Mexican Americans will excel in all levels of American life with admirable results. This is not a biography, but the study of a unique American community that used political power as a means to improve conditions and assume a rightful place in society. Step by step it protected its interest.

Social change is the central theme of this study. Social change is rarely precisely defined. In this case, social change is interpreted here as the desire to reorganize a group political structure and behavior that lead to equal opportunities and benefits as Mexican Americans and Latinos increased representation in local government. The change is not chimerical, certainly not minimal. It's real transformational change.

A noted social scientist rightly observed: "The facts of the need for change are not enough; they must be accepted properly by the groups if they are to become an effective basis for change."[3]

A Note on Methodology

Part narrative, part polemic, this work is based on reports, summaries of minutes of city council meetings, personal notes of official meetings, staff reports. New stories of city council meetings are factual accounts of events as they actually occurred. They are public record and are taped recorded. Also, its work is based on city ordinances and resolutions, U.S. Census data, oral histories, in-depth interviews, programs and exhibits sponsored by the local museum of arts and history, social scientist scholarly studies, community meetings, workshops, conferences, and newspaper accounts of local issues. Family-owned periodicals are very popular in small cities because they cover specific issues and events of importance to local residents. People have easy access to the editors. Publishers of these newspapers often take political positions that may influence their readers. Also of particular importance to this study is the author's observation as a longstanding resident of the city, educator, and participant observer throughout a segment of the period under discussion as community activist, city planning commissioner, and as city councilman and mayor of San Fernando. The narrative is written in the third person from the author's particular method of analysis. Chicano and Latino community influence were witnessed as they unfolded in San Fernando and Los Angeles over 44 years of consistent community civic activities.[4] This is a development analysis of Mexican American cooperation in the founding and growth of the city, with special emphasis on their struggle to regain their rightful place in the city dominated by Anglo Americans. The significance of this study is not theoretical; rather it is a documentary of a case showing organizations and their leaders utilizing social and political principles in their efforts to understand and resolve community problems. The following is helpful to an understanding of the characteristic uses of the single case study as described by Glenn Paige: "A single case is taken to be a body of factual statements at a low level of abstraction pertaining to a single unit of analysis or number of interacting units and limiting conditions which the researcher considers relevant for the explanation of a particular outcome.... A single case is a 'construct' whose empirical boundaries vary with the analytical choice – explicit or implicit – of the observer." [5]

Location and City and Political Structure

The locale of this case study is San Fernando, California, located 23 miles north of downtown Los Angeles at the northern tip of the San Fernando Valley (colloquially known as "The Valley") that bears its name. It is 2.4 square miles in size with a population of 25,000 of which 90 percent are Latino, 8 percent white, and 2 percent Asian, black and other groups. Although San Fernando is a small city, it is freeway close to just about everywhere in Southern California. The city is surrounded by Interstate 5 (Golden State Freeway), Interstate 210 (Foothill Freeway) with a moving panoramic view of the San Gabriel Mountains, and State freeway 118 (Ronald Reagan Freeway). It remains today one of the few U.S. tidy cities to be completely surrounded by another city. In the 2010 census, 43 percent of the city's residents were foreign-born and the percentage keeps growing.[6]

The compact city is completely surrounded by the city of Los Angeles and Valley communities of Sylmar, Mission Hills, and Pacoima. Its municipal affairs are con-

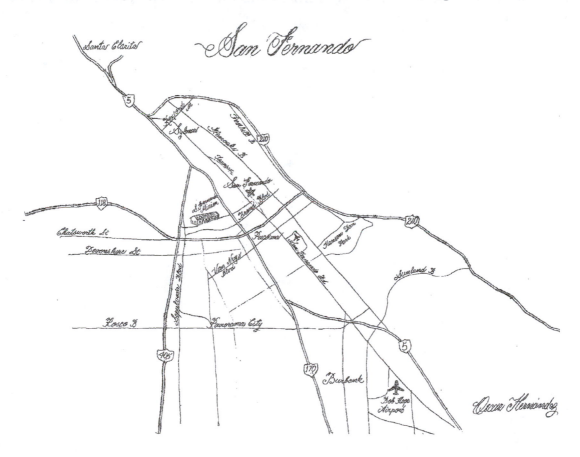

---

strained by the state general- law cities code unlike charter cities such as Los Angeles and Long Beach which have greater power over their civic affairs. California charter cities have a constitution (charter) which guides them. A general-law city such as San Fernando is regulated by laws handed down from the state. For example, general-law cities are generally governed by a city council of five members and a city treasurer elected every four years, and an appointed city clerk. Its five city council members are elected to four-year terms in staggered nonpartisan elections on the first Tuesday in March of every odd-numbered year. Unlike Los Angeles, San Fernando part-time city council chooses the mayor and mayor pro tem for a one-year term. The general-law cities code authorizes the city council to appoint a city administrator and other department heads who are appointed at will. Zoning and taxation policies are highly restricted by the code. The state limits the pay of council members in general-law cities. The restrictions are based on population and range from $300 to $1,000 a month. In charter cities, state law does not limit the salaries councils can set for them.[7]Critics feel that general-law cities' political activities are ministerial and seldom excite the public. But this is not the case in San Fernando as the reader will note in the following chapters.

ACKNOWLEDGEMENTS

First and foremost, I would like to pay tribute to all the students and faculty of San Fernando Valley State College (now California State University, Northridge) for their bold stand on issues vital to them and their community. In the late 1960s, lack of quality education, the demand on campus for a Chicano Studies Department, and an identity crisis were contentious issues for them and for the college's administration. They fought for these issues on campus and on to the communities from which they came. I am grateful to Dr. Rodolfo Acuña, founder of Chicano Studies at San Fernando Valley State College, who was responsible for inducting me to the Chicano Studies academic discipline in 1969. As a teacher of Barrio Studies (Community Studies) and with a deep professional interest in citizen participation, I took this unusual opportunity to observe and participate firsthand in community activities in Los Angeles and in San Fernando where I lived and served as city planning commissioner, councilman and mayor of San Fernando for 18 years.

This book is intended for college students in Chicano Studies and related areas, political science, urban studies, and history classes. My concern in writing as in teaching has been to help students understand the political world in which they live and to give them some general knowledge about local public policy and real Latino politics in social affairs. In order to achieve this goal, I became actively involved in "street activism" and engaged in public service to have an impact on people's lives. Thus, this narrative is the product of 44 years of consistent community activity and government service. Throughout these years there were many participants and friends who contributed to the stories in this book. I want to acknowledge a debt to them.

I am particularly grateful to my compatriots of Chicano Roundtable – José de Paz, Héctor de Paz, Xavier Flores, Ruben Rodriguez, and Everto Ruiz – former students and a colleague, who founded Pueblo y Salud, Inc. a major voice of the people. They ran my first campaign for city council of San Fernando in 1990 with Héctor de Paz as campaign manager. He ran the campaign from my garage with a large army of families and their children walking the precincts.

Thanks to all those who contributed information in the first part of the narrative about Mexican Americans' early role in San Fernando. The information was important in that it served as a backdrop to the study. Also, there were many more who gave generously of their time to support and share triumphs and political hazards with me, so many that it was impossible to adequately express my gratitude, particularly to members of the Save Our City Committee of San Fernando and students and faculty of Mission College, who stood behind me during my darkest experience in politics; to friends of the César Chávez Commemorative Committee, who helped me convince the council to construct a memorial for the great humanitarian.

I also want to give particular thanks to Xavier Flores, political masterstroke, who I have worked with in many community efforts, and who has advised me in various ways during my political career: Ruben Rodriguez, executive director of Pueblo y Salud, Inc., and Professor Everto Ruiz for their support and intelligent judgments. There is not enough space to express my personal gratitude to many more genuine leaders who were part of these stories.

I was assisted by a host of colleagues and friends in the preparation of the manuscript. I wish to express my greatest gratitude to Dr. Francine García Hallcom, Professor Emeritus of Chicana /o Studies, California State University, Northridge, whom I am personally indebted for her generous editing of the manuscript and for sensitive reworking of some of my statements. She was a cheerful editor who made my work less difficult. I am also obliged to San Fernando City Clerk Elena Chávez and Executive Secretary to the San Fernando City Administrator Julie Fernandez for assisting me in locating particular minutes of city council and redevelopment agency meetings, and to Senior City Planner Fred Ramirez for assisting me with questions on city redevelopment projects; to Virginia Megerdichian, David Casillas, and Martha R. Amaya who provided computer support, and especially Timothy Petlin for his technical assistance. I must thank Oscar Hernández for his artistic contributions to the book cover and the city location map. I also greatly appreciate the art works of Ignácio

Gómez and Anthony Juárea as well as photographers David P. Jiménez and Richard Arroyo for helping to improve the form and quality of the book. I must also thank Kendall Hunt publishing Project Coordinator Elizabeth Cray and Author Account Manager Christine A. Bochniak and their Associates for making the publication of the book possible. Thank you. They were indispensable in helping me get through this task. I want to acknowledge and thank Julie Sylva for reading several chapters and submitting helpful comments. She was San Fernando former city attorney.

Finally, I want to express my profound thanks to my wife, Carol O'Brien, and my two daughters, Moira and Annie and their families, for sticking with me during my dark instances in politics. They had warned me to quit politics while I was ahead.

Notes

1. 1. There is no single name for U.S. citizens of Mexican heritage. In past years, the term "Mexican" was widely used. In the early 1970s, the term "Mexican American" was coined by Los Angeles journalist Ruben Salazar in a series of articles written for the *Los Angeles Times*. The term "Chicano" took on a political tone in California and Texas during the student uprisings of the late 1960s and early 1970s. The term "Latino" is conveniently used by the media to lump Mexican Americans with other Latin Americans living in the United States. Currently, the term "Chicano" is losing ground to the term "Latino." The term "Hispanic" is rejected by Chicano activists who prefer to call themselves Latinos, a term less associated as European. In this study, the terms Mexican, Mexican American, Chicano, and Latino will be used interchangeably. There is also disagreement over the preferred terms "white" and "Anglo American." These terms as used herein refer to non-Hispanic whites. The reader may wish to read further about the issue of Chicano identity in Rodolfo F. Acuña, *Anything but Mexican: Chicanos in Contemporary Los Angeles,* New York: Verso Press, 1996. See also a brief description of this issue in Gregory Rodriguez, "Where Have All the Mexicans Gone?" in *Sunday Los Angeles Times*, November 12, 2006, M4.

2. For this study, a progressive is described as "one believing in moderate political change and especially social improvement by government action." This is borrowed from *Webster's New Collegiate Dictionary*, Springfield: G. & C. Merriam, 1981, 913. It is a description that fits the use of the term throughout the study of San Fernando. The "old guard" was the white political and economic elite who for years had a monopoly of power over San Fernando city government and economy and who had refused to share the government with Mexican Americans or Latinos. Mexican Americans had always been an integral part to the development of San Fernando since its founding.

3. This was briefly the conclusion of his study. See Dorwin Cartwright, "Achieving Change in People," *Human Relations*, 4 (1951), 381-392. The literature on social change is extensive. Because of the nature and scope of this work, the description provided by W. K.

Barger and Ernesto M. Reza is used herein. *The Farm Labor Movement in the Midwest: Social Change and Adaptation Among Migrant Farm Workers,* Austin: University of Texas Press, 1994, 6. A list of scholarly works on social change is covered on the subsequent pages.

4. The reader may wish to read further about this method of research in Nicholas Babchuk, "The Role of the Researcher as Participant Observer and Participants-Observer in the Field Situation," *Human Organization,* XXI (1962), 225. See also Arthur J. Vidich, "Participant Observation and the Collection and Interpretation of Data," *American Journal of Sociology,* LX (1955), 354-360.

5. Glenn Paige, "Problems and Uses of the Single Case in Political Research," 6-7, found in Steven L. Ashby, *Political Science the Discipline and Its Dimensions: An Introduction,* New York: Charles Scribner's Son, 1970, 157.

6. *U.S. Bureau of the Census, Census of the Population: 2010 Subject Reports, Native Origin and Languages.*

7. See *California General Law Cities Code, Chart: General Law Cities v. Charter Cities Code Sections 36501 and 53725.*

INTRODUCTION

San Fernando has a rich history and culture. The community was founded in 1874 and incorporated as a separate city in 1911. Its motto "Mission City" reflects the city's historical relationship to the San Fernando Mission. Named after the Spanish Saint and King Ferdinand, it grew out of the ranching activities surrounding the mission. In 1794, Franciscan missionaries led by Father Lausen established Mission San Fernando. The Tatavian Indians, the original residents of the San Fernando Valley region, built the mission where thousands of local Native Americans were converted to Catholicism.[1] They worked on the mission grounds as they remained captives in their own land by Spanish missionaries rule. (Historians have different views on this observation.)

Mexican influence in San Fernando is embedded in the fabric of its history. In the 1800s, Catalina López, daughter of the former San Fernando Mission administrator, and her husband Geronimo López, purchased 40 acres of land north of the mission and established a general store known as López Station. The couple is also credited for founding the first public school in the Valley and for establishing the first post office. Geronimo served on the first school board in 1875. In 1881, Catalina's brother Valentin López built a two-story adobe home. It became known as the López Adobe and is the oldest structure in San Fernando. Pedro López, son of Valentin and a nephew of Geronimo, served as the first constable for several years.[2] This information is of vital importance to the Chicano/Latino community, for it demonstrates, particularly to its youth, that their ancestors were pioneers of the early settlements in California and other states. (The first full-fledged university in what is now the United States, was established in San Augustine, Florida, in the mid-1500s.) Their Latino contributions to the development of the country need to be told.

Many people in the United States think that Mexican Americans are foreigners. To most Americans, knowledge of Mexican Americans steeped in U.S. history is an enigma, rarely taught in history or civic lessons. They have not been taught that Mexicans were already in California 100 years before 1848 when the United States "acquired" California after a war with Mexico planned by President James Polk when the Mexican government refused to sell California and New Mexico territories for $20 million. In the Treaty of Guadalupe that ended that war in 1848, Mexico surrendered California, Texas, Utah, Nevada, and parts of Colorado, Wyoming, New Mexico, and Arizona. Following the conquest, the status of Mexicans who decided to remain in the region changed. Although they technically became U.S. citizens, they were relegated to a subservient social, political, and economic position. They were excluded from the protection of the American political process. Their distinct physical appearance, culture, and language also made more difficult their acceptance with the Anglo American group, a problem that Mexican Americans had to tackle for years.[3]Notwithstanding, they saw strength in their culture and in their community which values love of family, hard work, respect, and integrity. Rodolfo F. Acuña in his perceptive discussions of the importance of community mutual cooperation correctly says in his book, *Anything but Mexican: Chicanos in Contemporary Los Angeles*: "Without a sense of community and a sense of history as a community, people become vulnerable to the plans and whims of the dominant group which can not only displace them but control them in other ways as well."[4]

Hence, these historical developments are mentioned because they provide a crucial frame of reference for the reader. Against this backdrop, the reader will have a clearer view of the rise and growth of Chicano actions as they tried to resolve their basic dilemma of citizen participation.

Other Major City Developments and the Role of Mexican Americans

There are two major events that contributed to the growth of San Fernando. They are (1) a railroad track that went through the city, and (2) the completion in 1913 of the Los Angeles Aqueduct which diverted water from the Owens River in the Sierra Nevada to Southern California. Adding water to the fertile soil of the Valley earned the region a reputation as a major agricultural and related business center.

This caused a rapid widespread expansion of economic activity and jobs in local towns and communities. In 1874, the Southern Pacific Railroad Company built a line through the city with labor composed mainly of Mexican and Chinese hands. San Fernando became an important central stop where the company serviced its cars and engines. There was a huge turnaround track and shops on Brand Boulevard and San Fernando Road. The turnaround was used as a terminal for the rail trolley cars that ran up Brand. The railroad structure at Maclay Street, next to the railroad tracks, was a passenger depot and had a freight loading dock alongside it. This was a busy place at that time. Fruit and vegetable packing houses dotted the area along the rail line employing local residents including many Mexican laborers. That year (1874) Charles Maclay, a landowner and former state senator, submitted a township map to the Los Angeles County recording clerk and soon the San Fernando community was incorporated as an independent city in 1911.[5]The new source of water flowing from the Owens River gave the city of Los Angeles an enormous power over the various communities in the San Fernando Valley, forcing them to join the Los Angeles Municipality. However, San Fernando prided itself with its own water wells, thereby keeping its independence from the metropolitan giant that surrounded it.

Before World War II, most of the city's Mexican residents lived in the south side of the railroad tracks by design. The community was segregated by housing policy and realtors' directions. Mexican workers and their families lived on 25 by 100 foot residential lots. Government discouraged this segment of the population from moving across the tracks to the north side of town where the newer and more spacious houses were located in Anglo American neighborhoods. Mexican children were even prohibited from using South Brand Boulevard sidewalks, the premier entrance to the city on the southern part of town. While Mexicans were kept in their place, many worked on the "other side" of the tracks as domestics and fruit pickers for growers who lived in the foothills overlooking the city lights.[6] The working families also encountered racism in the church they loved. A longstanding resident once recalled: "I tried to enroll my children at St. Ferdinand Catholic Grammar School but the priest referred me to Santa Rosa Catholic Church located in the barrio where he explained we should belong."[7] At that time, St. Ferdinand Church, the city's oldest religious place of worship, served the area's Italian faithful who did not wish to share the joy of Holy Communion with their Christian brethren. Similarly, Mexican and Mexican American children were put in separate "Mexican" schools on the south side of town. San Fernando and O'Melveny elementary schools were only two blocks apart, but children with Spanish surnames attended San Fernando while white youngsters went to O'Melveny. During the 1950s, people with Spanish surnames or those who spoke with a Spanish accent weren't allowed to swim in the San Fernando Park pool on days when it was used by whites. Jenaro Ayala, high school teacher who grew up in the area, thought "that this was the way it was."[8] As he puts it: "I didn't realize until I started getting more involved in the Chicano community – that this was a practice of segregation." Job discrimination at the local mall was also a problem. "At Kress's and Woolworth, the five-and-ten stores in the San Fernando Mall, only whites worked there, but at the time we didn't know they were discriminating," said Guadalupe R. Ramirez of Pacoima.[9] The past is never dead for those who have experienced exclusiveness in their lives.

Advocacy of a Social Philosophy

Much more will be said in the following chapters about the different standards that were applied to San Fernando Mexican Americans affecting their quality of life, and how the Chicano community responded. This involved, for example, efforts in organizing into self-support groups such as San Fernando Community Improvement Council (CIC), San Fernando Democratic Club, La Raza Unida Party, the Mexican American Political Association (MAPA), Latin American Civic Association (LACA), Movimiento Estudiantil Chicano De Aztlan (MECHA), Pueblo & Salud, Inc., and other social service organizations. Association participation is of great importance to Mexican Americans. Their traditional norm emphasizes cooperation and self-sufficiency. Voluntary associations where there are nonpartisan elections have been used as substitutes to the major political parties. They have the strength to resist the power elites.[10]

Researchers of community studies have found out that nonpartisan local elections weakened major political parties, leaving the average citizen victim to political control by local merchants. Organized business used their wealth and time most effectively to control elections since there was no other basis of organization from which to elect candidates to public office. Nevertheless, only voluntary organizations associated with labor groups were strong enough to challenge the influence of business interest groups.[11]

Chicano leaders and their organizations labored harmoniously and diligently to change the status quo, using the Saul Alinsky approach to community organizing. They drew upon their lives and the lives of their parents. Their road to political self-determination and empowerment had been a long and disappointing one. They adapted the view that society's negative assumption about Mexicans and other people of color as well as an unfair structure were the main impediments to their success. Meanwhile those on top tended to blame Mexicans' lack of personal initiative for their bad outcome. After a series of community study workshops assembled in San

Fernando, community activists learned the stark fact that the only means by which change could ever come about was through politics. They were a new brand of community activists, college professors, teachers, and students who were well versed in history, economics, and philosophy. To them, politics dealt with the exercise of power. Power builds self-respect and confidence. Those who exercise power determine the quality of life of a community; hence self-rule became their sine quo non, an indispensable cause. These ideas were not new.[12] They are deeply rooted throughout Western history and have become part of American ideals and principles. Power has been accepted as the key component of the U.S. political process at any level of government, especially in the local level. Finally, these community leaders had a blueprint that laid out the bedrock of an egalitarian ethos: the removal of the source of inequality in a city they loved. They, then, focused on securing access to city hall, a tiresome and long battle ahead of them. According to the advocacy group, city hall was ground zero for changing things. People live and work in local communities, and that's where change first happens.[13]As the old adage says, "All politics is local."

Notes

1. This is based mainly from "Saluting the 100th Year City of San Fernando," a special edition of the *San Fernando Valley SUN*, March 5, 1975. The edition commemorates the 100 years of the birth of the community in September 16, 1874, the first in the San Fernando Valley.
2. Ibid.
3. For the leading scholarly treatment of this subject from the perspective of a Chicano historian, see Rodolfo F. Acuña, *Occupied America: The Struggle Towards Liberation,* San Francisco: Canfield Press, 1972. Again, see Adolfo F. Acuña, *Sonoran Strongman,* Tucson: University of Arizona Press, 1974. A most important historical analysis of this period is found in Richard W. Alstyne, *The Rising American Empire,* New York: Oxford University Press, 1960; and Glen W. Price, *Origin of the War with Mexico,* Austin: University of Texas Press, 1967. In this study, Price writes that the U.S. House of Representatives went on record by voting that the war had been "unnecessary and unconstitutional" when President Polk sent the U.S. Army across the border into Mexico inviting a confrontation with Mexican soldiers.
4. See Rodolfo F. Acuña, *Anything but Mexican*, op. cit., 20. See also, "Principles and Ideals of Chicano Mutualism," in José Amaro Hernández, *Mutual Aid for Survival: The Case of the Mexican American,* Malabar: Robert E. Krieger Publishing Company, 1983, 84-98.
5. This interesting information was called to the attention of the present writer by Manuel D. Flores, former director chairman of Cabrillo State Bank and former councilman and mayor of San Fernando, elected in 1966. He lives with his wife Sally in Palmdale, California.
6. This position was made in an interview with longstanding townspeople who congregate regularly at Chacon Barber Shop, a popular meeting place in the middle of the barrio (the oldest Mexican neighborhood in the city).

7. Mary Louise Zamora made this statement to the present writer who was her next-door neighbor. She and her husband Frank Zamora raised three children who attended local Catholic schools and graduated from top Catholic colleges. Earlier in the 1980s, Mary Louise and the present writer were appointed to a parish committee that introduced Spanish-language Masses and other services to the growing Latino population in the Church. Currently, St. Ferdinand Catholic Church and St. Ferdinand Grammar School are predominantly Latino members.

8. Jenaro Ayala expressed this point perfectly in Ivette Cabrera, "Latinos Forced to Walk a Long, Difficult Road to Gain Equality," *Daily News*, September 15, 1977.

9. Ibid.

10. The Sociedad Progresista Mexicana (Mexican Progressive Society) was founded in 1911 with lodges throughout California. The purpose of this group was to provide support for Mexicans in need and to promote the Mexican culture in the membership. Lodge No. 56 of San Fernando was the organization's oldest in the Valley. For a description of Mexican and Mexican American associational life in the United States, see José Amaro Hernández, *Mutual Aid for Survival*, op. cit. See also Alvin Zander, *Effective Social Action by Community Groups*, San Francisco: Jossey-Bass Publications, 1990.

11. This is the conclusion arrived at by Oliver P. Williams and Charles R. Adrian in "The Isolation of Local Politics under the Nonpartisan Ballot," *American Political Science Review*, 53 (December 1959), 1052-2062.

12. To Professor José Amaro Hernández a.k.a. José Hernández, one of the reform leaders in San Fernando and author of this study, power was fascinating. It became the underlying theme of the book, *Mutual Aid for Survival*, op. cit. Engrossed with the works of the great Western thinkers such as Plato, Aristotle, St. Augustine and St. Thomas Aquinas, Machiavelli, and Hobbes, the author became especially enlightened with the ideas of Thomas Hobbes who advanced the notion that it was impossible to achieve any larger social good without a consideration of political power. Power was an essential agent of social change "to improve conditions within which people may assume a respected place in life, for the value of any man's life stand on parity with the life of any other man." For a comprehensive examination of these complex philosophers, see Andrew Hacker, *Political Theory: Philosophy Ideology, and Science*, New York: The Macmillan Company, 1961. For community power structure studies, see Floyd Hunter, *Community Power Structure*, Chapel Hill: University of North Carolina Press, 1953; Philip Green and Sanford Levinson, Eds., *Power and Community Dissenting Essays in Political Science*, New York: Vintage Books, 1970; and William H. Form and Joaan Rytina, "Ideological Beliefs in the Distribution of Power in the United States," *American Sociological Review*, XXXIV (February 1969), 19-31.

13. This idea runs parallel to the position advanced centuries ago by Aristotle in *Politics*, that the city is the single greatest hope for families and the larger society to achieve their full potential. See an analysis of *Politics* in Hacker, op. cit., 69-114.

CHAPTER 1

The Evolution of Mexican American Citizen Participation and the Slow Deterioration of the Anglo American System of Domination

In the preceding summary it was mentioned that Mexican families were founding members of San Fernando. They helped to build the railroad and develop the area's agricultural business. They worked in the fields picking olives, oranges, and many other fruits and vegetables. They worked in poultry farms, and in packinghouses. In short, they did the hard work Anglo Americans did not wish to do. Mexicans, Chinese, and Indians did most of the hazardous labor, using picks and shovels as they constructed the rail lines across the Valley. Nonetheless, they remained second-class citizens in their land. Mexicans were not allowed to live in white neighborhoods. Racism had been a San Fernando Valley tradition for years. However, more than any other Valley town, San Fernando accepted Mexican families although they were confined to a section of town called "el barrio."[1] The barrio became a port of entry for new arrivals. According to U.S. Census figures, 21,000 people lived in the Valley in 1920.[2] San Fernando at that time was the biggest town with 3,204 residents while Burbank was the second really populous town with 2,913.[3]

The main objective in this chapter and the following will be to examine particulars of history and biographies that gradually eroded the system of Anglo American domination in San Fernando. They were (1) the continual influx of Mexican immigrants, (2) the 1910 Mexican Revolution, (3) World War II and subsequent wars and the G.I. Bill of Rights, (4) the changing San Fernando Valley economic structure, (5) the mobilization of the San Fernando south side business community, (6) the farm workers grape strike and boycott and the Chicano grassroots community activism of the late 1960s and early 1970s, (7) the war on poverty, (8) the emergence of the Mexican American Civic Association (MAPA) and LA Raza Unida Party in San Fernando, and (9) the rise of Jess Margarito, a pugnacious politician and favorite son of the Chicano community who placed the old guard on the defensive mode in the 1980s setting the stage for a larger government role in the lives of people.

The Steady Flow of Immigrants

One of the most important of these historical events is the steady flow of legal and undocumented workers to California and other places in the Southwest. San Fernando was a prime destination of many working-poor families who came to work and start a new life in California. It's common knowledge that immigration, internal or external, responds to economic needs – the "push" and the "pull" forces that are manifested during economic cycles.[4] From the very beginning of the economic development of California and other parts of the country, American farmers and manufacturers have depended on cheap Mexican labor. Mexican miners in Arizona developed the rich mining industry in that state.[5] Mexico's economic instability and political crises have had a tendency to force its citizens to leave their country.

The Mexican Revolution of 1910–1920

A new wave of immigrants began in 1910. At that time, the Mexican Revolution of the same year created a state of upheaval and instability in the lives of Mexican families and businesses who found themselves in the midst of a fierce factional battle for control of the republic.[6] The dissenting armies were confiscating private property, destroying farms and communities, and sexually assaulting the women. As the violence got out of hand, thousands of Mexican families fled to safety on the American side.[7] Among those were working-poor families and near-middle-class merchants and professionals. Reyes Pérez was brought by his parents to San Fernando from the state of Guanajuato, Mexico, circa 1914 at the age of two.[8] They traveled in "vagones" (Mexican railway boxcars) packed with families and their children, escaping the war-torn countryside. They were robbed en route to Ciudad Juarez-El Paso, Texas (the main port of entry to the United States) by General Pancho Villa's ragged soldiers. The families feared Pancho Villa for his relentless attitude towards controlling his soldiers who were destroying private property, ransacking homes, and abusing women.[9] Reyes Pérez grew up in San Fernando as a young man, attended local schools and worked at various agricultural jobs in the Valley. In 1943, he returned to Valle de Santiago, Guanajuato, Mexico, where he met Evangelina Tinoco. They married in 1943. In 1953, they moved to San Fernando with a child. Reyes Pérez found employment at the Van Nuys General Motors plant two days after their arrival in San Fernando.[10]

San Fernando became the final destination of these immigrants in San Fernando Valley. The city was an established older community with a rich Mexican cultural ambient and a Mexican style of living. They had relatives and friends here who welcome them. They were particularly drawn to San Fernando and the Valley because of the ample jobs awaiting them. Agriculture had become the culture of the Valley in the 1920s. Their labor was much in demand in the growing economy.[11] The new residents scraped together what little money they had with them, and as their earnings in the fields and packinghouses allowed, they put down-payments on a two-bedroom house, saved more to buy a "terreno" (a piece of land), and/or purchase two or three additional houses as investments.[12] By the early 1900s, San Fernando Valley including San Fernando were made up of wheat fields, citrus and olive groves, and ranch land. The city population as elsewhere in the Valley began to grow when agriculture drew thousands of local people, Mexicans from other states and Mexico to work in the fields and packinghouses.[13] The city population in 1920 was 3,204. In 1930 it went up to 7,567, a 132.2 percent increase. In 1940 the population was at 9,094, a 20.2 percent increase. In 1950 the city had 12,922 residents, a 42.1 percent increase.[14]

Cornelio Carrillo came to California in the early 1900s with his mother and brothers. Because of the Mexican Revolution, the Carrillo's left Jalisco, Mexico, looking for a safe place to live and work. Cornelio worked on the construction of the roads in the Sunland/Tujunga area before settling in San Fernando in early 1924. He found work picking fruit in the local orchards. His wife Micaela Reyes Carrillo worked at the Sunkist packinghouse. Cornelio was a member of Laborers Local 300 Union for 56 years. He also worked as a gardener at Sombrero Ranch for J. B. Stetson, maker of the famous Stetson hat in Sylmar, California. Leandro Durán who lived on 1214 Mott Street was the majordomo of Sombrero Ranch. Cornelio was born on February 2, 1896 in Jalisco, Mexico. He resided on Hewitt Street for 75 years of his almost 102 years of life. Cornelio and Micaela Carrillo were the proud parents of twin brothers Julian and Albert and daughter María Carrillo Alba. The twins joined the U.S. Navy at the age of 17 while still attending San Fernando High School. The twins will be the subject of the following sections.[15]

Miguel Arevalo, Sr. and his wife Refugio Silva came looking for work in the San Fernando Valley orchards from Michoacan, Mexico, in 1918. They found a place to live in "Pico Court," an immigrant settlement in Mission Hills and an extension of the San Fernando barrio. The immigrant neighborhood was located behind the grounds of Andres Pico Recreation Park on Sepulveda and Brand Boulevards. (Later, Pico Court served as living quarters for "Braceros," Mexican agricultural laborers contracted by the federal government to work in the fields during World War II when the military draft depleted the U.S. labor force.) In 1925, Miguel and Refugio moved to San Fernando at 1310 O'Melveny Street where they raised 13 children.[16] Their sons Ascension, Mike, and Luis served in Europe during World War II. These servicemen and others will be the topic of Chapter II.

Mateo González who came from Mexico in the early 1900s and a friend of Miguel Arevalo, Sr. lived on Hewitt Street between Mission and Kalisher. Mateo and his daughter Mary Jane worked at the Tomato Canary of San Fernando. Mary Jane was a shift manager at the cannary located on Maclay and Pico where the present St. Ferdinand Church Hall is now situated. Mary Jane was an active volunteer in her community. She was an avid worker helping the nuns to raise funds for the construction of Holy Cross Hospital in the 1950s. She was also a nurse's aide at Olive View Hospital in Sylmar, California, during the tuberculosis epidemic outbreak that hit San Fernando and the northeastern San Fernando Valley in the 1930s.

Many San Fernando families bonded together by intermarriages. Mixed marriages were between whites and Mexicans. Mixed marriage between blacks and whites was uncommon. John Brooks worked as a freight car loader for Sunkist Packing Company during summer months while attending Glendale City College. Sunkist, a main employer of local men and women, was located on Brand and Sepulveda Boulevards by the San Fernando Mission. John Brooks was of mixed heritage. His mother Isabelle Villegas Brooks was the granddaughter of Geronimo and Catalina López, a pioneer family of the city of San Fernando. John grew up on 1716 Hewitt and 705 South Brand Blvd. He served in the National Guard as a radar operator during the Korean War. After his release from military duty, he worked with the San Fernando Lumber Company. He put in 50 years as a volunteer San Fernando Police Reserve officer.[17]

Teresa Cruz worked on the assembly line at an early age packing fruit for Sunkist until the 1940s when she became ill. She later went into business by herself and introduced the first tortilla press in the region. The tortilla press enabled her to produce tortillas in large enough numbers for wholesale distribution to local markets. The tortilla press, built by an East Los Angeles manufacturer, preceded the tortilla factory as it is known now. Teresa Cruz's little tortilla store was located on Mission and Woodworth Street. Teresa's grandparents, José Ynes Real and María Ygnácia Durán, came to California in the mid-1860s from Sonora, Mexico. They found employment working the orchards at Rancho Camulos in Piru, California. Teresa and another cousin, Victoria Real, were raised by their aunt Luz Real while living in Piru. Luz and her husband, Gabriel Ruiz, moved to San Fernando in the 1920s. Victoria Real, who married Edward Lyon on January 05, 1923, at the original St. Ferdinand Catholic Church in San Fernando, also was a packer.[18] Edward Lyon's brother, Arthur, was employed in a San Fernando orchard after serving in the Army during World War I. Arthur and his brother Edward were the sons of Henry and Emelia Estrada Vega Lyon. Emelia Vega was descended from an early "Californio" family from Mexico. (Californio is a term used to identify a Californian of Hispanic ancestry during the period when California was part of Spain or Mexico.) Henry Lyon's father, Cyrus, came to California in 1849 from Machias, Maine. Cyrus and twin brother, Sanford Lyon, owned a stage-coach station and rest stop on the northern end of San Fernando Pass. Lyon's Station was the first American settlement around the location of present-day Eternal Valley Cemetery. Henry Lyon's mother, Nicolasa Triunfo, was part Indian and was also descended from one of the 11 original families from Mexico that settled the Pueblo of Los Angeles in 1781. A main street was named in Santa Clarita after the early California prominent entrepreneur family.[19] Arthur Lyon stayed on nights in the orchards keeping the fruit warm in cold weather. He was a "smudger." When Vickie Carrillo Norton, granddaughter of Ed and Victoria Real Lyon, was asked what a "smudger" was, she explained that a "smudger" was a farm hand who maintained the smudger's pot in which oil was burned to protect the orchard from frost. The following sections of this study will have more on the Lyon family.[20]

Immigrant Farm Labor

The fortune of many San Fernando Mexican workers also started to decline in the late 1940s and early 1950s. They were having trouble finding suitable work in the area as the fertile Valley soil was being turned into subdivisions of newly built houses. For example, a large tract of land surrounded by Nordhoff, Zelzah, and Devonshire Streets in Northridge used to be an orange orchard, and now is the home of California State University. The school has preserved portions of the campus orange trees as a tribute to the Valley's golden years of agriculture.[21] Jesus and Amalia Ruiz and their four children, like many others families from San Fernando, Sylmar, and Van Nuys, worked in the Valley orange groves. Ironically, one of the youngest children of Jesus and Amalia, Everto Ruiz, later became a professor at the university. The Ruiz family was eventually forced to find work elsewhere. They traveled to the Santa Clara Valley in northern California where they found work every summer. They packed their Chevy truck with their four children and worked hard in the burning sun of the Santa Clara county area for several years. They returned to San Fernando in time for their children's school. Education was of prime importance to them, and they made sure the children never missed a day of school when they got back. Jesus and his family, like many other immigrants who came before them, came from Sonora, Mexico, in 1906, settling first in Piru, California. Amalia and her family also came from Sonora in 1925. Jesus and Amalia were married in 1930 and settled in San Fernando in that year. They put their hard-earned money into a house. Their goal was to provide a safe and stable environment for their kids. Their household was always lively and happy for they loved their music. Amalia had a beautiful voice, passing her love for music to the children. Hard work, education, and music were the legacy passed on to their growing boys and girls.[22]

Trinidad Govea of Guanajuato, Mexico, came to San Fernando in 1915 and found employment as a migrant seasonal farm worker following the crops in the Fresno area in northern California as did other San Fernando residents during the harvest season. Lucía Corral of Chihuahua, Mexico, came to San Fernando in 1920. Trinidad and Lucia were married in 1925. They had 10 children—5 girls and 5 boys—who all worked in the fields. The youngsters obediently turned in their earnings to their mother and she in turn distributed a portion of the earnings back to them according to their needs. Their son, Joe Govea, and other Mexican American war veterans will be discussed in the following section of the study.[23]

Anastacio and Delfina Bórquez established their roots deep in San Fernando when they arrived in town in 1919 from poverty-stricken Mexico. They found ample employment picking oranges and working for Sunkist Packing House. They had crossed the border at Nogales, Arizona. Their son Anastacio, Jr. and his wife Frances also worked for Sunkist, but Anastacio's last job was with General Motors Company. They raised four outstanding boys who proved to be a credit to the city. Their story will be discussed in the next section of the study.[24]

Jesus and Lorenza Chacón came to San Fernando in the early 1930s, "a la pisca" (to pick fruit). Initially, Jesus was brought by his parents to Brawley, California, at age two from Leon, Guanajuato, Mexico. He grew up in Brawley where he married Lorenza. For years the family picked fruit in the Valley until Jesus opened Chacón Barber Shop in February 1951.The barber shop became a popular business place on Kalisher and Woodworth Streets in the center of the barrio, providing many services besides haircuts. It made shower space available for the piscadores (fruit pickers). Day laborers hoping for offers of work waited in front of the business shop where crew chiefs would pick them up early in the morning and transport them to the farms. Jesus and Lorenza bought several apartments on Kalisher Street to provide for their retirement. When Jesus retired, he passed on the business to his son Arturo Chacón who was born at San Fernando Hospital on Mott and Chatsworth Drive. Chacón Barber Shop remains a friendly setting where friends meet and talk about the "good old days." Arturo married Ofelia López in1954.[25] She and her parents migrated to San Fernando in 1953 from Torreon, Coahuila, Mexico. Rosa Tejeda, Ofelia's mother, is 103 years old, active, and in good health. Ofelia and Arturo praised their parents for the wonderful cultural values bestowed on them.[26] Families like these and many others that followed them set the standard of family conduct in San Fernando. The family was the keystone of social life, the bedrock upon which the city was built. They maintained the family, the dignity of labor, and the beauty of the Spanish language and culture.

World War II and Subsequent Wars

A change of course in American life occurred in 1941, principally to San Fernando families who were a young population.[27] Immediately after the Japanese attack on Pearl Harbor, many young men were called for military duty. Many volunteered, including women as well as other Mexican Americans from San Fernando who served with pride and distinction in all branches of the Armed Forces. They were proud of their uniform and the units in which they served. They fought shoulder to shoulder with Anglo Americans and other buddies in all parts of the world. Mothers also bore the heaviest burden of World War II and subsequent wars. Some lost their sons; others had entire families serving in uniform. There seems to be a lack of proper recognition for those mothers and families of fallen heroes as well as those who had a husband, son, or daughter serving with distinction.

When the veterans returned home, there were new jobs waiting for them in the new Valley industrial economy.[28] They found ready employment in the Valley building boom joining Laborers Local 300, a workers' construction union that was becoming more and more Chicano/Latino in membership. Many San Fernando Mexican Americans veterans applied the skills they learned in the service to civilian life. Many found jobs with the U.S. Postal Service and other government agencies. Others took advantage of the G.I. Bill of Rights vocational training programs or attended colleges or universities paid by government funds. The young veterans married and bought homes in traditional San Fernando white neighborhoods and in newly developing white housing tracts in Mission Hills, a community adjacent to San Fernando. They purchased their new homes on 30-year low-mortgage rates guaranteed by the veterans administration under the G.I. benefits program. No down payment was required.

The following is a sample of Mexican American men and women of San Fernando who fought valiantly during World War II and subsequent wars for the love of their country. Some did not make it home. A partial list of the fallen heroes is forthcoming.[29]

The first San Fernando World War II casualty was young Salvador Castro who was lost in a submarine assignment. He enlisted in the Navy with his parents' blessing when he was only 16 years of age. They lived on Celis Street. Alfred W. Hasty, grandson of Geronimo and Catalina López San Fernando pioneers, also disappeared in a submarine during World War II. He was born at San Fernando Hospital located at Chatsworth Drive and Mott Street. Alfred joined the U.S. Navy Submarine School about a month after graduating from San Fernando High School. After his submarine training, he was assigned to the submarine U.S. *Corbina*. The submarine was reported missing on its first run in January 1944.

Edward A. Mula, a white soldier originally from New York, entered the Army immediately after the Japanese bombing of Pearl Harbor in 1941. He served his country three years as an infantryman before he was killed in combat. He was awarded the Purple Heart posthumously given to his wife Emma Nemback Mula at their 609 Chatsworth Drive home. Emma was the granddaughter of Henry and Emelia Lyon.

Other U.S. servicemen from the barrio who were killed in action in Europe during World War II included Raymond Durazo of O'Melveny Street, Trinidad Ramirez of Pico and Workman Streets, Salvador López who lived on the 1200 block of Mott Street, Salvador Cortéz of Kewen Street, Tom López of Mott and Kalisher, Gustavo Romero of Kewen Street, and Cruz Fernandez of Amboy Street. Frank Tresierras, Jr. who lived with his family on Acala Street was killed in action in the Pacific Theater on the last day of the war. Other barrio youth killed in action during World War II were Willie Granado and David Landín Ortiz. Willie Granado was Frank Tresierras' neighbor on Acala Street on the southern edge of Kalisher Street. David Landín was a cousin of Manuel Landín, a San Fernando businessman. Frank Tresierras had two other brothers who served in World War II. James was with the U.S. Army and Dan in the U.S. Navy. Dan was with the shore patrol in Guam and Saipan Islands. A third brother, Richard, served with the U.S. Coast Guard during the Korean War.

Raymond G. Durazo took part in the invasion of France with the 22nd Infantry of the "Famous Fourth" Division and was killed on the Siegfried.line in Germany, September 17, 1944. He was buried in an American military cemetery in Belgium. This is a partial list of San Fernando natives who died defending their country during World War II.

Servicemen who almost didn't make it home to their families.

Manuel Ruiz was in the Normandy Invasion with the 941st field Artillery Battalion. The invasion in Normandy France in June 6, 1944, by U.S. and Allied forces was by far the largest amphibious operation in history.[30] The strategic goal of the invasion was to establish a beach head on the Western European front. The United States lost 1,465 of its soldiers and 5,138 were wounded or captured. Corporal Ruiz whose family lived on 1026 Woodworth Street was awarded the European Medal with two battle stars.

 U.S. Army infantry rifleman Joe C. Govea was wounded on two occasions. He fought in the 1944 Battle of the Bulge in Belgium with the 26th Regiment, 1st Infantry "Big Red One" Division. This battle was a major German counteroffensive launched in December 1944 catching the United States and its Allies by surprise. The operation was mounted by Hitler's elite SS Panzer Army groups in a gamble to split the British and American Allies, forcing them to negotiate a peace agreement. The German counteroffensive is believed to be the single biggest and bloodiest battle that the United States encountered in World War II.[31] The field combat was fought under extreme cold weather for the foot soldier on both sides. The United States suffered 19,245 casualties, 47,500 wounded, and 23,000 captured or missing out of 89,746 U.S. troops in the field. Joe C. Govea's childhood friend, Fernando García of a prominent San Fernando family, nearly didn't make it home to San Fernando either. He was captured during the fierce combat in the Battle of the Bulge and held in a German prison for five months In an interview with Joe Govea he could not explain how they survived in the midst of the hard-fought Battle of the Bulge when their buddies were being killed to the right and left of them. British Prime Minister Winston Churchill told the House of Commons following the Battle of the Bulge: "This is undoubtedly the greatest American battle of the war, and will, I believe, be regarded as an ever-famous American victory."

Joe Govea received the following awards as an infantry rifleman: the Combat Infantry Badge, Bronze Star, Purple Heart, the European Medal with two battle stars, Victory Medal, American Campaign Medal, Good Conduct and the Commemorative Battle of the Bulge Medal. Additionally, he received a certificate of appreciation from the French government for his war efforts in Northern France, Belgium, and Germany. He was inducted in the Army when he was 18 years old along with his barrio friends Fernando García, John Contreras, Frank González, Frank López, Robert Acebo, Mickey Alvarado, Armando Magdaleno, and many others from San Fernando, and David González from Pacoima. David went to local school with Joe Govea and took basic training together in the Army before being shipped out overseas. David González received various commendations from the Army for bravery including the Congressional Medal of Honor. He was the first Chicano to receive the nation's highest honor in Southern California. A Los Angeles County park—Camp David M. González at Calabasas, California, and a City of Los Angeles housing project, David González Housing Project—were named after the Pacoima war hero. David gave his life rescuing three fellow soldiers. (It is not a stretch to say that Mexican Americans/ Latinos have earned an impressive 42 Congressional Medals of Honor, more than any other ethnic group in the country.)[32]

Daniel Govea, Joe Govea's brother, served in Korea with the 3rd Armored Division. Joe Govea worked part time with San Fernando Heights Lemon Association before he was drafted. After his honorable Army discharge, he used the G.I. Bill to take classes in construction, worked a few years in the construction industry, and at age 40 landed a job with the City of Los Angeles as building inspector. The Purple Heart and Bronze Star hero retired from the City of Los Angeles as a principal building inspector and currently lives with his wife Shirley in Northridge, California.

Other San Fernando Mexican American youths who were wounded in World War II and awarded the Purple Heart Medal included José García who was an artillery gunner from 1944 to 1945 when he was wounded in combat in the Western Europe offensive drive. He stayed in the military as an infantryman from 1948 to 1966 when he retired from the Army. Staff Sergeant Armando Ballesteros was also awarded the Purple Heart when he was wounded while serving with the 91st Infantry Division during World War II.

Army rifleman Mike Zamora was wounded during U.S. offensive in Italy. He is the recipient of the Purple Heart and the U.S. Infantry European African Middle Eastern Campaign Medal. He entered the Army on November 24, 1942. His brother Joe Zamora served in the South Pacific Theater against Japanese armies. Luis Arevalo, from a well-known San Fernando family, received a couple of Purple Heart Medals and other commendation medals for bravery as he single-handedly captured seven German soldiers. His other two brothers, Mike and Ascension Arevalo, also served in Europe with the U.S. Army during World War II. The boys lived at 1013 O'Melveny Street with their parents before they were inducted in the military. Ascension ("Chon") Arevalo married Lupe Borboa after he returned from the war and settled on 1214½ Mott Street where they raised their family. Albert Chacón was wounded in Vietnam while fighting the Viet Congs with the U.S. Army. He was awarded the Purple Heart after he left the service. His wife Rosa was elected to the San Fernando City Council in 1992 becoming the first Chicana to hold that post in San Fernando. Alberto's father, Larry Chacón, was stationed in Iceland with the U.S. Army during World War II. After his tour of duty in the military, Larry returned to San Fernando to his wife Esperanza. They bought a house on the corner of Workman and Pico Streets where they raised six children. He worked in construction and became actively involved in Chicano politics.

Some San Fernando veterans have unique experiences—little known to others. The following is an unusual story about a San Fernando resident who perhaps is the only veteran in California to provide military service for two separate governments. Juan Casillas was born June 24, 1924, in Cook County, Illinois. At the age of 2, he and his sister moved to Jalisco, Mexico, where they were raised by their father. At the age of 20, he moved back to Illinois after fulfilling his military service in Mexico with the rank of sergeant (although he was a U.S. citizen). He worked in the Chicago steel mills where he was inducted to the U.S. Army in 1950 serving two years in Korea. He received the Purple Heart and the Silver Star for bravery in the frontlines as a platoon sergeant. In 1953, he went to Mexico and there he married Olivia Lucero, age 16, in Santiago, state of Durango, Mexico. Thereafter, they settled in San Fernando where they raised six children. Juan retired from the Van Nuys General Motors plant in 1986. More of Juan Casillas and other San Fernando residents who worked for General Motors will be discussed in Chapter II.

A remarkably talented painter, Artist Frank Martínez was an Army medic with the 103rd Evacuation Hospital Unit, present when the American forces stormed the beaches of Normandy France in 1944. He also took part with the unit in four other major battles in the European theater. An acclaimed Southern California painter, some of his works expressed the experience of that event in his life. He is a husband, father, grandfather, and mentor to many of the younger artists. He currently resides in Pacoima and is a humble man when he talks about the war. A sentient person, he gets very emotional when he talks about the courage and caring of the medics of his units and about the men who died or suffered severely in battle. Frank was born in Los Angeles in 1924. His father Hilario Martínez of Najari, Mexico and mother María Alonzo of Guanajuato, Mexico came to Los Angeles in 1910. Hilario and María married in Los Angeles and settled in "Palo Verde," a community located in what is now Dodger Stadium. In 1929, Hilario and María moved to "Pico Court," an extension of the San Fernando Mexican community, across from the San Fernando Mission. While Helario picked lemons in the field, his wife María was a packer working for Sunkist Packing House. Frank went to San Fernando Elementary School. He also attended San Fernando High School with American war hero David González of Pacoima. Frank remembers attending school with Alice Lyon Carrillo of San Fernando, too. He never finished high school as he enlisted in the army in 1943 at the age of 18. Notwithstanding, at the conclusion of the war he attended Borough Polytechnic Art Institute in London, Chouinard Institute, and Otis Arts Institute in Los Angeles. The Frank Martínez Art exhibit in 2009 at the San Fernando Museum of Arts and History was a tribute to his community. It attracted large crowds of art lovers. Among the pictures exhibited at the museum was a mural depicting the founding of the Pueblo of Los Angeles and the role that the Catholic Church played in its early development commissioned by the Smithsonian Institute, a mural for the 1984 Olympics that is located at the site for the field hockey event at East Los Angeles Community College, and a mural executed in hand worked ceramic tiles located in the main lobby of the Sky Harbor Airport in Phoenix, Arizona—to name a few. Justly indeed, Artist Frank Alonzo Martínez is proud of his military service, his art and culture.

Four generations of an early California family of mixed heritage served their country well in four wars. Henry and Emelia Estrada Vega Lyon's sons Edward and Arthur served in World War I. Arthur was part of an expeditionary force sent overseas to France. Edward Lyon's son Edward Lyon, Jr. served in the South Pacific in World War II, and grandson Thomas E. Lyon was in Vietnam with the U.S. Marines. Thomas Lyon's daughter Corporal Kaitlan Lyons also served with the U.S. Marines. Henry and Emelia Estrada Vega Lyon's other grandsons served in World War II. William F. Miranda served in the European Theater and South Pacific. Robert J. Gutierrez served in the South Pacific and was wounded in action. He received the Bronze Star and Purple Heart medals. After World War I, Edward Lyon worked for San Fernando Lumber Company as a clerk and delivery man. He was also was a volunteer fireman for the City of San Fernando for many years. Edward and his wife Victoria Lyon saved their money and later went into business. Their role and others in the Mexican American business district will be the subject of Chapter II.

It's not uncommon for an entire family to be serving in the military. For example, Joe Govea's brother-in-law Luis Contreras fought in Normandy with an Army tank battalion. Luis's three brothers—Jess, Joe, and John—also served their country in the Army with distinction during World War II. Undoubtedly, this was a distressful experience for Justina Contreras, who like all war mothers waited restlessly to hear from her boys. The Contreras family resided on the 1000 block of Kewen Street.

Twin brothers Albert and Julian Carrillo, born April 18, 1927, dropped out of San Fernando High School and immediately enlisted in the U.S. Navy when they were 17 years old. They both served in the same LST (Landing Ship, Tank) during World War II before brothers were prohibited from being assigned to the same naval vessel. After their discharge from the Navy, the twins returned to finish their high school education. They then opened Carrillo Barber Shop near the corner of Kalisher and Pico, but later moved to Mission Boulevard on Carrillo Plaza. Albert Carrillo married Alice Lyon, daughter of Edward and Victoria Real Lyon.

Three local brothers—Jess, John, and Joe Espinoza—fought against Nazi soldiers in Europe. Jess and John were in the infantry while Joe served in the U.S. Navy. Their parents Luciano and Nieves Espinoza lived on Hollister and Workman. Their next-door neighbor

Clemente Ferrer, who played with the Espinoza boys as kids on barrio streets, joined them in the Army during World War II. Clemente's parents were Felipe and Tranquilina Ferrer. Another neighbor Wilfred Negrete served with the Army in the Pacific Theater at that time. Robert Acebo, Sr. served with the 28th Army Division in Germany during World War II. His family resided on Mission Boulevard. He now volunteers with local veterans organizations. Robert Acebo's son, Robert Acebo, Jr., served with the Army in Vietnam.

Robert Bórquez and his brothers Eddie and Manuel Bórquez saw action with the U.S. Army during World War II. After the war, Eddie and Manuel Bórquez worked for General Motors at Van Nuys retiring after 30 years with the company. Manuel Bórquez's house on 1117 Mott Street is currently occupied by his widow Martha Bórquez and their daughter Martha. Bob Bórquez made his career working for Thrifty Drug Store in San Fernando rising to the position of store manager. He is an active member of San Fernando Kiwanis Club. Rudy Bórquez, the younger brother, worked until retirement with Lockheed Aircraft Company in Burbank. Robert Bórquez's son Edward served with the U.S. Airborne (paratroopers) in Vietnam. Indeed, this is a remarkable family with deep roots in San Fernando.

Joe A. Negrete of San Fernando and his children, moved by the love of their country, enlisted in various branches of the military. Senior Joe A. Negrete served during World War II with the U.S. Marines. The siblings followed in their dad's footstep by enlisting in the military during the Vietnam War: Specialist Joe Negrete, Jr., U.S. Army; Corporal Leonard Negrete, U.S. Marines; Irene Negrete, U.S. Army Women Corps; Specialist Abel Negrete, U.S. Army; and grandson Adrian J. Carlon, U.S. Air Force. Joe A. Negrete, Sr. and Wilfred Negrete who lived in the Hollister and Workman neighborhoods are cousins.

Richard Ysais and his brother Felix both served in Vietnam. Richard was awarded the Purple Heart while fighting with the 1st Infantry Division. Felix served with the 1st Cavalry Division. The boys are related to the Negrete family. Wilfred Negrete is their uncle. Richard resides with his family on South Brand Boulevard in San Fernando.

The Quijada family had servicemen in the three branches of the Armed Forces. Sergeant Louis Quijada was with the 8th Air Force in World War II. His brother Ray "Reno" Quijada was in the Army during that period. Ray's sons Army First Lieutenant Frank J. Quijada and U.S. Navy Capitan Edward J. Quijada both served in Vietnam. Delfina Tresierras Quijada still lives in the house at the 400 block of Newton Street where she raised her children. She comes from a family rich in military history. Delfina's brothers' tours of military duty were cited in the earlier paragraphs of this section.

Following is a partial list of other San Fernando residents who served their country with distinction.

Joe Villegas was an Army medic with General George Patton's Tank Division in Europe. He is the son of Inocencio Castro Villegas and grandson of Geronimo and Catalina López, founding members of San Fernando. Joe Villegas is buried in the Veterans Cemetery in Westwood, Los Angeles. Another combat medic, Staff Sergeant Herman H. Rodero, was in New Guinea and the Philippines campaigns in the Pacific Theater in which he received the Asiatic Ribbon with three bronze stars. His parents and several other families from Spain migrated to San Fernando in the 1940s and 1950s. They once owned an auto repair and paint shop on Workman and San Fernando Road.

Manuel Flores enlisted in the Army in 1944 at the age of 16 with his parents' permission after graduating from San Fernando High School. He joined the Army medics and served in the Pacific during World War II. After his military service he attended college under the G.I. Bill earning an engineering degree from the University of California at Los Angeles (UCLA). His name will appear in other sections of this paper.

John Britt, a good friend of the Fernando García family and of the Mexican American community, deserves to be mentioned here, too. Lieutenant John Britt was a chief motor machinist mate with the U.S. Navy stationed at Pearl Harbor. He survived the Japanese surprise attack that forced the United States into World War II in the Pacific. He also was in the Battle of Midway and served in the Battle of Guadalcanal where his PT boat squadron was patrolling with Lieutenant John F. Kennedy's famous PT 109. The highly decorated hero was discharged from the Navy on May 17, 1946. In 1952, he moved with his young wife Marjorie Gould (Marge) from Rhode Island to San Fernando. A job was waiting for him as a machinist with Lockheed Aircraft Company of Burbank. Upon arrival in California they were confronted with their first Valley racist attitude when a realtor asked them as they were purchasing their house in San Fernando, "Why do you want to move into a Mexican town?" In the late 1950s Marge, a member of the Young Women Christian Association (YWCA) board, supported the suggestion of the board president that a black woman be invited to join the group and represent the growing black residents of Pacoima. The next morning there was a burning cross in the Britt's front lawn. Marge admitted being frightened, but she said it made her stronger in her personal belief that everyone be treated fairly regardless of race, national character, or status in life. The role of this fine San Fernando family will be taken in the following chapters.

Louie Guiza, a local boy, was called to duty with the Army during World War II. He served in the Pacific where he caught malaria during his tour of duty there. He suffered from this disease throughout his life. He and his wife Jenny lived on 622 South Brand Boulevard. He retired from the city's public works department.

Louis J. Najar enlisted in the Navy in July 1942 and served in the Pacific area, taking part in the Leyte and Attu campaigns. A member of the Najar family has served in every war and conflict since World War II. Fred de la Cerda, another member of a prominent San Fernando family, entered the service on March 29, 1943, participating in numerous campaigns including the Marshalls, Gilberts, Marianas, New Guinea, Iwo Jima, and Okinawa.

Richard Tresierras served with the U.S. Coast Guard during the Korean War. His brother Frank Tresierras, Jr. was killed in action during World War II.

Staff Sergeant José Amaro Hernández volunteered in the then U.S. Army Air Force after high school serving from 1950 to 1954, spending two years with the 315th Airborne Troop Carrier Wing, Survival Training and Equipment unit in Japan and Korea from 1952 to 1954. Discharged from the Air Force in November 1954 at Maxwell Air Base, Montgomery, Alabama, his unit commendations include the Korean Service Medal with three bronze stars, Republic of Korea Presidential Unit Citation, United Nations Service Medal, the National Defense Service Medal, and the Good Conduct Medal. He earned bachelor and masters of art degrees in economics from St. Mary's University, San Antonio, Texas, and Ohio State University, Columbus, respectively, under the G.I. Bill and a doctorate degree in political science from the University of California, Riverside. He is a Professor Emeritus of Chicana/o Studies at California State University, Northridge. José and his wife Carol O'Brien came to Northridge in 1969 from Cincinnati, Ohio. They moved to San Fernando in 1971, where they raised daughters Moira and Annie on 652 South Brand Boulevard, a house bought under the G.I. Bill. The children attended local Catholic schools and Stanford University, and are medical doctors. Dr. José Hernández was councilman and mayor of San Fernando for 16 years.

Paul Arroyo served with the U.S. Navy in Vietnam. He is the grandson of Paul Cruz, a retired San Fernando city employee. Jess Margarito, former councilman and mayor of San Fernando, was inducted in the Army in 1966 along with a dozen other local boys. Nine went to Vietnam and the others went to Germany and Korea. Jess Margarito was sent to Germany serving there from 1967 to 1968. Julian Leon, an Army officer during the Vietnam War, was a former city park recreation leader at Las Palmas Park. He graduated from San Fernando Valley State College (now California State University, Northridge). Robert Villafaña also a graduate of San Fernando Valley State College served in Vietnam with the Army infantry. His wife Diana and daughter Rebekah received graduate degrees from the Northridge campus.

By 1946, peace had returned to the world and veterans were returning home. The children of immigrants had served their country well. At home, they found San Fernando's white-controlled government still closed to Mexican Americans and Latinos. Notwithstanding, they found greater opportunities in the growing Valley housing boom, manufacturing and business economy after they returned home. Before they joined the service, their parents were locked in working pools in agriculture and other low-wage jobs. As has been observed, the U.S. Armed Forces provided a major avenue of upward mobility for returning Mexican American veterans who had been traditionally on the frontlines in time of war. The G.I. Bill was an important watershed for many service men and women including Mexican Americans/Latinos who took advantage of veterans' benefits in education, job training, business loans, and purchase of homes in wholesome neighborhoods. Disabled veterans' benefits were extended for their children's education. The returning Mexican American veterans were in a better position to press for local political participation, better city services, neighborhood improvements, equity in civil service jobs, and better education for their children. Whites controlled the city council, the police station, school board, and school curriculum. Whites controlled the local financial institutions and the Democratic Party.

Notes

1. For a superb and readable treatment of the growth and development of the San Fernando Valley, see Kevin Roderick, *The San Fernando Valley: America's Suburb,* Los Angles: Los Angeles Times Books, 2002.
2. Ibid., 74.
3. Ibid., 60.
4. Although the causes of international migration are complex, most experts point to push-pull factors. A good assessment on this issue is found in Hans P. Johnson, "Illegal Immigration," *At Issue,* San Francisco: Public Policy Institute of California, April 2006; and Gilberto Hinojosa, "Immigration an Economic Issue," *San Antonio Light*, San Antonio, Texas, July 2001.
5. This is recounted in Carey McWilliams, *North from Mexico: The Spanish-Speaking of the United States,* New York: Greenwood Press, 1968; and in José Amaro Hernández, *Mutual Aid for Survival*, op. cit. In addition, see Rodolfo F. Acuña, *Anything but Mexican: Chicano in Contemporary Los Angeles*, 112-116, op. cit. This study concludes that in bad times when Mexican labor is not needed, Mexicans are rounded up by immigration agents and deported to Mexico. This occurred during the Great Depression years when the government resorted to forced repatriation of Mexican nationals and their native-born children to Mexico. From 1931 to 1934, thousands of Mexican families were sent in train loads to Mexico without the benefit of legal counsel. They were blamed for massive unemployment during the economic crisis of the 1930s. This inhumane act was deeply felt in communities in Texas and California, especially in Los Angeles when 13,000 Mexicans were taken to the

Los Angeles train station and deported. Dr. Acuña also maintains that the current anti-immigration rhetoric (that undocumented workers cause unemployment and take scarce resources from Americans) is a political siren song and finger pointing of a complex national issue. The vast flow of Mexican and other foreign labor continues because it is profitable to U.S. businesses, to American residents, and to Mexico. If the flow of cheap labor is no longer profitable, it will stop coming. Mexico would lose millions of U.S. dollars sent home by immigrant nationals. See Rodolfo F. Acuña extensive work, *Corridors of Migration: The Odyssey of Mexican Laborers, 1600-1933,* Tucson: The University of Arizona Press, 2007. The contribution of foreign labor to the U.S. economy is also recounted by a recent study commissioned by the Cato Institute reported in *Newsweek,* August 23-31, 2009.

6. The literature on this political issue is extensive. The reader is referred to Aviva Chomsky, *They Take Our Jobs,* Boston: Beacon Press, 2007. Also see Michael C. Meyer and William L. Sherman, *The Course of Mexican History,* New York: Oxford University Press, 1995.

7. As a point of interest it should be noted here that Mexican border crossings were not considered illegal at the time of the Mexican Revolution until new laws imposed barriers to entry in 1917 and 1924. During the early part of the 20th century, C. M. Goethe, head of the Eugenic Movement in California, Chancellor David Stern Jordan of Stanford University, and Eugenic professor Samuel Holmes of UC Berkeley led by *Los Angeles Times* founder Harry Chandler and other civic leaders argued that Mexicans were an inferior race and the least competent minority group entering U.S. borders. Hence, they pressured the government to impose quotas to reduce the immigration of "Mexicans" to California, and called for their exclusion in American life. They instructed real estate brokers to cease selling properties to them. This so-called "scientific justification" led to the passing of the Immigration Acts of 1917 and 1924 when the first U.S. Border Patrol agency was established to keep "genetically inferior" Mexicans out of the country. Very little of this information is known openly. For more detailed arguments on this position, see David Dorado Romo, "Crossing the Line," *Los Angeles Times*, February 27, 2006. He is also the author of *Ringside Seat to a Revolution: An Underground Cultural History of El Paso and Juarez, 1893-1923,* El Paso: Cinco Puntos Press, 2005.

8. This section is based on an interview with Evangelina Tinoco Pérez, age 86, wife of Reyes Pérez on June 16, 2009, at the San Fernando Las Palmas Nutrition Senior Center. She was kind enough to share her family experience. Reyes passed away in 1948.

9. Children of the Revolution have many stories to tell about this difficult period. Another example, Minerva Fuentes Hernández never romanticized the exploits of Pancho Villa (as some do) in dealing with a complex struggle over the future course of the Revolution. To her, Pancho Villa was no different from the lawless "federales" (government troops) who terrorized and plundered rural communities in northern Mexico, and who rewarded themselves with any woman they could get their hands on. At the age of 16, she experienced a heroic escape with her parents, three sisters, and four brothers as they swam across the Rio Grande into Eagle Pass, a border town in southern Texas, as "federales" soldiers pursed them to the riverbank. Her parents were concerned, rightly so, that their girls would be captured and taken away by the soldiers.

10. Evangelina Pérez, op. cit.
11. Roderick, op. cit.
12. Evangelina Pérez, op. cit.
13. *San Fernando Valley SUN*, op. cit.
14. U.S. Bureau of the Census, *1950 Census of Population,* Volume II, *Characteristics of Population,* Parts 5 & 6, California.
15. Vickie Carrillo Norton, granddaughter of Cornelio and Micaela Carrillo, provided this information on September 12, 2009.
16. The information for this paragraph and the following was contributed by Martha Arevalo González, granddaughter of Ascension and Refugio Silva Arevalo.
17. John Brooks assisted with this information on September 4, 2009.
18. Alice Bacon, daughter of Teresa Cruz, provided this information on September 19, 2009.
19. Vickie Carrillo Norton shared this information on September 2, 2009, at a meeting held at the San Fernando Museum of Arts and History.
20. Ibid.
21. Roderick, op. cit.
22 This is an excellent account of a little known episode of the lives of some San Fernando families as recounted by Professor Everto Ruiz on July 2, 2009.
23. This was based on a conversation with Joe C. Govea, who was raised in San Fernando.
24. Robert Bórquez provided this information by telephone on July 2, 2009.
25. Arturo and Ofelia Chacón assisted in this section on July 4, 2009, as they love to tell the story of their proud parents.
26. *Birthday Journal,* State Farm Insurance Publication, November 26, 1906.
27. The medium age of San Fernando population was 29.2 according to the U.S. Bureau of the Census, *1950 Census of Population Characteristics,* Volume II, Parts 5 & 6, California.
28. Roderick, op. cit., 119-127.
29. This section was made possible with the assistance of war veterans who spoke during the inauguration of the veterans exhibit honoring veterans and fallen soldiers at the San Fernando Museum of Art and History on November 11, 2007; the veterans exhibit supervisor, Elvira Orozco; and Manuel Flores, Robert Bórquez, Vickie Carrillo Norton, Marjorie Britt, Albert Chacón, Olivia Casillas, Martha Arevalo González (daughter of Ascension and Lupe Borboa Arevalo), Delfina Tresierras Quijada, Artist Frank Martínez, and Richard Ysais. In particular, this section is indebted to Joe C. Govea for his invaluable contribution and personal knowledge of many of the barrio servicemen mentioned herein. He is a "walking encyclopedia" of knowledge about his San Fernando neighborhood and about his experience in World War II. Another valuable source of information for this section was the *Black and Gold Year Book* published by the Associate Students and San Fernando High School, San Fernando, 1950.
30. The Battle of Normandy has been the topic of many historic accounts, films, and television miniseries. See, for example, Stephen Ambrose's HBO special "Band of Brothers," and *Saving Private Ryan*, a 1998 film directed by Steven Spielberg and starring Tom Hanks. For a brief summary of the invasion of Normandy, see Guy History Web Site on WWII, "The Invasion of Normandy (1944)."

31. For a thoughtful appraisal of war veterans in World War II, see Robert Dole, *One Soldier's Story*, New York: Harper Collins Publisher, 2006; also see Trevor N. Dupuy, et al., *Hitler's Last Gamble: Battle of the Bulge, December 1944 - January 1945*, New York: Harper Collins Publisher, 1994, and *American Experience: The Battle of the Bulge*, PPBS Documentary produced by Thomas F. Lennon.
32. To support this statement, see Roy Benavidez and Oscar Griffin, *The Three Wars of Roy Benavidez*, San Antonio: Corona Publishing Company, 1986; and Raul Morín, *Among the Valiant: Mexican Americans in World War II and Korea*, Los Angeles: Valiant Press, 2002.

CHAPTER 2

Structural Change in the Economy and New Job Opportunities in the San Fernando Valley

During the 1950s, Chicanos became urban dwellers (over 50 percent moved to U.S. metropolitan centers) leaving agricultural-related businesses for manufacturing, service, and construction job opportunities.[1] In the 1940s and 1950s the Los Angeles region experienced a vibrant period of prosperity as a result of increased growth of defense industries, manufacturing, and service occupations. The Valley, once a major player in the California citrus industry, became the center of new industries (e.g., aircraft companies, auto, big motion picture studios, and financial institutions, just to name four).[2] The new economic structure and the growth of industries attracted a new wave of demographics to the region. New residents moved in as they rode this period of prosperity and job opportunities, including second- and third-generation Mexican Americans from rural communities in Texas and New Mexico. As in the past, they settled in East Los Angeles, Van Nuys, Panorama City, Sylmar, and San Fernando. These communities served as magnets for native Mexican Americans as well as immigrants from Mexico. The Valley had become more diverse: a mixture of working class, middle class, and professional.[3]

San Fernando, leader in the Valley elementary school movement, also was first to provide high school instruction there—a great factor in the Valley's growth and prosperity. San Fernando High School, which was originally housed in the current middle school on North Maclay Street, later moved to its current site on O'Melveny and Fox Streets in 1952 when it joined the Los Angeles Unified School District. San Fernando

High School played an important role in the Valley's new economic scenario with its young and productive force. The city's residents mostly Mexican Americans rushed to apply, landing coveted spots in the various industrial, manufacturing, and service sectors of the local economy. Anastacio Cisneros, for example, began working at Lockheed Aircraft Company at Burbank in 1942 after working many jobs in the Valley field and packing houses in Mission Hills and San Fernando. He came to San Fernando in 1918 from Michoacan, Mexico and lived in San Fernando for the rest of his life.[4]

Manuel Flores was hired by Lockheed in 1950 as an engineer right after his graduation from UCLA's School of Engineering.[5] Years later, he was appointed Lockheed Aircraft Company's equal employment representative and state affirmative action director. He retired from Lockheed in 1983 and then went into business in San Fernando. Native-born Virginia Barragán, daughter of Anastacio Cisneros, also worked at Lockheed in 1953 and retired there in 1991.[6] She started as a typist, promoted to executive secretary, and later to a publications coordinator in the publications department. Her husband Joe Barragán, a Korean War veteran, worked at the Van Nuys General Motors plant as an office administrator. A steady job with employees and family benefits permitted the Barragáns to live a fuller live and to enjoy precious time with their children's school activities. The family devoted many years to community improvement programs in the city. They became an important voice on issues of importance to their community. Robert Bórquez's younger brother Rudy also worked for Lockheed building war aircrafts during World War II. After his retirement, he died from cancer related to his work inside aircrafts.[7] He and his family lived on 802 Mott Street, San Fernando.

After World War II, factories continued to grow in the Valley's dynamic economic expansion. Jobs became plentiful. Mexican and Mexican Americans worked in all the major industries and business institutions. The Van Nuys General Motors plant opened in 1947 employing at one time over 5,000 autoworkers from the Valley, including a significant number of Mexican Americans from San Fernando. Hard work and dedication to their jobs were their strength as they competed for jobs. Cirilo Cruz Tejeda, Juan Casillas, Fred Rodríquez, and Reyes Pérez of San Fernando were happy working for General Motors. The company was praised as a good employer for employing thousands of assembly workers from the Valley and San Fernando and for providing them with a good life. They credited the company and the union salary for their houses, their family security, and a comfortable retirement. The employees' good salary generated sales and property taxes to local government agencies. Pete Beltrán, political director of the United Auto Workers Union, was also praised for representing the autoworkers at the plant. It has been good for Juan Casillas's son

Rene, too, who works in the auto parts department of General Motors in Fontana and who is retiring soon. Juan Casillas's other son David is traveling coordinator with the internationally popular rock English group Duran Duran.[8] Juan Casillas and his wife Olivia have four other grown children.

Juan Casillas, who loved baseball and played organized baseball in Mexico, volunteered his spare time teaching children in Sylmar and San Fernando the mechanics of baseball as a pastime. Fred Rodríguez was a co-founder of Little League San Fernando Braves. Reyes Pérez and his wife Evangelina were avid supporters of Head Start in San Fernando. In addition, they were active in leadership roles in Chicano community organizing. They provided community support in the founding of the California State University, Northridge Chicano Studies Department. Their children attended four-year colleges earning degrees in various professional programs.

Many of the new employees moving to Valley manufacturing and construction positions settled in the San Fernando and immediate vicinity, a haven for family-oriented couples seeking small-town values and joyful backyard family experience. Many bought new three- and four-bedroom homes built across from Brand Park and San Fernando Mission on Brand Boulevard, and San Fernando, replacing white owners. John Menchaca married Olga in 1953 as soon as he received his honorable discharge from the Army.[9] He immediately found employment with Van Nuys General Motors, bought their home on Brand Boulevard where they raised their children and sent them to college. These parents and others engaged in decisions about how their children's school should be run. They augured a new era of community development in San Fernando and other communities.

Pursuing new jobs, higher wages, better working conditions and home ownership was a positive development for Mexican Americans and other working-class citizens of San Fernando. The newlywed couple Elvira Camarillo and Angel Orozco of Pacoima moved to San Fernando in 1954 to a new housing subdivision on Pico and South Huntington Streets. The area on the southern side of town had been used for farming as the orange groves were "knocked down for the new housing development."[10] Elvira and Angel raised their children in the Pico neighborhood. Angel worked for General Motors. Elvira later became the San Fernando city treasurer. Lockheed Aircraft engineer Manuel Flores and his wife Sally were having trouble buying a house "across the tracks" on the northern section of the city. According to Manuel Flores, the north side was out of reach to Mexican American families. Realtors had declared it a "redlined district." They would not show properties for sale to prospective Mexican buyers. But Manuel Flores grinned as he explained how he "pulled the rug" under the racist realtors by going beyond them, straight to the seller.[11] Hence, he made a deal and bought a house in 1956 on North Lazard Street. During the interview, Mr. Flores claimed that he was the first Mexican American to purchase a house on the exclusive side of town. He bought the house under the G.I. Bill housing program. When asked if there was any other form of racism in town he hastened to add that "Mexican Americans were not allowed to sit among whites on the first floor of movie theatres. They could only sit on the balcony to enjoy a movie."

Ironically, the spatial pattern of discrimination in San Fernando and other places in the Valley strengthened the cultural identity of Mexican Americans because it kept them culturally insulated. In addition, this racial attitude tended to anger the Chicano youth who later took part in the late 1960s to early 1970s student uprisings against the status quo. The development of interrelationship between the two communities was fundamental to the incoming generation of the newly emerging youth consciousness. They cried out "Ya Basta" ("Enough is Enough").

Homeownership, a pinnacle of the American Dream, gave Americans access to the conditions that contribute to overall well-being: ergo, access to wholesome neighborhoods, including school quality, neighborhood safety, recreation facilities for children and seniors, and quick response by government agencies. Children from stable neighborhoods have a better chance of staying in school.[12]

San Fernando men and women took advantage of all job opportunities available from installing Sears garage doors to delivering Sears washing machines and dryers to households, to administering huge finances for banks. Sewing companies moved to First Street and employed many Mexican women because they could sew in their own houses at low wages. San Fernando Electric Manufacturing Company also located on First Street prided itself on the number of local residents working for the firm.[13]

John González and his wife Mary came to San Fernando in the 1900s to work in the orchards but discovered that there were many other job opportunities upon their arrival in town. John picked fruit and worked with a railroad crew for a number of years. He then traded jobs for one with the General Motors plant at Van Nuys in the 1950s. His last place of employment was with the Los Angeles Department of Water and Power where he finally retired. John and Mary González used to live in front of the old Santa Rosa Church on Kalisher and Hollister Streets.

Carmen Rocha was an employee of Price-Pfister, one of the nation's largest plumbing fixture manufacturers in Pacoima, until the company moved to Mexico in the 1980s. Her son Gil Rocha was a band frontman for the Silhouettes, a garage rock-and-roll band that played with Richie Valens (a.k.a. Richard Valenzuela), the rock pioneer of the 1950s. Richie Valens was best remembered for his love ballad "Donna," a popular hit of Fifties Rock. The song came from Carmen Rocha's garage on 653 Chatsworth Drive where the band and Richie Valens practiced the song. The garage was a happy site where they composed and rehearsed their music. They frequently used Carmen's upright piano.[14]

The 1950s was also a good period for builders and construction workers. The construction industry was the pillar of the Valley economy in the 1950s and 1960s housing boom.[15] Construction union jobs paid higher wages with real benefits for the family. San Fernando Mexican Americans were often hired in construction represented by Laborers' Local 300 Union.[16] In the 1960s, Local 300 union member Frank Martínez and his wife Mercedes bought a house along picturesque, Mexican palm-lined Brand Boulevard. Earlier Mexican, Japanese, or African Americans were prohibited from purchasing property on that street. His daughter Marisela Torres attended UCLA and is a teacher's aide at St. Ferdinand Grammar School. She served several years as San Fernando city planning commissioner.[17]

The housing boom not only affected construction jobs, it also brought an outside effect on the Valley economy; that is, it created a ripple effect for people working for companies that provided financial and real estate services, building materials, home improvement and related businesses such as plumbing, electrical, roofing, moving, and the like. Most of these new businesses did not require a college education. Consequently, many of the jobs were filled by San Fernando Mexicans who did not have a high school diploma, but who were eager to work, punctual and protective of the job opportunities offered. These were splendid personal traits that led to job security at that time.[18]

While union construction provided higher paying jobs, the work was tough, strenuous, and exhausting. Roberto Pulido worked on many union contracts. He is now retired and resides with his wife Francisca on Third Street. His son José Pulido helped his father on some side construction jobs as a teenager, and noted in his experience that it was the "hardest work" he had ever done. A UC Berkeley and UCLA graduate, José Pulido served eight years as San Fernando city administrator.[19]

Francisco Arrizón, Sr. also worked for many years with Laborers' Local 300 union labor contracts.[20] He retired early from the union. He and his former wife Guadalupe (Lupita) opened a tidy deli/restaurant, Tortilleria La Talpense on North Maclay Street. The restaurant is popular for its fine Mexican home cooking. In particular, it is famous for its Menudo soup, a delight to its Mexican/Latino patrons and connoisseurs of exquisite Mexican food. The soup is made of the lining of a cow's stomach (tripe), pig's feet, and hominy.[21] A great deal more on the Mexican soup is found on Chapter X. Additionally, Francisco Arrizón, Sr.'s sons own Arrizón Bros. Trucking. Francisco Arrizón, Jr. is the current organizer/public sector representative of Laborers' Local 300 of Los Angeles. The Arrizón story is about a blue-collar family who look at themselves as good citizens whose success is due to personal qualities such as hard work, initiative, strong family ties, and thrift. They have made an important contribution to the development of San Fernando.

Another San Fernando notable is Sergio Rascón, a rising star in the labor movement of Southern California. He is business manager of Laborers' Local 300 of Los Angeles. He and wife Flora raised their children in San Fernando. They now reside in Sylmar. Mike Quevedo of San Fernando is union president of California Laborers for Equity and Progress whose office is located in El Monte, California. Mike comes from a long line of family unionists. He and his wife Rebecca reside in their home on North Huntington Street in the northern part of town. Mexican Americans and Latinos have a proud history in their leadership role of strengthening labor relations in the nation's labor movement.[22]

It is quite evident from the foregoing observations that Mexican Americans were in the position to generate considerable labor and political strength at this point in time as will be seen in the following chapters.

The Mobilization of the South Side Business Community

There was another interesting development in San Fernando during the 1950s and subsequent years as an expanding proliferation of small businesses appeared in the Mexican American section of town. These included grocery stores (tiendas de abarrote) and meat markets, bakeries, restaurants, bars, hair dressers and barber shops, repair shops, gasoline stations, and other small retail stores. Mission Boulevard (name changed to San Fernando Mission Boulevard) and Kalisher Street became the major Mexican business district making Mexican Americans less dependent on south side white businesses. These streets were lined with retail stores advertising their products onto the sidewalks. Kalisher Street became impacted with establishments selling beer and liquor, and billiard halls, and little market stores. The business district included independent-owned "tienditas" (little mom-and-pop stores) that provided personal and cheerful customer service. They were owned by business men and women who had a flair for small businesses. Some of the business families were of mixed heritage (Anglo and Mexican Americans). They worked together in unison. Although their businesses were limited (e.g., they could not get a loan), they never lost their entrepreneurial spirit. Some of the small businesses graduated into larger business enterprises. They had the essential ingredient for financial responsibility and economic independence. There was a high degree of willingness to cooperate amongst themselves and a desire to assist the poor.[23]

José Sierra owned a small shopping mart on Mission and Pico, a beer saloon, a billiard hall, and a barber shop. José Sierra, whose family migrated from Spain and settled in San Fernando, ran the grocery store while the other stores were leased. His brother Ed Sierra converted his house on Mission Boulevard and Hollister Street into his restaurant "Ed Sierras's Spanish Café" in 1932 which became a popular eating spot for Hollywood movie stars from the 1930s to the 1960s. Gil Jaramillio bought Sierra's Spanish Café from his father-in-law, changing the name to Sierra's. The restaurant was noted for its fine Mexican cuisine. Gil Jaramillo was the founder of Mission Brand Tortillas of San Fernando. The entrepreneurial Mexican American learned to manufacture authentic tortillas in large quality and quality whose business developed into a successful tortilla distribution network in California and Mexico. He later sold the Mission Tortilla Company in the late 1970s to a multinational corporation from Dallas, Texas, so he could pursue the restaurant business. He opened up another Sierra's restaurant in Canoga Park, California, and then introduced "Mission Burrito." The Mission Brand Tortilla is now advertised as the "World's best-selling Tortilla."

After World War II, Edward and Victoria Lyon owned and operated Lyon's Market on Mission and Kewen for almost 20 years. Lyon's Market was a convenient neighborhood market that provided fresh meats, produce, and everyday staples. Their store extended credit to families trying to make ends meet before credit was an accepted institution. Keeping records was not an easy task for small businesses, but store records nevertheless showed that they did not expect poor families, who were struggling to feed their children, to pay their bills. Alice Lyon helped her parents in the everyday operation of the market. She married war veteran Albert Carrillo who owned a barber shop with his brother Julian in the Mission Boulevard business district. Ed and Victoria sold their grocery store to Jess and Ramona Arevalo Franco at which time it became Franco's Liquor. Jess and Ramona Franco also owned a Hancock gasoline station on Mission and Celis Streets where Jack-in-the-Box is now doing business. Their daughter Mary Ann Rose worked as a receptionist for the City of San Fernando in the 1950s. Ramona's sister Isabel Arevalo (no relation to Miguel Arevalo's family) was the city's first Miss San Fernando of 1930. Their brother Abe Arevalo served with the U.S. Army during World War II.

After World War II, twin brothers Albert and Julian Carrillo opened their barber shop near the corner of Pico and Kalisher, later moving their business to Mission Boulevard. The business did well over the years. Then Albert Carrillo and his wife Alice Lyon Carrillo bought the major part of the business block on Mission and Hewitt in the early 1960s and named it Carrillo's Plaza. Albert and Alice followed the example set by their parents Edward and Victoria Lyon; that is, work hard, save, and invest, buy other properties and become major landlords in the city.

Further north on Mission and Hollister Carmelita Vásquez managed her own grocery store. She was noted in the Valley for her fine reputation for handmade corn tortillas ("hechas de mano").

Ernesto Martínez came to California at the age of 16 in the early 1920s to pick oranges. According to his son John Martínez, his dad decided that picking oranges was not his forte, so in 1941 he went into business putting a "cantina" (beer bar) on Mission and Kewen Street. In 1949, he owned and managed a Flying-A gasoline station and auto mechanic shop on Mission and Griffith Street. This auto mechanic shop is now run by his son John Martínez. When asked what kind of businessman his father was, John stated clearly: "My father came to this country to work and raise a family. He was an enterpriser; he sold fertilizer by the truck load in his spare time."[24]

Manuel Martínez (no relation to Ernesto Martínez) was a major landlord in San Fernando. He owned valuable building properties near downtown including a hotel on the corner of Brand and San Fernando Road on the San Fernando Mall. Another Hispanic businessman Manuel Alcala owned a jewelry store on the Mall. At that time many of the jewelry and clothing stores were owned by Jewish businesspersons who lived out of town. Manuel Castro was the baker and owner of a bakery located on Pico and Kalisher. Louis González operated his small shoe shop in a little place on the corner of Kewen and Kalisher. At the edge of town on Kalisher and Woodworth is the Chacón Barber Shop where old friends still get their haircuts and tell stories of their past.

The business district also included well-known business men and women who were community activists such as José Aranda who owned an Arco gas station on Mission. He ran unsuccessfully for city council on various occasions. In 1980, José Aranda and others were involved in a lawsuit against the city at-large election which put the Mexican community at a disadvantage. *José Aranda, et al. vs. Van Sickle, et al.* was considered by the U.S. District Court and the Ninth Circuit Court of Appeals in connection with similar cases from other states. Aranda lost. The case was resolved in favor of the City of San Fernando. The courts decided that citywide elections were more suitable to small cities like San Fernando. More on this will be discussed on Chapter IV.

In the middle of the barrio was the popular La Mexicana grocery and meat market owned by Narcio García. His sons acted as sales clerks and butchers providing friendly service to nearby households. The prominent García family was actively involved in Chicano politics. Beer was an important sales commodity in all grocery stores in the barrio.

The Frank Yudico family, longstanding residents of the San Fernando barrio and committed community activists, had a grocery store and meat market on busy Kalisher and Hewitt Streets. These folk business establishments were located within walking distance of family households. They sold groceries and fresh meats, folk remedies, perfumes, clothing, the Spanish-language *La Opinion*, and other household goods. In short, the business district was a center of Mexican life. It was festive with loud music flowing from the stores. These little Mexican stores were forerunners of today's popular 7-11 minimarts. The Usebio Landín family ran a convenient confectionary store and magazine stand next to the Yudico market. They shared customers. Usebio published a weekly reporter *VIVA* about family and neighborhood news. Manuel Landín, son of Usebio Landín, was manager of the San Fernando Valley Savings and Loan Association located in San Fernando. The Manuel Landín family supported and worked every year at the St. Ferdinand Church fund-raising fiesta. La Perla grocery store and meat market on Kalisher and Woodward Streets, owned by Louis Mendoza, was across from Chacón Barber Shop. La India Market, owned by World War II veteran and Purple Heart recipient Armando Ballesteros, was located on Kalisher and Mott Streets, a frequent site of "Los Polviados" (well-groomed young men inspired by the Los Angeles "Pachucos" style of clothing—a trim black zoot suit and wide-brimmed feathered hat—and mannerism of the mid-1940s). The Pachuco character was portrayed in Luis Valdez's hit play "Zoot Suit." The mass media described them as gangsters. San Fernando Polviados were not gang members.[25] They took pride in showing off their fine clothing and new identity. They did, however, have some skirmishes with a rival group that congregated on the Kalisher and Woodworth intersection called "barrio de la Rana (frog)" This was a small district within the main barrio. The district got its name because during the rainy season, running water on the dirt streets created a "charco" (a pool of standing water) in the intersection that lured frogs to the pond. Chacón Barber Shop was in the center of the small district, a niche where the boys of both groups got their haircut. They respected Arturo Chacón, the barber and the owner of the place. The respect was reciprocal.

Alberto Padilla, a former city councilman, was the proud owner of a "tiendita" on Workman and San Fernando Road. Mr. Padilla won the hearts of the Chicano community for his generosity on Church support and to his community. He was popular at Church festivals as a singer of Mexican love ballads. He was married to Anita Real and was uncle to Everto Ruiz. He later became a realtor, assisting Mexican Americans buying into once prohibited white neighborhoods. He was recalled from public office by a special interest group. More of this relationship will be found in the following chapter.

Father Luis Valbuena, the pastor of Santa Rosa Catholic Church, was troubled that the Mexican /Mexican American community was not getting the needed financial service from local banks. As a start, he established a credit union in the Church grounds facilitating small loans to the parishioners. But he went further. He urged the community to demand better financial services (i.e., checking, savings, and loans) that the growing barrio community directly needed.[26] Father Valbuena was the visible clergyman in the social issues of the local church community. As a result of his activism, a San Fernando business group led by former Lockheed engineer Manuel Flores, who had a knack for starting a business, answered the call for action. They applied for a chartered Hispanic state bank which was approved as Cabrillo State Bank. The bank's first officers included Manuel Flores as chairman and director. Other original charter bank directors of Hispanic origin included Raul Aragón, Sr. (owner of Aragón Plumbing) and Dan E. Tresierras (family owner of Tresierras markets).[27] Dan Tresierras's father Frank Tresierras, Sr. and his family, who had opened a small grocery store in Pacoima and built it into a chain of supermarkets throughout the northeastern Valley, originally lived in Acala Street on the southern end of Kalisher Street. Raul Aragón and his brothers Frank and Rudy were busy at work in construction. Raul Aragón, Jr., son of Raul Aragón, Sr., was a student activist at San Fernando Valley State College (California State University, Northridge) in the 1960s, helping to found the Chicana/o Studies Department at the school. Later he became an outstanding student counselor at the university.

The Cabrillo State Bank located on South Brand and Hollister changed ownership over the years. It is now part of Citibank which is located on the same Cabrillo State Bank premises. Manuel Flores was also president and director of the Hispanic-chartered Camino Real Savings and Loan Association on Mission and Hollister. There was no information available about the present status of this financial institution. However, Pacific Western Bank currently occupies the Camino Real Savings and Loan Association former building on 400 South San Fernando Mission and Hollister.[28]

Finally, what was unfolding during the decades of the 1950s and 1960s was a sophisticated Mexican consumer who discovered a new strength as his or her purchasing power was being noticed by the profit-oriented white economic elites, and a host of smart Mexican American/Latino business men and women. Businessman Manuel Flores summed it up neatly when he said, "These new businesses were filling a void in the Hispanic community, emphasizing helpful and cheerful personal customer service that appealed to the Mexican/Mexican American clients. As their purchasing power increased, they demanded better service and quality merchandise."[29] Another interesting aspect of their growing purchasing power was less concern about white acceptance. In short, a social and economic shift was occurring in San Fernando and Los Angeles that would fundamentally change the cities' political and social landscape. As Hector Barreto, Sr., founder of the U.S. Hispanic Chamber of Commerce, succinctly put it, "When I came to this country, I was a second-class citizen. I want to make sure my children will be first-class citizens."[30]

Notes

1. The reader may wish to read further about the urbanization of the Chicano in David R. Díaz, *Barrio Urbanism: Chicanos, Planning, and American Cities,* New York: Routledge Publisher, 2005.
2. See Roderick, op. cit., 143-146, 162, 176; and "Valley Generations of the Century," *Daily News*, November 16, 1999.
3. Ibid.
4. *The San Fernando Valley SUN*, op. cit., 56.
5. This information was obtained on August 19, 2009, during a conversation with banker Manuel Flores at James Restaurant in San Fernando.
6. This is in accordance with the information provided by Virginia Barragán on August 13, 2009.
7. The elder Robert Bórquez provided this information to the present writer.
8. This and the following paragraph were drawn from Ofelia Chacón, daughter of Cirilio Cruz Tejeda on July 2, 2009, and Evangelina Pérez and Olivia Casillas on July 16, 2009.
9. John and Olga Menchaca were interviewed by phone on August 14, 2009.
10. These were the actual words of Elvira Orozco on August 14, 2009, as she described her earlier experience in San Fernando.
11. This was the conclusion of Banker Manuel Flores in the interview held on August 19, 2009.
12. Of owner-occupied property, 57.3 percent of the property was considered high for San Fernando for a blue-collar community in the 1950s. This figure is taken from the *1950 U.S. Census of Housing,* Volume 1, *General Characteristics,* Part 2, California. The Bureau of the Census has not been able from 1930 to 1970 to enumerate accurately the Mexican American population of the United States.
13. *The SUN*, op. cit.
14. Carmen Rocha shared this information with the present writer. They were neighbors. He would take her "champurado," her favorite Mexican hot chocolate, when she was bed ridden. Carmen passed away in 2009. For a brief summary background on the life of Richard Valenzuela, see Beverly Menaheln and Richard Valens, *The First Latino Rocker,* Tempe, AZ: Bilingual Press, 1987; and Roderick, op. cit., 143-144.

15. Roderick, op. cit.

16. For a detailed history of the Laborers Union, see Bill Talbitzer, *The Laborers in the West: A History of the Laborers' International Union of North America*, 2nd ed., Sacramento: Pacific Southwest Region, Liuna, AFL-CIO Publishers, 1994.

17. Marisela Torres shared the information on her parent's background on October 9, 2009.

18. Based on the 1950 U.S. Census, San Fernando, the medium school completed was 10.4. The 1950 U.S. census figures did not provided a breakdown of the number of Mexican Americans in town. The city population at that time was 12,922, of which 5,488 were listed as foreign born. See *1950 Census of Population,* volume II, *Characteristics of the Population,* Parts 5 & 6, California.

19. José Pulido provided this information on August 25, 2009.

20. This section has benefited as a result of discussions with Lupita Arrizón and Francisco Arrizón, Jr.

21. For the secret of the "magical powers" of the traditional soup, see the *Los Angeles Times,* November 20, 1999, and the *San Diego Union Tribune,* November 5, 2000.

22. Bill Talbitzer, op. cit. See also Kenneth C. Burt, *The Search for a Civic Voice: California Latino Politics,* Claremont: Regina Books, 2007, 7-52.

23. This section was made possible by the following informed citizens who shared their notes on the background of these businesses: businessman Manuel Flores, former city treasurer Elvira Orozco, Joe C. Govea, Alice Bacon (daughter of Teresa Cruz), Delfina Tresierras Quijada, former councilman and mayor of San Fernando Jess Margarito, businessowner John Martínez of Martínez Auto Shop, the Jaramillo and Sierras family websites, and Vickie Carrillo Norton (granddaughter of Ed and Victoria Lyon) whose insightful knowledge of San Fernando businesses is very interesting. Arturo Chacón who grew up in Kalisher Street provided a personal insight of barrio life at that time.

24. John Martínez was interviewed at his auto mechanic shop on July 24, 2009.

25. *Los Angeles Times* journalist Frank Del Olmos was concerned about the negative impact Zoot Suit fictional characters might have on Chicano youth's mode of behavior. See Magdalena Beltran-Del Olmo and Frank O. Sotomayor, eds., *Frank Del Olmo: Commentaries on His Columns from the Los Angeles Times.* Los Angeles Times Books, 2004, 126-129.

26. Elvira Orozco made this fine point. Initially, she was a volunteer consultant to the Santa Rosa Credit Union.

27. Interview with Manuel Flores.

28. Ibid.

29. Ibid.

30. Quoted in "Latinos Old Guard Passing the Torch," *Los Angeles Times*, September 15, 2009, 6.

CHAPTER 3

Decades of Progressive Citizen Participation

Introduction

The preceding chapters showed that the Mexican American community of San Fernando had roots sunk deeply in the history of San Fernando and had helped to develop the city and the San Fernando Valley agricultural industry. It recognized the family as the center of community life and the main institution for preserving its cultural values. Patriotism was also central to the Mexican American perspective as demonstrated by active participation in combat in times of war, and winning the highest war medals. The veterans returned home with an aura of hope, optimism, and possibilities of new job opportunities and mobility via politics and leadership. They looked ahead to increasing the role of Mexican Americans' civic life. Home ownership and education by Mexican Americans were facilitated by Veteran Administration benefits. During the 1950s, Mexican Americans worked their way to better jobs and business ventures, generating considerable visibility in the white-controlled city.

Chapter III will focus on the Chicano grassroots community activism of the 1960s and 1970s and analyze the beginning of the progressive era of San Fernando. It was a period of significant historical events that paved the path for Chicano empowerment in San Fernando. A case in point: The War on Poverty, federally-funded program, was a meaningful factor in San Fernando and elsewhere in that it created job opportunities for Chicano/Latino and other activists who staffed community organizations designed to improve the community life of residents.[1] These organizations served as training grounds for future Chicano leaders. Many young and older citizens served as board members of organizations acquiring skills in organizing, planning, and administrating programs that assisted communities by providing social needs. They gained knowledge of the city power structure and how public policy was made. Independent of local government control, the federally sponsored organizations teamed up with a host of other self-support groups in San Fernando and Los Angeles such as the Latin American Civic Association (LACA), Mexican American Political Association (MAPA), United Farm Workers Union (UFW), United Auto Workers (UAW), and other groups concerned about the Chicano protracted struggle for a rightful place in American society. This study refutes the generalization that Mexican Americans and Latinos have a lower level of political participation than other groups.

A Summary of a New Era of Increased Political Fight for Social Reform in California

A social crisis confronted the nation in the decade of the 1960s. Racism and xenophobia persisted. Riots and demonstrations swept the country's major cities in 1965.[2] In California, the Chicano movement for civil rights and equal opportunity began in 1966 with the start of the farm workers grape strike against DiGiorgio farms.[3] The strike focused on organizers César Chávez and Dolores Huerta's fight to organize farm workers in Delano, California. It was the first of many other confrontations with the established order. César Chávez who had been active in Los Angeles as general director of the Community Service Organization (CSO) left in 1961 to work with farm workers in Delano. The strikers got sympathetic support in the urban centers of the nation. The working-class city of San Fernando like other Mexican American communities became a center for organizing activities in the Valley. Many of its citizens marched with the strikers, planned fund-raising campaigns for the farm workers, and opened their homes for out-of-town union organizers. They educated their children about the plight of the workers and their families, who made their living working in the field under extreme hardships. It was no accident that San Fernando became a stronghold for farm worker support when many of its citizens had made their life working in the fields.

Chicano students used the power of protest to force decision-makers into action. The youth, a primary engine of change, also criticized the previous generation of Mexican American community leaders for not being sufficiently militant against the status quo. On campus, they walked out of their classes demanding a change in school curriculum that was relevant to their needs: bilingual-bicultural programs, Mexican history and culture classes, Mexican American teachers and counselors, as well as a friendly administrative environment that would welcome their parents to school. Roosevelt and Garfield High Schools were central to the historic 1968 walkouts, followed by a series of student protests throughout Los Angeles. The "walk-outs" of East Los Angeles schools were joined by students from Valley schools, including San Fernando High School led by United Mexican American Students (UMAS) student leaders and teachers. They took to the "walk-out" protest form because that was the only vehicle of participation open to them. Indeed, the students with the support of their parents were an influential power in the Chicano movement particularly in California and Texas. They were the backbone of the 1960s and 1970s organizing political activities for social justice. The young activists vowed not to take a back seat in their demands for better schools, while rightly addressing the school board. Subsequently, their earnest appeals were denied. Change was in the horizon.

The United Mexican American Students' (later named Movimiento Estudientil Chicano de Aztlan, or MECHA) organization had participated in the 1966, 250-mile religious procession, along with about 10,000 other supporters, from Delano to the state capitol in Sacramento, California, publicizing the workers' demand for collective bargaining rights with growers. They followed César Chávez, the prodigy of the Chicano movement, who they believed represented the best in a human being. The organized students also participated in the 1968 Robert Kennedy California primary for U.S. president. A Viva Kennedy headquarters in San Fernando with volunteer-driven Chicano youth was run by San Fernando community activist Ralph Arriola. He was on leave from his job as an organizer for the United Auto Workers in Van Nuys, California. Chicanos suffered their greatest disappointment when Kennedy was assassinated in 1968 in Los Angeles after he had won the California presidential primary with Latino community support.

Demand for Chicano studies that reflect all aspect of the Chicano experience was first introduced to the San Fernando Valley State College (now California State University, Northridge) administration in 1968 by reformed-minded Chicano students on campus and developed by Professor Rodolfo F. Acuña (a.k.a. Rudy Acuña) who became the first chair of the Chicano Studies Department (later changed to Chicana/o Studies Department). Campus students who initially backed Dr. Acuña's negotiation with the administration for the department included from San Fernando Raul Aragón, Jr., Frank Lechuga, Mike Verdugo, and Everto Ruiz who later became a professor at the institution; campus students from Pacoima and other Valley communities were Irene Tovar, Pete Barboza, Jr., Becky Vallejas, and Manuel Jacquez. San Fernando community supporters of the new department included Reyes and Evangelina Pérez, and Valley activists Nellie Parra, Juanita Morales, Guadalupe Ramirez, and Louie García. Nellie Parra was a former United Auto Workers (UAW) union organizer who later attended the Northridge campus where she received a teaching credential in bilingual elementary education. Irene Tovar also served on the Chicano Studies Faculty–Community Committee. San Fernando and Pacoima were the organizational base for community support for the new department. In 1969, San Fernando Valley State College had only 50 Chicano students. By 1996, it had over 3,500. In 2013, Latino student enrollment in California State University, Northridge jumped to 15,000 or 38 percent of the university student enrollment. The Northridge campus Chicano Studies interdisciplinary program attracted talented students and professors and evolved as the nation's finest and most innovative academic experiment and a model for other college ethnic studies programs to emulate.[4] Angelina Tovar of San Fernando was one of the first Chicana students to graduate from the Chicano Studies, Operation Chicano Teacher (OCT), a Ford Foundation program that trained students to teach in barrio schools. First in the family to attend college, many of these students benefited from Affirmative Action and the state Education Opportunity Program (EOP) which provided direct grants to students of working families. Richard Montes was one of the first EOP students from central Los Angeles to attend San Fernando Valley State College in 1969. After graduation, he married a local woman, Aida Casillas, daughter of Juan and Olivia Casillas. Richard and Aida raised their family in San Fernando. Violeta Quintero, a talented local musician, was another EOP student who enrolled in the first Chicano Studies class offered in 1969. Bobby Arias graduated with the first EOP Class of 1972. In August 1969, Professor José Hernández was one of the first professors hired by Dr. Acuña to teach at the Northridge Chicano Studies Department. He had been an instructor at Miami University of Ohio. Other professors hired in the program at that time, included Dr. Carlos Arce, Dr. Rafael Sandoval, Dr. José de Anda, and Professor Gerald Resendez. Professor Jorge Garcia and Dr. Richard Romo were hired in 1970. In 1971, Dr. Francine Hallcom, Dr. Carlos Navarro, Dr. Raul Ruiz, and Professor Everto were added to the department teaching staff.

California State University, Northridge (CSUN) Professor Everto Ruiz and students Ruben Rodríguez and Roberto Bernal started a food cooperative at a place on Kalisher Street, providing its membership fresh fruits and vegetables at affordable prices. Everto Ruiz, music professor at the school, started the first Mariachi music youth programs in the Valley. Over the years many schools formed Mariachi bands and their youth earned popular acclaim throughout the state and nation. Mariachi music is derived from Jalisco, Mexico. Eduardo Palacios founded Immigration Service of Santa Rosa in 1970, offering free immigration service to people seeking legal status in the United States. He was a student of Professor of Chicano Studies Jorge García, who later became dean of CSUN School of Humanities. To date, the Immigration Service of Santa Rosa is the most consistent and most successful immigration service agency in the Valley. It has served as a model for other community self-help organizations offering immigration services to hundreds of people who wish to reside legally in the United States. Its current executive director is former councilman and mayor of San Fernando, Jess Margarito. CSUN Professor of Chicano Studies José Hernández served on the board of directors of the agency for several years. Also, Professor Hernández started the first Mexican youth folklore dance program in the city. Chicano Studies student Virginia Diediker was the co-founder and first dance instructor. Classes in Mexican folklore dance are still offered at Las Palma Park Recreation Center as the program celebrates its 39th anniversary in San Fernando. Chicano Professor José Hernández was also the founding member of various drug and alcohol prevention programs in the Valley. He was a member of the first board of directors of El Proyecto del Barrio, a drug abuse prevention organization which also became a national model for other self-help drug prevention groups. One of the professor's earliest students, Xavier Flores, became a leading expert in alcohol and tobacco abuse prevention programs. Also, for 13 years Professor Hernández and his students provided free income tax service to low-income families at Mary Immaculate Catholic Church in Pacoima. Students Hector Barragán and Ruben Rodríguez were two of the first students who assisted in this project. Hector Barragán graduated with an accountant degree and now owns his own accountant business. Hernández and other Chicano Studies professors gave time and hard work to many other organizations at that time, helping them to organize and in decision-making processes, to incorporate, and in doing ordinary work, as well as being a valuable resource. On some occasions, Professor Hernández represented workers before the state Industrial-Labor Board. He helped workers file grievances for owed employment compensation, preparing the material before the court, and defending the workers before the state presiding judge. In October 1982, he and Professor Rodolfo Acuña joined the Coalition to Save the Van Nuys General Motors plant from closing. The company was planning to shift plant operations to Canada. The coalition of labor, business, educators, religious and community leaders successfully negotiated an agreement with the company executive officer to keep the Van Nuys assembly plant open for 10 years, avoiding a severe economic blow to the Valley until the Los Angeles Redevelopment Agency planned for the economic development of the company property. The coalition used political and economic tactics, mobilizing community support and threatening a boycott of General Motors cars in the Los Angeles area if the company shut down the plant. The Valley at that time would have lost nearly 5,000 jobs, top blue-collar positions in Southern California impacting the lives of auto workers and their families many who lived in San Fernando and immediate areas. At stake were thousands of homes, college educations, and a stable middle-class lifestyle created by decades of hard work. It wasn't just auto workers being affected, but suppliers, teachers, nurses, doctors, bankers, and the like who would also bear the financial pain. A huge shopping center offering a variety of stores now has replaced the historic makers of the Camaro Chevrolet. This was a sign of the times starting when well-paying manufacturing jobs were being exported to other countries and replaced with lesser compensated retail positions.

Making a Difference

There are many more amazing Chicano stories during this period that came out of the Northridge campus. One more needs to be told here. In 1971, Bert Corona, a community, civil rights, and labor leader of California, joined a campus demonstration on educational opportunity programs. Alongside him in the march was a little baby girl being pushed in a stroller taking in all the protest. As the notable leader pointed to her, he said: "I have been fighting for years to make life better for her and future generations." Coincidently, 34 years later that little baby grew up to become one of Bert Corona's attending physicians while he lay seriously ill in a Los Angeles hospital. When the young doctor told the patient this story, as relayed to her by her father, the labor leader reflected for a moment and then he smiled satisfied.[5] Young people today need to know that other people have fought for them to have an equal education, and for the principles which guided them.

The National Chicano Moratorium

The most violent confrontation against the Chicano community occurred on August 29, 1970. During the National Chicano Moratorium against the War on Vietnam as 30,000 or more participated in a peaceful demonstration against the war, hundreds of people were hurt and some jailed as the police disrupted the families and children gathered to listen to speakers. Ruben Salazar, news director of Los Angeles television station KMEX, Channel 34 and former columnist for the *Los Angeles Times,* who was covering the event, was killed by a Los Angeles county sheriff's deputy as the reporter sat inside the Silver Dollar Café. Nothing came out of the investigation of the unruly police crashers of the Chicano Moratorium's peaceful forum. Salazar's friends and other community activists suspected foul play by the Los Angeles County Sheriff's deputies. Salazar had been critical of local police in his *Los Angeles Times* columns and radio reports. California State University, Northridge Professor Raul Ruiz watched as he took pictures of the deputies firing tear-gas canisters through the restaurant's front door. He was prevented from entering the building after the display of police fire power. Salazar was found dead later at the bar of the restaurant. A final Sheriff Department report released in 2011 concluded that the deputies had employed poor tactics and made mistakes that resulted in the reporter's death. To this date, Professor Ruiz is not convinced that Salazar was killed by a deputy tear-gas projectile. Chicana activist Irene Tovar was a member of the National Chicano Moratorium Committee representing the Valley. Some of the principal leaders of the National Chicano Moratorium Committee were ostracized by government authorities and had to appeal to the courts for redress.[6]

The decade of the 1960s moved Mexican and Latino people into the spotlight of American politics. Phil Soto, a former La Puente city councilman, was elected to the state legislature in 1962, becoming one of the first Mexican Americans elected to the California governing body in this century. Latino voters came out in great numbers in 1964 voting for Edmund G. "Jerry" Brown for governor of California. Consequently, many talented Latino men and women were appointed to major state positions of responsibility. The increased civic and political activities provided them with a greater optimism that change would come to their community soon. They realized that politics was a tedious and hard-headed process that required persistent citizen involvement; hence, progress was to be made one step at a time. To them, time was their valuable resource. In 1967, Dr. Julian Nava was elected to the Los Angeles School Board. In 1980, President Jimmy Carter appointed him U.S. ambassador to Mexico. Raised in the barrio, he went on to earn a doctorate degree at Harvard University and taught history at San Fernando Valley State College (now California State University). By the 1972 presidential elections, the Mexican American community was a stronger political force in California. Local communities were electing Mexican Americans as mayors and city council members throughout the state, including Monterey Park, Montebello, La Puente, and Norwalk in Los Angeles County; Carpenteria, Coachella, Colton, and Riverside in Southern California; and Dinuba, Delano, and Parlier in the Central Valley. Ruben S. Ayala was San Bernardino county supervisor. Major groups such as the United Farm Workers, the Mexican American Political Association, Raza Unida Party, the G.I. Forum, Community Service Organization (CSO), and United Auto Workers union with a strong Mexican American membership emerged as main actors in the California political scene increasing the role of Mexican Americans in civic life. In Los Angeles, the Raza Unida Party, which consisted mostly of MECHA activists, was dissatisfied with the two-party system. It sponsored young radicals such as Professor Raul Ruiz to run against Chicano Democrat liberals for public office. *El POPO* (short for Popocatepeti Mexican volcano) *MECHA,* the campus newspaper edited by Professor Raul Ruiz of California State University, Northridge, took pot shots at Chicano liberals, kindling the fire to address issues critical to the Chicano/Latino community.[7]

Profesor José Hernández on the picket line, Air Traffic Controllers Strike, LAX Aug. 10, 1981

The City of San Fernando

In San Fernando the city population grew from 12,922 in 1950 to 16,093 in 1960, an increase of 24.5 percent. According to the 1960 census conducted by the U.S. Bureau of the Census, 5,333 residents were foreign born. Of this, 75.5 percent came from Mexico and spoke Spanish at home. The medium income of all families in San Fernando was $6,613, below the medium income of Los Angeles County families. Of those 18 years or older, 64 percent did not complete four years of high school education.[8] Although in this census there wasn't a breakdown on the general characteristics of minority language groups, it was clearly evident to local educators and administrators that children of newer immigrants were not succeeding in school. Their parents, who also lacked adequate educational levels, were concentrated in low-paying jobs, which in turn led to high poverty levels. They were unable to help with their children's homework. The academic achievement gap was evident when Mexican American children first entered school and continued through the primary grades. They were left to make their way in the public schools, and more likely placed in a nonacademic schedule than were other students.

The Emergence of the Latin American Civic Association and Other Groups

Concerned about the poor state of education and related problems in their community, a small group of middle-class Chicano educators and community leaders—specifically, Reseda High School chair of foreign languages Edward Moreno, as well as Reseda High School historian Dr. Rodolfo Acuña and linguistic teacher Dr. Rafael Sandoval, and State Board of Education member Dr. Miguel Montes—banded together in 1963 and formed the Latin American Civic Association to address issues that determined the future of their community. As Mexican Americans achieved social mobility, they sought to improve the lives of those left behind. As labor leader César Chávez said thoughtfully: "We cannot seek achievement for ourselves and forget about programs and prosperity for our community."[9] Dr. Montes was a San Fernando dentist and his office was located at 501 South Brand. The following also played an important role in the founding of the self-help organization known as LACA: Rose Hernández, Anne González, Antonia Tejada, Pete and Carmen Barraza, Joe and Connie Barboza, and Louie Flores. Rose Hernández served as LACA secretary. Anne González taught pre-school and Antonia Tejada was a successful Valley realtor. Pete Barraza was a general contractor and his wife Carmen held the position of secretary for the Los Angeles Unified School District. Joe Barbosa was a general contractor while his wife Connie, an activist on women's issues, also served as an auxiliary pre-school member. Louie Flores worked for the state unemployment office, now state human resource department. At their first press conference, speaker Richard Tafoya, a former representative of Los Angeles, Mayor Samuel Yorty, spoke on the need for "building up the image of betterment of the Latin American in a quiet, constructive way, improving educational, political, social and economic status of the Latin American and focusing attention on the rights of every Latin American to share in the growth and equal opportunities that exist in this country."[10] Antonia Tejada, president of the Latin American Civic Association, reported on the need for adequate housing for poor families who were living in crowded conditions. Eduardo Quevedo, another invited speaker and kingpin of Chicano politics in California, spoke on the various state legislature matters. They all saw the need for LACA leaders to work in the education field to combat school dropouts and school failures.

LACA leaders felt that education was the key factor in improving the quality of life in poor communities. They challenged the school district to no avail for its indifference to better train the Chicano child. Consequently, they turned to greater political involvement. For only through political participation did they hope to be heard. It was their belief that if they had the right people in public office, they could better shape educational policy and all other issues. Thus, political involvement superseded education. Impressed by LACA's enthusiasm about helping people, Irene Tovar, a teenaged Valley Community College student, joined the self-help community organization. She was eager to help her communities of San Fernando and Pacoima. She directed the organization's voter registration project as her volunteers registered 1,000 new voters in the North East Valley. This was by far the most ambitious voter registration project undertaken by an organization in the Valley. Also, the newly registered voters helped James Gorman win reelection in a highly contested campaign for the seat of the 28th Congressional District. Now the community leaders were ready to talk about education with the congressman.

Dr. Miguel Montes, Edward Moreno, Louie Flores, and Jim González (an instructor at Glendale Community College) met with Dr. Rudy Acuña at his house where they worked on a proposal for federal funding of a Head Start program in San Fernando. A series of position papers by the area's most respected Chicano scholars provided the intellectual impetus as the basis for the proposal. The anti-poverty regional agency in Los Angeles was consulted for advice before the proposal was forwarded to the Department of Health and Human Services in Washington. Operation Head Start, the center piece of the War on Poverty, was one of many government-sponsored anti-poverty programs of the Economic Opportunity Act of 1964, designed to intervene in the poverty cycles of poor families. Its goal was to expose children of poor families to a variety of pre-school literacy activities. The objective here was to raise the children's low average pre-school literary rates so they could compete in the primary grades with their peers of more affluent households.[11] The LACA program proposal mirrored the Little School of the 400, a pre-school curriculum developed in 1959 by the League of United Mexican American Citizens (LULAC) of Texas. The "escuelita" as it was called in Texas taught Spanish-speaking children a working knowledge of 400 English words before they entered the first grade so they could complete the first grade successfully.[12]

Finally the LACA pre-school proposal was completed in 1964. Using his personal funds, Dr. Miguel Montes took the papers to Washington for funding. When he made contact with several Department of Education officials about his proposal, he was surprised to find that the officials had no knowledge of poverty in San Fernando Valley since they considered the region a middle-class white suburb of Los Angeles. The proposal was delayed. It was finally approved after U.S. Congressman James Gorman intervened on behalf of San Fernando children. Ethel Norvid, who was in charge of the congressman's Van Nuys office, was also very helpful in accommodating the group's community improvement efforts. LACA Head Start began operation in 1965 at its first classroom rented at Las Palmas Park Recreation building. The classroom was full of anxious students. Head Start also offered medical, dental, mental health, and nutritional services. Parent involvement was required through both volunteer participation and employment as Head Start staff. According to LACA co-founder Ed Moreno, San Fernando Head Start, designed and administered by Chicanos, was by far the most ambitious educational project undertaken in Southern California.

In 1966, LACA leaders won another social victory; that is, it received federal funds for a program called Joint Venture located in San Fernando. Many community organizations developed out of this program including San Fernando Community Improvement Council (CIC). CIC raised thousands of dollars through the sale of fireworks and other venues to assist needy college students with their school fees and books. It also took pride in improving declining neighborhoods. Following Saul Alinsky's method of community organizing, the organization succeeded in removing a cattle slaughterhouse from a residential neighborhood bordering San Fernando.[13] After five unsuccessful years of fighting Los Angeles City Council to remove the city's last slaughterhouse from their backyards, the community made up chiefly of lower income working Mexican American homeowners went to court. In October 19, 1969, a county superior court ruled in favor of removing the cattle slaughterhouse from the residential area. The plant owned by Globe Packing Company had been operating on that location since 1915. Since then a neighborhood grew around the plant. About 500 cattle were being killed and butchered every day. Residents complained constantly to the authorities about the bad smell and about the heavy traffic of speeding truckloads of animals and their drippings on Chamberlain Street leading to the plant. The victory to remove the slaughterhouse was a clear example of how low-income citizens, when mobilized, can influence decisions that matter to them. CIC and its leaders were ahead of their time.[14] In the 1960s, the concept of environmental justice was not fully developed. The concept of environmental justice now concludes that minority and low-income communities deserve to have the same consideration as everyone else when decisions impacting the environment and public health are made.[15] Pioneer community activist and former United Auto Worker union organizer Nellie Parra directed the initial development of the group. She later became an elementary school bilingual teacher. Her parents came to Arizona in 1915 from Sonora, Mexico.

El Proyecto del Barrio primarily worked with volunteers who took an interest to find a cure for the effects of dangerous drugs. El Proyecto won national recognition as an innovative self-help drug abuse program that had successfully aided adults. The project now serves as a multipurpose social center in the Valley. Roberto Castro, an ex-convict, was the organization's first executive director. He laid the foundation for the extraordinary success of preventing drug abuse in the Mexican American and black communities. Also, Joint Venture was one of the organizers of Parents-Advisory Council conferences in the Valley and on school campuses—the first in the nation. Parents-Advisory Councils advanced the concept of neighborhood schools. Thousands of adults attended and participated in workshops, representing numerous Valley communities.

LACA served as an umbrella for the Northeast Valley Health Corporation (NEVHC), a medical unit covering the health needs of indigenous people of the area. NEVHC has evolved into a major provider of health services to poor people, including the undocumented. Robert Villafaña at the age of 23 was the first chairperson of the organization's board of directors, the youngest head of a large—non-profit agency in the Valley.[16]

Volunteers in Service to America (VISTA), another anti-poverty domestic program, placed citizens with community-based organizations to work towards the empowerment of the poor, and Upward Bound, which assisted students from poor households enter college, were administered by LACA staff. In San Fernando there were other federally-funded programs charged with helping the poor become self-sufficient, including programs centered on the growth and development of youth leadership. The Unity Workshop conducted seminars for both Mexican Americans and Blacks on critical issues to them as well as classes on civic awareness and community responsibility. It also served in social gatherings. The program director, Professor Warren Furamoto, was a fine role model for youth like Everto Ruiz, Jesus Lechuga, Grace and Delia Pérez, daughters of Reyes and Evangelina Pérez—just to name four. LACA provided space, materials, buses for field trips, and other amenities for groups who wished to use LACA resources.

The original staff of LACA consisted of Louie García as executive director. Suad Cano, a respected Iraqi American educator, was the assistant administrator. Her husband Gonzalo Cano who worked for the U.S. Department of Justice was a valuable resource to LACA innovators. The other staff members were consumer advocate Horacio Martínez, businessman Gerardo Martínez, American Indian Ed Olivas, and Tatavian Indian Chief Little Bear Rudy Ortega. Antonio Flores (Tony) became a member of LACA in 1965. He was a longtime local activist, a math and shop teacher at San Fernando Junior High School, and an active member of the local Mexican American Political Association. Other contributors to LACA were Nellie Parra, Mary Martínez, Ernie Cortéz, and East Los Angeles College President Ed Avila.

LACA progressive leaders and their volunteers took on political issues such as Proposition 14, a realtor-sponsored referendum that discriminated against minorities in the housing market. They joined Mexican Americans, Blacks and other progressive groups in defeating the 1964 proposition. In 1967, they campaigned and helped

Dr. Julian Nava win a seat in the Los Angeles Board of Education.[17] He was the first Mexican American elected to that position in Los Angeles. They continued to conduct voter registration in Latino neighborhoods and successfully assisted Edmund G. "Jerry" Brown to become governor of California in 1974. In 1975, the governor appointed LACA volunteer Irene Tovar to the State Personnel Board which supervised the civil service component of government. In 1981, she was appointed to the Public Employment Relations Board, a quasi-judicial agency that mediated disputes. They successfully lobbied U.S. Congressman James Gorman to appoint Gil Manriquez to the position of postmaster of San Fernando Post Office. LACA Women Auxiliary offered scholarships to Latinas who sought a college education. They supported César Chávez's union grape boycott and provided busses loaded with people to go to Sacramento to lobby for farm workers to demand collective bargaining. The Head Start program expanded to other communities in Pacoima, Van Nuys, and Panorama City. Additionally, a housing project was constructed with federal funds for Valley low-income families. For the first time of its existence, the Latin American Civic Association suffered from an internal discord in 1993. Irene Tovar, a board member of LACA during its inception, was appointed executive director of the organization replacing Ralph Arriola, the previous executive director, amid allegations of mismanagement and noncompliance of the group's policy and procedures. As stated by longtime community leader Jess Margarito, Ralph was pressured by the Los Angeles County Office of Education (LACOE) to resign. LACOE oversees federally funded Head Start projects in Los Angeles. Ralph Arriola resigned because the issue was impacting his ability to manage the non-profit corporation programs.[18]

The Emergence of the Mexican American Political Association (MAPA) and the San Fernando Democratic Club in San Fernando

The statewide flutter of Chicano political progress in the mid-1960s inspired San Fernando Hispanic businessmen to challenge the guardians of the unpopular status quo when a chapter of the Mexican American Political Association joined by the San Fernando Democratic Club activists began to organize. Sam Córdova, the Hispanic transplant from New Mexico, provided invaluable guidance helping to empower Mexican Americans in San Fernando, and later in Los Angeles.[19] The politically active members felt a deep grievance about being left out of the West Valley Democratic Party hierarchy. They also criticized the Democratic Party for being insufficiently supportive of Hispanic issues. Particularly, they were disappointed with Assemblyman David Negri who had won the 41st Assembly District seat with a hard-fought campaign led by MAPA and Democratic Club volunteers. While in office Assemblyman

David Negri, a Sephardic Jewish attorney from San Fernando, became more interested in West Valley politics than with the needs of the increasingly Latino residents of his Northeast Valley district. Consequently, Sam Córdova and Bill García led their group in a campaign against his reelection to a second term in the Assembly. They threw their weight successfully in support of Republican Hank Arklin to represent the 41st Assembly District. In 1970, MAPA and Democratic Club members helped James Keysor, a liberal Democrat, to replace Assemblyman Hank Arklin in the state legislature. Assemblyman James Keysor appointed Ralph Arriola of San Fernando as administrative assistant of his office.

In 1971, Assemblyman James Keysor pushed successfully in Sacramento for the construction of Mission College. San Fernando MAPA and San Fernando Democratic Club assisted by the *San Fernando SUN* newspaper, San Fernando Chamber of Commerce, as well as the Sylmar Democratic Club, Sylmar Chamber of Commerce, and other college advocacy groups from Sylmar had lobbied the state legislature for a much needed community college in the East and Northeast Valley. After the state legislature approved funding for the new school, a controversy ensued over the location of the new campus. Four prominently West Valley Jewish leaders split over the issue of where the college should be built. State Assemblyman Howard Berman and his political partner Henry Waxman with strong connections with the Valley Democratic Party insisted that the new college be built on the west end of the Valley where area students would have easy access to higher education although the West Valley already had a major four-year university, and two additional community colleges in close proximity. Nevertheless, MAPA's coalition to bring a community college to the Northeast Valley had the support of West Valley Jewish businessman Richard Katz, a friend of San Fernando, who later was elected to Northeast Valley 41st Assembly District. More importantly, San Fernando and Sylmar received the school support of Monroe Richman, president of Los Angeles Community College District Trustees. Dr. Richman got the community college district to sell a 10-acre district-owned land in Northridge and used the land revenues as seed money for the new campus on Hubbard Street and Eldridge Avenue, by the beautiful San Gabriel Mountains. Indeed, it pays to have friends in positions of power. Without political power, Latinos like any other contending special interest group, could not compete for resources vital to their existence. Political power, argued the Chicano political advocates, is the key to community improvement. This is the theme that is pivotal to the study of San Fernando.

Guadalupe Ramirez, grandmother and active member of the League of United Latin American Citizens (LULAC), was also a major driving force behind the efforts to bring higher education to the Northeast Valley where the Latino population more than tripled in the 1970s. Through her persistence the college trustees agreed to choose

Sylmar as the Mission College site. Educator Andrés Torres and community leader Roberto Villafaña of San Fernando, and many more, assisted Mrs. Guadalupe Ramirez in getting community support for the school. Professor Andrés Torres was one of the first professors hired to teach in the new institution. He was a speech professor. Professor Art Hernández was appointed acting president and was credited for finding the permanent site of the main campus in Sylmar. In the beginning, classes were scattered throughout San Fernando and Pacoima until classroom buildings were constructed in the new grounds of the school. The Guadalupe Ramirez Child Development Building now serves as an outward sign of the unwearied efforts of an elderly lady to bring first-class college education to the blue-collar communities of East and Northeast Valley. She is affectionately known as the mother of Mission College. Other steadfast supporters of Mission College included Thelma Barrios, editor and publisher of the *San Fernando SUN*, and writer Betty Franklin who both played a crucial role in promoting the college in their local paper.

On February 9, 1971, the Sylmar-San Fernando area was struck with a major earthquake. It was a day people will not forget. The Sylmar-San Fernando earthquake struck early in the morning throwing people in the air from their beds. Building walls fell out and power lines came down flashing with fire. Appliances tipped down and some people were pinned down from falling furniture. The Los Angeles County Olive View Hospital in Sylmar was destroyed. The loss of a first-rated county hospital in the Northeast Valley deprived working-class families of much needed health care. Further, several patients died as a result of the magnitude 6.5 tremor. Los Angeles County Supervisor Baxter Ward adamantly opposed community request that the hospital be rebuilt. Notwithstanding, the San Fernando Mexican American Political Association activists together with the San Fernando Democratic Club and a coalition of advocacy groups for community improvement played an important role in restoring Olive View Hospital. First, they had to get rid of Supervisor Baxter Ward.[20] They mounted a vigorous campaign to oust Mr. Ward from office and succeeded to elect Michael Antonovich as the new supervisor representing the northern San Fernando Valley. In 1978, Mapistas Sam Córdova, also Valley district director of the League of United Latin American Citizens, and Bill García who was appointed to supervisor administrative staff, traveled to Washington on their own expense and lobbied U.S. Congressman Jim Gorman for a $40 million startup funding for the new hospital. With federal and county funds Los Angeles County Olive View Hospital was rebuilt providing first-class medical services in the region.

As stated earlier, Mexican Americans and Latinos attached great importance to citizen participation. The dedication and energy that they invested made their communities better for children to play, learn, and grow as good citizens. Furthermore, the decades of community activism marked a crucial milestone in the Mexican American drive for an identity and visibility considered essential for community empowerment.

Notes

1. For a good assessment of the War on Poverty programs, the reader can read Marshal Kaplan and Peggy L. Cuciti, *The Great Society and Its Legacy: Twenty Years of U.S. Social Policy,* Chapel Hill: Duke University Press, 1986; and Lyndon B. Johnson, *My Hope for America,* New York: Random House, 1964.

2. For a detailed assessment of these tumultuous years, see Joseph Boskin, *Urban Racial Violence in the Twentieth Century,* Beverly Hills: Glencoe Press, 1969.

3. A well-documented account of a new era of California Chicano political activism in the 1960s, plus a brief review of the birth of California Latino politics are found in Kenneth C. Burt, *The Search for a Civic Voice: California Latino Politics*, op. cit. Also, a popular account of the historical events described in this section of Chapter III is found in a series of episodes produced by the National Latino Communication Center and Galan Productions, Inc. in association with KCET-Los Angeles, 1966. These VHS videocassettes are recommended as follows: episode l: *Quest for a Homeland*, episode 2: *The Struggle in the Fields*, episode 3: *Taking Back the Schools*, and episode 4: *Fighting for Political Power*.

4. See Rodolfo F. Acuña, *Anything But Mexicans*, op. cit., 311. See also Rodolfo F. Acuña, *The Making of Chicana(o) Studies,* New Brunswick: Rutgers University Press, 2011.

5. The baby, Moira O'Brien Hernández, daughter of Carol and Professor of Chicana/o Studies José Hernández, graduated from Stanford University, and University of Southern California (USC) where she received a degree in internal medicine. Moira's younger sister Anne also graduated from Stanford University, and University of Illinois where she received a degree in veterinary medicine.

6. The following is a partial list of students, teachers, and community leaders from San Fernando and Valley communities who attended the historic National Chicano Moratorium on August 29, 1970: Ignacio Gómez, Sergio and Diane Velarde Hernández, José A. Hernández, David Jiménez, Paul Luna, Art Moreno, Charlie Pérez, Pat Reynosa, María Reza, Olivia Ruiz Robledo, Everto Ruiz, Gilbert Salazar, Sylvia Suárez, Irene Tovar, Ramona Tovar, and Miguel Verdugo.

7. These and other Chicano advocacy groups were cited as major Chicano political players in California during the period under discussion in *The Search for a Civic Voice,* by Kenneth C. Burt, op. cit.

8. Data of this sort were found in the U.S. Department of Commerce, *Bureau of the 1960 Census,* volume 1, *Characteristics of the Population,* Part 6, California.

9. This section was made possible with the assistance of LACA co-founder and scholar Edward Moreno.

10. Quoted in "Latin Americans Unite to Improve Standards," *The Valley News and Valley Green Sheet*, November 28, 1963.

11. See Marshal Kaplan and Peggy L. Cuciti, *The Great Society and Its Legacy*, op. cit., and Lyndon B. Johnson, *My Hope for America*, op. cit. Refer to Internet Explorer, search *Operation Head Start*.

12. For a good appraisal of the Texas Spanish-speaking Little School of the 400 research, see Benjamin Márquez, *The Evolution of a Mexican American Political Organization LULAC*, Austin: University of Texas Press, 1993, 51-52. For other barriers to Chicano education, see Barbara Schneider, et al., "Barriers to Educational Opportunities for Hispanics in the United States," in Martha Tienda and Faith Mitchell, eds., *Hispanics and the Future of America*, Washington, D.C.: National Academies Press, 1990, 179-227.

13. Saul Alinsky held that mass organization be built on issues of prime importance to the membership and on those that were easily obtainable. Further, he believed that an organized community must see some tangible evidence of success for its efforts before mounting another battle. See Saul Alinsky, *Reveille for Radicals*, New York: Vintage, 1969.

14. Other CIC members who assisted Nellie Parra in the removal of the cattle slaughterhouse from the Chamberlain Street neighborhood included her sister, Mary Martínez, Ralph Arriola, Everto Ruiz, and José A. Hernández, to name a few.

15. "Environment justice is the fair treatment and meaningful involvement of all people regardless of race, color, national origin, or income with respect to the development, implementation, and enforcement of environmental law, regulations, and policies," United States Environmental Protection Agency.

16. Professor Everto Ruiz and Irene Tovar contributed to this section.

17. Burt, op. cit., 239.

18. This statement was made by Jess Margarito and LACA co-founder Edward Moreno on January 19, 2010.

19. The information of this paragraph and the following were suggested by Sam Córdova when he was asked to review Chapter III for his comments. The reader also is referred to Yvette Cabrera, "Latinos Forced to Walk a Long, Difficult Road to Gain Equality," *Daily News*, September 15, 1977, 3.

20. A partial list of MAPA and Democratic Club membership is provided in Chapter IV Notes #5.

CHAPTER 4

The Search for a Civic Voice in San Fernando

To better understand Mexican American efforts at seeking representation in local government, a storied past of a long, hard journey of political participation is presented in this chapter. In 1950, the San Fernando white-run government was still closed to Mexican American and Latino citizens. That position changed (at least for a while) when Alberto Padilla, a businessman and a folk hero to the parish of Santa Rosa Church, was elected to the San Fernando City Council in 1950 offering Mexican Americans the first shot at political representation in the city. Mr. Padilla was able to expand the grounds of Las Palmas Park and its recreational activities for the area youngsters. Additionally, he appointed several Mexican Americans to commissions, a milestone in San Fernando. Nonetheless, his political career did not last long. The steady, restrained, and gentle councilman ruffled some feathers when he criticized the chief of police for not correcting his officers for harassing law-bidding citizens of the south side of town. Police abuse was fashionable at that time. Councilman Padilla explained to his colleagues and to the public that mutual trust between police and the Mexican American community was the key to successful crime prevention in the city. "He was a straight arrow fighter for the victims of police misconduct," said Jess Margarito, executive director of Immigration Services of Santa Rosa, Inc. He continued, "Councilman Alberto Padilla really took that position to heart causing the loss of his Council seat."[1] The criticism of the chief did not bode well nor did calling for change in the attitude of police officers toward Mexican Americans. The conservative voters who controlled political life in San Fernando rounded enough signatures to recall him in 1951, along with colleagues council members Charles A. Schofield and Marion F. Smith. A local newspaper editorial made a strong point that Chicano political activist José Aranda backed Smith, Schofield, and Padilla. The editorial also stated that José Aranda, president of a civic betterment league together with Lee Ward, Sam Richardson, Gilbert Dodson, Robert Martínez, and John Anderson had signed an official notice of intention to recall Herb Martin "…one of the city's finest city councilman."[2] Alberto Padilla was the first Chicano elected to the San Fernando City Council and the first of his community to be recalled from public office.

In 1958, voters elected David Calderon to the city council apparently feeling obliged to have a Mexican American representative to their liking on the council. Calderon, unlike Padilla, was less threatening, more like a guy the white economic and social elites would like to have over for dinner.[3] He spoke good English and socialized with well-off white merchants functioning fully in the economic and political life of the city. He was not the bristled type of person to challenge the old guard position. Unlike Padilla, he was Mexican in name only, for he seldom identified with the city Mexican population. There is no knowledge that he tried to represent the views of Mexican Americans in the city council though he appeared with Latin American Civic Association members in a picture of the *Valley News and Valley Green Sheet* in a November 28, 1963, press conference.[4]

The politically active San Fernando Mexican American Political Association (MAPA) and San Fernando Democratic Club ran Manuel Flores for a seat in the 1966 city council elections.[5] Manuel Flores was a key member of the conservative Hispanic middle-class MAPA organization of San Fernando. He was an ideal candidate to run a smart campaign in the city controlled by commerce and a Republican-oriented local government. He was a former Lockheed aircraft engineer and a successful banker in San Fernando. His volunteers went door-to-door recruiting new voters and creating a new presence in the heavily white precinct on the north side. Further, they asked Mexican American voters to vote for only one in a contest for three on council vacancies. To vote for three would cancel the vote of their choice. The strategy worked. Businessman Manuel Flores won a seat in the selective city council in 1966.[6] On "Election Night" when election results were being posted in city hall council chambers, there were two factions, specifically jovial MAPA and Democratic Club sympathizers, and a undercurrent resentment toward Manuel Flores.[7] The council gadflies were there, too. Councilman Manuel Flores learned quickly that winning an election and governing were two different challenges. These are distinct challenges in American politics. As a council member, he couldn't get a second from his colleagues for almost anything. He went to city hall to do great things for the community. What he found was that government was a slow, sticky process. The guarded council missed out on his expansive expertise in engineering and business—a loss to the residents of San Fernando. His greatest accomplishment, however, was to get influential Chicano businessman Joe Aranda to a city commission, a big political development in the 1960s. Manuel Flores served only one term in office. He said that he wanted to spend more time with his wife Sally and his businesses. He stayed involved in community volunteer work, particularly with the Santa Rosa Catholic Church Scholarship Committee. Subsequently, he joined the Republican Party. As he put it, "I didn't leave the Democratic Party, the party left me."[8]

La Raza Unida Party in San Fernando

In 1972 a new political party, La Raza Unida Party, began to be active in San Fernando supported mainly by California State University, Northridge (CSUN) MECHA students and professors.[9] The third party accused the San Fernando Valley Democratic Party of often ignoring or defining the needs of the Mexican/Latino communities. La Raza Unida Party stood for a broad social vision of equity and justice such as community empowerment, district elections, bilingual/bicultural education, affordable housing, neighborhood improvement, and public safety. It also advanced Mexican cultural values as family solidarity, cultural pride, honesty, and service to others. It supported Jess Margarito and Richard Corona as candidates in the 1972 San Fernando City Council election. The young Chicano candidates for city council office had sound family upbringings and strong community ties. They were proud of their city and hoped to bring a new voice to government. However, their candidacies provoked a great reaction from voters of the north side of the city. Prior to the election, La Raza Unida Party had conducted an extensive voter registration drive. The city clerk issued a statement concerning alleged voter registration irregularities, followed by a press release issued by the incumbent mayor stating that the activists were attempting to gain entry to "our houses of government and create chaos in our orderly governmental processes."[10] The mayor was referring to La Raza Unida Party students who were conducting the voter registration drive. The idealist young candidates lost the election. They were vastly outvoted as white voters stormed the voting booths to protect their government. The election loss, however, did not discourage Raza Unida Party rank and file for Andrés Torres, a speech professor at a local college ran for city council in 1976 under the banner of La Raza Unida Party. The party employed a new strategy the old-fashioned way; to wit, it submitted only one candidate. The politically engaged students registered new voters and went door-to-door telling voters to vote for only one. There were three vacancies on the ballot. French politician and historian Alexis de Tocqueville underscored the importance of civic participation in America as far as the early 19th century when he wrote: "It is not possible to achieve any social good without people involvement."[11]

Los Angeles Police and Social Change

The 1976 city election has an interesting story that needs to be told. The president of the La Raza Unida Party chapter in San Fernando, José Ramirez, was an undercover agent of the Los Angeles Police Department disguised as a Chicano activist trying to help the Mexican American community achieve representation in the city. MAPA leaders and volunteers as well as the candidate were not aware that the police officer was covertly placed there to spy on MECHA activities and to undermine MAPA's efforts to duly elect Professor Andrés Torres to office. The police officer purposely failed to get out the vote on precinct 16. The Mexican American precinct was the largest in the south side and José Ramirez was in charge of assigning volunteers to get out the vote on that area on the day of the election. Instead, he threw a party all day for the volunteers, providing beer and drugs.[12] Dr. Rodolfo F. Acuña in his perceptive discussion of this problem in his book *Anything But Mexican* wrote:

> Throughout the 1970s and 1980s police authorities spied on community organizations, attempting to frustrate efforts for social change. As a result in 1978 the American Civil Liberties Union filed The Committee Against Police Abuse v. Los Angeles Police Department on behalf of 141 plaintiffs, including individuals and groups. The legal discovery process revealed extensive police spying. In one case, a police officer lived with a plaintiff for seven years and had a child with her so as to spy on her friends. Surveillance of Left groups such as the California State University, Northridge chapter of the Movimiento Estudiantil Chicano de Aztlan (MECHA) and the Chicano Studies Department at that institution was common. At least two LAPD officers, Augie Moreno and José Ramirez, infiltrated MECHA and took Chicano Studies classes. The Police Department's Intelligence Division (PDID) even turned over files on individuals to the Western Goals Foundation, an ultra-right wing group.[13]

It was difficult to break down the entrenched mindset of the police hierarchy who did this. It considered itself "an autonomous police force" at that time and in subsequent years.

Los Angeles settled out of court to cut its losses, paying out millions of dollars to the litigants. Furthermore, if the case would have gone to a jury, officials of the cities and institutions that cooperated with the Los Angeles Police Department spy network would have been embarrassed and would probably also have had to pay large sums of taxpayer funds. The LAPD's covert criminal activities in Northridge and San Fernando also disgraced the most cherished American Credo and strength of America, that anyone can grow up to be a good citizen and run for public office.

The Raza Unida Party candidate loss at the polls in 1976 did not end with a somber note. Still, it was sobering to the present writer to observe that the students and teachers acted responsibly at that time when they learned about the travesty of justice in San Fernando, and about their bad experience in a decaying order in Southern California. To them, the campaign to elect a responsible person to represent their views in government was far from over. La Raza Unida Party had a short life in San Fernando and elsewhere, but it inspired a broad generation of Chicano youths to get involved in politics. It created a new brand of social commitment for Chicano leaders to emulate, and pioneered voter registration drives that eventually led to the election of a large number of Chicanos and Latinos to public office. The Mexican American Political Association continues as a viable organization serving the Latino communities of San Fernando and North East Valley. The membership of the local chapter is now composed of progressive followers and is independent of the state MAPA organizational apparatus.

San Fernando Elect the First Mexican American City Treasurer

In 1972, Elvira Orozco was elected San Fernando city treasurer, the first Chicana elected to public office in Southern California. Fiscal conservative Orozco was first employed in 1960 as deputy city treasurer. In 1970 she was appointed acting city treasurer when then city treasurer Leona Paine resigned after she got married and moved.[14] Elvira Orozco continued to serve as a public servant of San Fernando continuously for over 43 years until she retired in 2005. She remains engaged in community activity assisting church and non-profit organizations with financial advice. She is co-founder of the San Fernando Museum of Art and History. Historic preservation is now her mainstay.

Population Replacement Modus Operandi

The 1970 U.S. Census revealed that there were 16,521 people residing in San Fernando, a 3 percent increase of the previous census count of 16,093. The census included in this report 8,104 persons with Spanish surnames, about 50 percent of the city's population.[15] The short increment of this census indicated that the in-migration of new residents to San Fernando had stabilized as second and third generations of Mexican Americans/Latinos reached a notch higher in social and economic standing and moved to more spacious Valley houses in Mission Hills, Granada Hills, Northridge, and Chatsworth communities. The destructive 1971 Sylmar-San Fernando earthquake hastened their departure. A process of population replacement was also going on as white retirees fled the city to their retirement destination, leaving their houses to newcomers to the city. The loss of San Fernando natives was replenished by working-class families from the inner city of Los Angeles and other corners of Los Angeles County seeking a slower pace and new job opportunities in construction, manufacturing, auto repair, and related occupations in the prosperous Valley economy. Many found employment in craftsmanship, clerical positions, health, and service industries. Very few were in professional, technical, and kindred positions. There were no teachers living in San Fernando during the census period.[16]

The population replacement in San Fernando in the decade of the 1970s is an interesting phenomenon to observe, and one that has been occurring throughout the nation's history—a racial, ethnic, or social class community replaced by another group or entity. Sociologists Ernest Burgess and Robert Park of the University of Chicago observed as far back as 1924 in a study of Chicago that during periods of rapid urban growth, the core city expanded outward creating separate functional zones representing business, manufacturing, and poor workmen's homes.[17] The zone of better residences, essentially the best place, attracted middle-class families. This zone consisted of large single-family houses, ample parking space, children's playgrounds, and good schools. Quality apartment buildings were allowed. Finally, the commuter zone functioned as upper-class workers' "dormitories," mostly of who commuted to work by public transit or car. These separate racial and social class communities became increasingly controversial during the nation's civil rights issues on housing and school segregation in the 1950s and 1960s. The model (theory) developed by Burgess and Park explaining the spatial organization of urban areas and distribution of social groups laid the foundation for college curricular programs on land-use planning.[18] Municipalities planning departments employ trained urban planners to design and monitor land-use pattern changes in their communities. State governments delegated broad land-use powers to municipalities to regulate the spatial environment of their communities.

In 1976, the San Fernando City Council looked like this:[19]

Lawrence W. Dick
Michael Y. Sagor
Perry R. Harris
Edward R. Díaz
Paul E. Macey
Elvira Orozco, City Treasurer

The city council typically composed of all-male business chums appointed Edward R. Díaz, a gardener by trade, to fill a vacancy on the council. He served until 1978. Nothing could be found specifically about his political activities in San Fernando. The city administrator and his line of staff were all male and white. No woman had been elected or appointed to the city council until 1982 when Carmillia Noltemeyer won a seat that year at the city elections.

Ralph Arriola Runs for City Council

Ralph Arriola, a typical mainstream individual with extensive community and government experience, ran for city council in 1980. As a former union lobbyist and an administrative assistant to Assemblyman James Keysor enjoying broad support from Latino businesses as well as influential white civic leaders, he presumed that he would win one of the three vacancies on Election Day. Instead, on April 8, 1980, Ralph Arriola received only 539 votes, compared to 814 votes for Patrick J. Modugno, and 807 votes for Daniel F. Mackin.[20] Arriola blamed the defeat on the Mackin Election Committee for a letter mailed to voters insisting that Arriola was being supported by militant nonresident elements of La Raza Unida Party. (He explained to the public that La Raza Unida Party refused to back him because he was not being sensitive to their cause.) The Mackin letter also asserted that Arriola was a party to a lawsuit against the city's election-at-large system of voting, costing the city thousands of dollars in tax funds. (He also tried to make it clear to the public that although he originally joined the lawsuit, he dropped out because of his political activities.)[21] The case *Jose Aranda v. J. B. Van Sickle* was being considered by the U.S. Ninth Circuit Court of Appeal in San Francisco with other similar cases from other states. (The Aranda case will be discussed in more detail in the following section. It needs only to be noted here.) Local elections in San Fernando required candidates to run in the entire city rather than in smaller districts. The suit claimed that at-large balloting made it difficult for a Latino to get elected.

Some political observers blamed the defeat of Chicano/Latino at the polls on the failure of Latinos to show up to vote. CSUN Professor José Hernández agreed that there was Chicano voter apathy at that time. He said in an interview with the *Valley News* that in campaigning house-to-house for Arriola, he encountered a sense of hopelessness among the voters that he believed was the result of "a history of exclusion."[22] He blamed bigotry for the exclusion of Latinos from the political process. "There is no doubt there is voter apathy," he said in the interview. "But that is because they can't foresee a chance of winning. Historically, Anglos have voted as a bloc."[23] In 1972, Jess Margarito was defeated in the council race charging that the police were called during Election Day to patrol voting sites. Two years later Andrés Torres lost by only five votes to Councilman Michael Meyers, liquor store owner in the barrio who catered mainly to Mexican Americans. The Chicano professor, however, added that Mexican and Latino Americans do not win political races because of "legal schemes" used by dominant groups against minorities. He was referring to at-large elections that favor majority bloc–voting residents (whites in San Fernando) as opposed to district-based elections. The latter system would divide the vote giving the minority a shot at electing a person of their choice linked to his/her constituents. Under the at-large election system, the election is held citywide, thus diluting the minority vote, and candidates run from any section of town. In San Fernando, it was not unusual for two council members to come from the same bloc of white precincts. Conversely, under the district system the city would be divided into wards or districts and voters restricted to vote in their corresponding districts. The candidates for city office must reside in the district they wish to represent. Under this plan, the Latino community would be entitled to two safe districts or two seats at the council table from the heavily Mexican/Latino census tracts on the southern portion of town.

Professor Charles R. Adrian, University of California, Riverside political scientist and expert on local government, wrote in 1987, "cities with a small number of Council members and with mixed racial groups, wealthy and poor, and professional and working-class persons inevitably left out some groups unrepresented." Furthermore he correctly observed: "The sense of access to Council members by ordinary citizens was muffled by at-large elections."[24] Hernández warned: "In the years to come, elections-at-large will work against the Anglo American community when Chicanos are the majority population." Finally he summed it neatly when he told the *Valley News* reporter: "We are not going to go away," he said. "Time is in our favor. Our population is young and it's being educated. We are not counting much on the Aranda case. In the long run, citywide elections will work in our favor."[25] A change in demography shifts the power position and thereby the policies of a community. There is a precedent to this development in U.S. cities and regions.

The *Jose Aranda v. J. B. Van Sickle* Case

In 1974, the Mexican American community and Chicanos who ran for office and lost brought a class action lawsuit against the City of San Fernando in U.S. District Court, Los Angeles under 42 U.S.C. paragraph 1983 alleging that racial discrimination in various forms including at-large election procedures used by the city were unconstitutional under the 14th, 15th, 19th, and 20th Amendments to the U.S. Constitution.[26] They also alleged racial discrimination in city services as a result of racial polarized geographical separate communities. Joaquín Avila, Mexican American Defense and Educational Fund (MALDEF) distinguished attorney, filed suit in U.S. District Court. The party to the lawsuit included José Aranda, Jess Margarito, Richard Corona, Andrés Torres, Héctor Barragán, and Roberto Villafaña. Roberto Villafaña paid the court registration fees. After reviewing all documents and holding hearings of both parties, the U.S. District Court ruled in favor of the city. The court declared that plaintiffs failed to prove their case that San Fernando at-large elections and other racial discrimination charges denied the Mexican American community equal protection before the law.

On May 17, 1976, the district court decision was appealed to the U.S. Ninth Circuit Court of Appeals (600 F 2d 1267) in San Francisco, California: José Aranda, et al., Plaintiff-Applicants v. J. B. Van Sickle, et al., Defendants-Appellees. Joaquín C. Avila of the Mexican American Legal Defense and Educational Fund, San Antonio, Texas and Morris Baller, Mexican American Legal Defense and Educational Fund, San Francisco, California (argued) represented the plaintiffs-appellants; John A. Lewis (argued), Lewis, Vani & Ghirardi, San Fernando, California represented the defendants-appellees who asked for a summary judgment on the case.[27] MALDEF, the premier Mexican American civil rights group, used the Voting Rights Act of 1965 as the legal foundation for creating district-based elections to replace at-large elections to city council. The organization claimed district elections to be more fair, equitable, and inclusive and that the at-large election system was an affront to the most basic principle of democracy that elections count. After three years of reviewing court precedents and hearings that related to the litigation of the Aranda case and other similar cases, the three-judge panel of the Ninth Circuit Court refused to accept the plaintiffs' contention that San Fernando Mexican American residents suffered from discrimination and therefore needed stronger constitutional protections. In June 12, 1979, the court declared that plaintiffs failed to establish that the at-large election was conceived as a "purposely devise to deny Mexican Americans access to political processes or further racial and economic discrimination."[28] It said that San Fernando had used at-large election schemes under Government Code Section 36503 in selecting the five-person city council since the city was incorporated in 1911. The court also said in a written statement that the 2.4-square-mile city was too small for partitioning into districts to the "effect that it would make it difficult for small cities to recruit candidates in every district."[29] While this position could have been plausible, the other statements made by the court blaming the exclusion of Mexican Americans from responsible administrative positions in government for their low education level, economic status, and civic awareness were based purely on the judges' philosophical views. If the city had been interested in diversifying its staffs, it could have tapped a pool of Mexican Americans/Latinos of professionals and clerical workers available in the Valley and Los Angeles.[30] The judges also questioned whether government was in the position to address social problems (see upcoming discussion). Mexican American advocates for social justice and equity have long argued that Mexican Americans, like many whites and any other special interests, supported the view that government does affect the quality of lives of citizens. In supporting this point, the political activists believed that citizen participation in the political processes was essential since those who held power determine the future of the community. As was pointed earlier, this idea is not new; it's embedded in the annals of American political science. Nevertheless, the court approved district elections on other similar cases. The following were the court's findings:[31]

* The City of San Fernando is not racially polarized, nor has it been at any time in the recent past.
* Mexican Americans can live anywhere in the city they choose to live.
* The concentration of Mexican Americans in the "barrio" cannot in any way be traced to city government, but is the result of individual desire of the Mexican American to associate with those of similar racial and economic status.
* The undesirable conditions in the barrio, such as old housing, unemployment, poverty, low levels of education, assuming they exist, are social problems which, to a greater or lesser extent, face all communities and are problems which arise because local governments have not always been able to successfully accommodate the economically and educationally disadvantaged who constitute a portion of their citizenry. In San Fernando, there is nothing on record to indicate that race plays any role in the matter; the underprivileged, be they white, brown or black, suffers the same unhappy fate.
* Although Mexican Americans constitute 48.7 percent of the city's population, the highest percentage of registered voters they were able to obtain was 28.7 percent in 1972.
* The failure of Mexican American voters to elect Mexican American candidates to the council in proportion to their population in the city is attributable, largely, to apathy of the Mexican American voter and not to racially polarized voters.

* The electoral process is open to Mexican Americans to the same extent it is open to others.
* There has been no racist campaign tactic against Mexican Americans either in the newspaper or by incumbent or anywhere else.
* The charges of voter registration irregularities by the city clerk in the election of 1972 were not directed at the Mexican American community and were made in the performance of the city clerk's duties as city clerk.
* The references to the Mexican American candidate activities in the election of 1972 were probably in reference to La Raza Unida Party and its efforts to register Mexican Americans in the barrio. An attack upon political activist organizations is no more evidence of racial polarity than an attack upon the John Birch society.
* There is no evidence of police harassment at the polls; if such incidents did occur, these were no more than a few isolated incidents which fall short of establishing a pattern for which an inference of voter polarization may be drawn.
* The concentration of Mexican Americans in nonprofessional categories with accompanying lower salaries in the city government is attributable to low levels of education and low civic awareness not to any racial discrimination.
* The small number of councilmen (three in the city's history) and commission members from the barrio is due to low civic awareness which is the result of high unemployment and low levels of education and not the result of racial discrimination.
* In response to the needs of the Mexican American community the city through the Redevelopment Agency was attempting to remove some of the blight in the barrio of which plaintiffs complained.
* The city government is not less responsive to Mexican American citizens than to other segments of the community.
* The reason for maintaining the "at large" election scheme set forth by City Administrator Robert James in a letter to Assembly James Keysor, to the effect that it would make it difficult for small cities to recruit candidates in every district which is necessary for a meaningful choice by the voters, is reasonable and not arbitrary or capricious as San Fernando is a relatively small, compact city covering an area of approximately 17,000 residents.
* The at-large election scheme in the City of San Fernando is such as to allow all persons irrespective of race to participate in the government process on an equal basis according to their wishes and ability.
* The failure of Mexican American registered voters to participate in the city government and elect members to the council in proportion to their population has been due to apathy, lack of education, training and experience, lacking economic support and other similar reason which are applicable to all persons irrespective of their race but who are otherwise similarly situated.

Thus, the Appeals Court held that the advocates' grounds about racial separation were out of date. It concluded that there was no substantial issue of fact which remained to be litigated and that the defendants were entitled to a judgment as a matter of law. The defendants' motion for summary judgment was therefore granted. The Chicano advocacy group for fair representation had charged correctly that the at-large issue was a symptom of a bigger problem that needed to be dealt with in a community split over special interests. Politics, the art of public funds distribution, was being challenged again in San Fernando. Notwithstanding, there was a silver lining to the Court Notice of Class Action released on June 12, 1979, as the reader will see in the succeeding chapters. "La lutte continua"—the struggle continues as the Italians so pervasively say.

Notes

1. This paragraph is based on a conversation with Jess Margarito on January 10, 2010.
2. *San Fernando Valley SUN*, June 8, 1951.
3. The views expressed in this paragraph are contributed by Sam Córdova on October 19, 2009. Sam Córdova was an active member of the Mexican American Political Association and the Democratic Club in their earliest days of political activity in San Fernando.
4. See *The Valley News and Valley Green Sheet*, November 28, 1963.
5. The following is a partial list of MAPA members: Ralph Arriola, Sam and Stella Córdova, Bill García, Fernando García, Manuel Flores, and Gil Sotelo. A partial list of San Fernando Democrat Club membership includes Raul Aragón, Sr., John and Marjorie Britt, Sam and Stella Córdova, Armando García, Bill García, Fernando García, and Richard and Mary Peña. Louie and Sophie García and Greg and Belia Medina were not formal members of the Democratic Club but were good friends of the group joining them on community volunteer work. Louie and Sophie García now live in Oxnard, California. Greg and Belia Medina still live in San Fernando. Belia is Louie's sister.
6. The information in this section was made possible with the assistance of Sam Córdova, Marjorie Britt, Jess Margarito, and Manuel Flores.
7. This statement was taken from an interview with Marjorie Britt, president of the San Fernando Democrat Club on January 20, 2010.
8. Manuel Flores made this statement in a discussion with the present writer on August 18, 2009.
9. This section briefly summarizes La Raza Unida Party political activities in San Fernando during the period under discussion with the assistance of MAPA member Jess Margarito on January 10, 2010. A partial list of La Raza Unida Party membership at that time included Genaro Ayala, Richard Corona, Marshall Díaz, Victor Ferra, Xavier Flores, José Galván, Gene Hernández, Richard Loa, Ray Magaña, Jess Margarito, Mary Martínez, Eduardo Palacios, Nellie Parra, José Luis Ramirez, Henry Romero, Ruben Rodriquez, Everto Ruiz, Ben Saiz, Andrés Torrres, Irene Tovar, and Roberto Villafaña.

10. This is quoted in the summary judgment of the José Aranda v. J. B. Van Sickle case (1979).

11. Alexis de Tocqueville, *Democracy in America,* New York: Alfred A. Knopf, 1947.

12. This was the conclusion of Jess Margarito who was deeply involved in his community to get Mexican American representation in local government.

13. For a good reading of this period, see Rodolfo F. Acuña, *Anything But Mexican,* op. cit., 262-264. See also the *Daily Sun Dial,* California State University, Northridge, February 23, 1984.

14. Elvira Orozco assisted with this information.

15. U.S. Department of Commerce, Bureau of the Census, *1970 Census of Population, Population Characteristics,* Volume 1, Part 6, California.

16. Ibid.

17. The celebrated perspective for studying cities known as the human-ecology approach in sociology is found in Ernest Burgess, "The Growth of the American City: An Introduction to a Research Project," Publications in *the American Sociological Society,* 18 (1924), 88-97. Also available is a brief summary of the early theories of human ecology in Chauncey D. Harris and Edward L. Ullman, "The Nature of Cities," in the Annals of *the American Academy of Political and Social Sciences,* 242 (1945), 7-17.

18. The present writer was head of the urban studies and urban planning program at California State University, Northridge in 1982-1995. He was also a San Fernando Planning Commissioner from 1996 to 1990. In 1990, he was elected to his first-term city council office.

19. This information was made available by City Clerk Elena Chávez.

20. This information is available at the city clerk's office.

21. For an analysis of the San Fernando City elections of 1980, see "Voting Fruitless Say Area Latinos," in *Valley News,* May 11, 1980. See also Letters to the Editor, *San Fernando Valley SUN,* May 21, 1980.

22. Ibid.

23. Ibid.

24. Charles R. Adrian, *A History of American City Government: The Emergence of the Metropolis, 1920-1945,* New York: Lanham Publishing Company, 1987, 488. Dr. Charles Adrian was the present writer's doctoral dissertation adviser and mentor in the Department of Political Science at the University of California, Riverside.

25. *Valley News,* op. cit.

26. The summary judgment of *Jose Aranda, et al. v. J. B. Van Sickle, et al.* is found on the Internet. Type *Jose Aranda v. J. B. Van Sickle* case, search, and a list of cases appear on the screen, including the José Aranda case under the Column Citation 600 F 2d 1267.

27. Jess Margarito, a party to the in-large election class action, assisted with this section.

28. José Aranda, et al., op. cit.

29. Ibid.

30. Hiring qualified city employees that fit the profile of the community it served was the priority of Dr. José Hernández (the present writer) in his first term as council member in 1990.

31. The Appeals Court findings of fact are listed as they appeared on the Notice of Class Action, Jose Aranda, et al., op. cit.

CHAPTER 5

The Historic Election of 1984

For years, as the record showed, race-based elections made sure that Mexican Americans were excluded from the city electoral process. Mexican American civic leaders wanted representation for their community in decision-making positions. Few presumed how to get it as a staunch all-white political machine was determined to prevent them each time from reaching their goal. That, of course, changed in 1984. Hence, the second part of the saga of San Fernando's changing race relations begins on this page.

The Dennis F. Webb Controversy

In December 24, 1979, San Fernando Police Officer Dennis F. Webb was gunned down during a robbery of a 7-11 convenience store located on Hubbard and Second Street. The robber escaped on foot along Workman Street in the barrio. The San Fernando police were called immediately. Officer Webb stopped a man on the corner of Woodworth and Workman Streets who was passing through the barrio towards Mission Hills and Los Angeles and who fit the description of the armed robbery suspect. During the questioning of the man, a scuffle ensued. The murder suspect shot the officer six times and fled in the police officer's car. San Fernando police swept the barrio neighborhood questioning Chicanos on the street.[1]

During the January 5, 1980, city council meeting while the council was considering to approve $10,000 in city funds for a Webb reward fund, Councilman Daniel F. Mackin made a remark that he hoped the officer's slayer would make a "Mexican escape" and meet with a speedy justice. He tried to explain that he was referring to a Mexican technique of law enforcement that allowed a criminal to escape and then take a shot at him. During a press conference held in front of the city hall, Mexican American and Latino community leaders were upset at Mackin's racial remark. They were more disturbed when Mackin added that he hoped that the reward money for information leading to the arrest and conviction of the slayer would not go to a "Mexican illegal." José Hernández, professor of Chicano Studies and Urban Affairs at California State University, Northridge, called Mackin's remark about "a 'Mexican escape' a Hollywood statement, which revealed his unfamiliarity with Mexican history."[2] He also was concerned by the Anglo community's slow reaction to the attack on the Mexican American community. Louis García, executive director of the Northeast Valley Health Corporation "hoped the controversy would raise a level of awareness in the Anglo American community, who by and large don't tolerate this kind of behavior." Ralph Arriola, who lost to Mackin in a recent city election, said: "As citizens of this city and local community, we are appalled that an elected official would use the tragic loss of Officer Webb as an opportunity to vent his racial slur on the Hispanic community."

Councilman Daniel F. Mackin dismissed the stinging criticism of his remarks as sour grapes. He blamed Arriola for masterminding the attempt to discredit him and called Arriola a "disgruntled, defeated candidate" who ran against him last year. The Latino advocacy group at the press conference rejected Mackin's suggestion that they were criticizing him because their candidate Arriola lost the election. "This is a historical battle—not something based on Mr. Arriola," responded Marshall Díaz, secretary of the board of directors for Proyecto del Barrio.[3] Apparently, Mackin's short debut in public office did not bode well.

The controversy became a cause celebre in the Mexican American community, arousing a heated public debate in the following council meeting in January. The angry protesters packed the council chambers and demanded that council members censure their colleague and others called for his resignation. After a long meeting in the night, the impassionate outcry failed to win the needed votes to censure Mackin. The council rejected a motion by Mayor Roy Richardson that Councilman Daniel Mackin be censured for comments made during the January 5 council meeting. Mackin, Councilmen Perry Harris, and Michael A Majers voted against a reprimand, while Mayor Richardson and Councilmen Patrick Modugno voted for it.[4] That did not surprise the protesters. Mexican Americans were accustomed to being either ignored or maligned in city hall. But the discontented protesters shouted as they were leaving the chambers, "Wait until next city elections." The most important consideration for Mexican American voters was to be treated with respect.

The Webb killer was caught a few weeks later on Sepulveda Dam on Burbank Boulevard off of Interstate 405 South (San Diego Freeway) where he had abandoned the getaway police car. The Anglo American suspect was convicted of Officer Webb's murder and sentenced to life without parole. California did not have the death penalty at that time.

The Changing Demographics of San Fernando

The face of San Fernando was changing; politicians who wanted to win elections took heed. Between 1960 and 1980 the Spanish-origin residents more than doubled from 30 percent to 63 percent. Of this, 93 percent were of Mexican heritage. Their medium age was 23.1 years.[5] The highest concentration of Latinos was located south of the railroad tracks in the city's eastern boundary. A change in demographics imposed tough realities on white politicians and their supporters in San Fernando and elsewhere. Candidates for public office who wished to reach out to the Latino electorate needed to have sincere and respectful personalities. They were expected to respond in good faith to their issues fairly and justly. The Latino electorate votes for representatives that best represent their goals and needs. This should not be viewed as politics of ethnicity. It's not about race; it's about performance. When whites voted as a bloc, their voting pattern was never described as ethnic politics.

The Rise of Jess Margarito

A development of major significance was the emergence of Jess Margarito, a popular Chicano community hero who placed the old guard on a defensive mode in the 1980s, setting the stage for the eventual decline of Anglo American domination over the local politics of the city. He ran again for city council in 1984. A resolute leader who had a reputation for being more effusive in challenging the status quo in San Fernando had to overcome doubts that he could win the election this time. He had to run a largely different campaign, focus on issues, and avoid harsh attacks on the establishment.

Selecting the Optimum Campaign Strategy

Jess Margarito appointed Emma Hernández as a paid campaign manager, the first in a Chicano campaign for public office in San Fernando.[6] Emma received a bachelor of arts degree in Chicano Studies from California State University, Northridge, and had worked as director of a Valley poverty agency. Corrine Sanchez, director of El Proyecto del Barrio, a drug and alcohol prevention program in Pacoima, and community activists Ruben Rodríguez, Héctor Barragán, and José Galván made up the core of Jess Margarito's city council campaign committee. José Galván, a graduate from CSUN, was studying law in another local university. Ruben Rodríguez was a key leader of the Latino Coalition for Fair Redistricting of the San Fernando Valley. Héctor Barragán was a student at CSUN studying accounting. In Jess Margarito's campaign for city council, Ruben alone registered 350 new voters. He was assigned to make sure that the new voters made it to the polling place. The committee plan of action included the following basic rules:[7]

1. Keep a low profile. Run a positive campaign on issues.
2. Do not agitate the public; be non-confrontational.
3. Use American flag–colored leaflets to state candidate's reason for seeking public office. Write a short summary outlining the candidate's family background, education, occupation, military service, and community volunteering experience.
4. Plan housing meetings.
5. Candidate must go door to door to meet voters.
6. Work on precincts that know the candidate best; avoid hostile precincts. Use time wisely.
7. Do voter registration on the spot at people's residences. People registered in shopping malls may not be from San Fernando.
8. Encourage voters early in the campaign to vote by mail. Appoint a volunteer worker to supervise a voter-by-mail campaign.
9. Organize phone banks and position precinct captains to bring out the voters to the polls.
10. Follow government strict rules on campaigning and fundraising.
11. Keep an accurate record of campaign funds and expenditures for public record.

In sum, the tone of Jess Margarito's 1984 campaign strategy was reasonable and commanding. Tactically, it was a wise strategy in a city with racial and ethnic tension. In the 1984 city elections, there were two vacancies in the city council. Incumbents Patrick Modugno and Daniel Mackin were running for reelection. Additionally, former Councilman Michael Majers and Jess Margarito were vying for a seat as well. Michael Majers had previously won in 1978, beating Andrés Torres in a heated campaign. The latter and Mike Majers's opposition to censure Councilman Dan Mackin for alleged racial remarks were still fresh in the minds of voters from Jess's neighborhood.

The campaign went smoothly until Dan Mackin, commander of Veterans of Foreign War (VFW) Post 3834 of San Fernando, used his position to advance his candidacy during VFW membership meetings and at Sunday breakfasts.[8] Some members in the organization who knew Jess was also a war veteran objected to the one-sided comments of their commander against Jess. They asked their commander to participate in a debate with Jess in a VFW meeting so that the other comrades could listen to both views. Mackin declined. On Election Day, Jess routed both Mackin and Majers.[9] When it was announced that Pat Modugno and Jess Margarito were the winners of the election, Jess supporters burst out with joy. It gave them an incredible boost to their confidence at the polls. For him to rise above his first loss in 1972 was inspiring to everyone in the Latino community. San Fernando had a lot to celebrate, too. The city's long-running civic drama about equal representation was appearing to be a reality. Indeed, the victory at the polls was a great historical breakthrough. His victory in 1984 strengthened the concept of democracy. This was, perhaps, his greatest contribution as a public servant. The political process, the indisputable orderly method to gain power, was now being opened for more citizens. He planted the seed for the first Valley Mexican Americans to win seats in the Los Angeles City Council, Los Angeles Unified School District Board of Education, the State Assembly and Senate, and U.S. Congress. Not until Jess Margarito was elected to the San Fernando City Council did Valley Mexican Americans begin to stir politically. His winning campaign strategy became the model for those who aspired to run for public office.

The main difference between the 1972 city elections and the 1984 elections was the sheer size of Latinos using the ballot box and the strong sense of community that was evident as the Mackin remarks stirred the community to action. Latinos in particular felt a deep grievance about being stereotyped. The Jess victory also raised ethnic confidence at the poll throughout the region. His victory at the polls created a ripple effect for others inspiring to run for public office. Population shifts, hard-fought political strategizing, and the rise of organized labor as a factor benefiting Latinos and other minority candidates moved them to the top in U.S. politics.

The 1980s were supposed to be the decade of the Chicano; it arrived early in San Fernando. The city had reached a mark of excellence. The world watched. A new chapter of Latino political history was unfolding in the city. There was an enormous excitement and interest around Jess Margarito's 1984 election and about his impact on the city's political structure. It was inevitable that there was going to be some backlash at the opportune time, for he shook up the city establishment.

The Rebel with a Cause

Despite his victory at the polls Jess Margarito, a popular figure in grassroots politics, continued with his crusade to help elect candidates for public office who could address Latino issues that had been ignored for decades. He had helped found the La Raza Unida Party, a progressive Chicano third party. In 1972, Jess lost the election after his first try running for San Fernando City Council in a campaign led by Raza Unida volunteers. In 1974, he and others sued the city of San Fernando over its at-large elections. The voting-rights complaint was rejected by the Ninth Circuit Court of Appeals in 1980. In 1984, he organized the Mission City Political Committee raising funds and providing volunteers to assist progressive candidates for the Los Angeles School Board.[10] The political committee supported the Tom Bradley Los Angeles mayoral campaign as well as Los Angeles Councilman Richard Alatorre. It reached out to other area elected leaders such as Congressman Howard Berman, a friend of farm workers. Jess Margarito used his political clout to support candidates who understood Latino issues. He supported the appointment of Richard Alarcón as Mayor Tom Bradley's liaison to the San Fernando Valley, making him one of the Valley's most promising Latinos in government. In 1993, the Valley voted Richard Alarcón the first Chicano to represent the Valley on the Los Angeles City Council. Later, he was elected as the first Chicano to represent the Valley in the California State Senate.[11] Before State Senator Alarcón and others stepped in the political arena, Jess Margarito was the only Latino who held unquestioned political power in the Valley.[12] In 1987, Councilman Margarito appointed CSUN professor José Hernández to the city planning commission, hoping to springboard his political career.

Councilman Jess Margarito's first priority was to govern. Additionally, he was now in a position to be more effective in encouraging and leading community improvement efforts. As a Latino, he was expected to do more for a community that had been neglected for years. On November 30, 1984, he met with community leaders to plan for the startup of a grassroots organization following Saul Alinsky's method as an education agent for members and as a pressure group committed to protect communities.[13] The organization eventually became known as the Valley Organization in Community Efforts, or VOICE. Those present at the Santa Rosa Catholic Church of San Fernando's preliminary meeting were Father Thomas Rush of Santa Rosa, Father Paul Mather of St. Ferdinand Church of San Fernando, Pastor Alfred Fields, City Councilman Jess Margarito, Professor Everto Ruiz, and Professor Dr. José Hernández—to name only six.[14] Father Rush stated "that the new organization will have the local government assistance on issues of affordable housing and other issues of the poor." Dr. Hernández acknowledged that "there are some organizations that once they win a community battle, they disappear." He hoped that wouldn't happen to the new group. In

Councilman Jess Margarito's view, "residents shouldn't tolerate abuse in neighborhoods that caused their communities to deteriorate." He added: "Until now we have seen a 70 percent reduction of drugs in the entire city, but we should be alert that the drugs don't return to our streets. This organization can see to that."[15] (The problem of alcohol abuse, however, remained a big problem in the city. This problem will be spelled out in greater detail in the following chapter as VOICE joins the community to fight off the proliferation of alcohol businesses in San Fernando.)

San Fernando, the Hotbed of the Valley Drug Trade

During the heroin epidemic of the 1970s and early 1980s, Kewen Street between Kalisher and Workman Streets was the epicenter of the drug trade. The street became a drive-through as cars and vans looked for drug dealers. Some vans were spotted with their business markings, including a public utility truck with a public logo. This popular drive through enterprise was dubbed the "hotbed of the Valley drug trade." That stretch of the street was a popular business spot for two restaurants—El Cinco Café and Rio Alto Café—that attracted many customers for their fine Mexican food and cold beer. A longtime and knowledgeable resident of the barrio made this observation, "White students from nearby high schools in Mission Hills and Granada Hills used their school lunch period to pick up their supply of weeds."[16]

During an interview, Jess Margarito was asked why the environment conditions persisted. He gave three straightforward explanations: "The previous City Councils didn't have the political will to clean up the drug trafficking nuisance in the business area integrated with family households. There was no interest in protecting the environment and public health of the Mexican neighborhood." He continued, "Moreover, the city code enforcement unit of the Community Development Department was practically nonfunctional. And also, the police didn't know how to handle a longstanding problem; they didn't know how to talk to the community either."[17] Consequently, he said he took over the lead in a community operations to drive the drug dealers out of business. He joined Vecinos Unidos (United Neighbors), a Santa Rosa Parish group headed by Salvador Ponce. Together they mobilized the neighborhood, held weekly meetings in the parish hall, and walked the streets in groups to discourage drug sales. Church leaders carried cameras taking pictures of automobiles on the streets. Jess Margarito knew the neighborhood well since he grew up there. He lived through some of the difficult problems that affected the poor. He knew the youngsters that were being used by the dealers as "spotters." Spotters were positioned on street corners to warn dealers when the police were in the area. The councilman talked the teenagers out of their jobs and helped them enroll in youth programs at Las Palmas Park. The free market of drug sales on Kewen Street was clearly a case of environmental injustice to a community of low-income families; nevertheless, it demonstrated how a city employee who fit the profile of a community can be more effective in the outcome of a community problem. This observation, however, is not always a consistent pattern as the reader will see in subsequent sections of the study of San Fernando.

In 1988, Jess Margarito was reelected to another term to the city council. During his first term in office, he worked well with his colleagues Pat Modugno, Roy Richardson, and Carmillia Noltemeyer. They worked together directly in a wide range of activities whether cleaning up neighborhood streets, demolishing abandoned structures, or beginning its deteriorated downtown improvements. They worked towards making neighborhoods safer, attracting new businesses that added revenues to the city coffers, and directing higher city revenue producing proposals.

The city Latino community made other political gains. Ray Silva was elected to the city council in 1986. He resigned in July 1988 to move to Central California to study for the ministry. Evelio Franco was appointed to fill his position. Dan Acuña was also elected to the city council in 1986. In 1990, Dr. José Hernández, who hailed from the "Chicano Power" movement of the 1960s and 1970s, was elected to the San Fernando City Council, followed by Rosa Chacón who was elected to the same office in 1992. Councilman Jess Margarito was credited for orchestrating the elections of Silva, Hernández, and Chacón to public office.

The shift in population and victories at the polls did not experience a smooth transition of power in San Fernando, as will be seen in the coming scenarios. Some elements of the public remained uncomfortable at the increasing accumulation of power of Jess Margarito and his supporters. They felt like they were losing control of their government.

Notes

1. Arturo Chacón, the barber of Kalisher Street, saw the commotion in the neighborhood of the murder scene from his barber shop on Woodworth Street He shared his knowledge of the event in an interview on February 19, 2010.
2. The statements in this paragraph and the following were taken from "Mexican Escape Remarks Still Anger Latino Groups," *Daily News*, January 15, 1981.
3. Ibid.
4. See "Censure Motion Killed," *Daily News*, January 21, 1981.
5. The decennial census counts found "Spanish-origin" residents made up the majority (12,219) of the city's population of 17,731. See the *1980 U. S. Census of Population, General Population Characteristics*, Volume 8, Part 6, California.

6. Interview with Jess Margarito on February 16, 2010.
7. The campaign committee sought professional advice from the William C. Velásquez Institute office in Los Angeles. The Institute conducts research aimed at improving the level of political and economic participation in Latino and other underrepresented communities. An off-shoot of the Southwest Voter Registration and Education Project, the Institute has conducted interesting research on Latino voting behavior.
8. Interview with Jess Margarito on February 16, 2010.
9. City of San Fernando: 1984 General Municipal Election Official Results available in the City Clerk office.
10. Interview with Jess Margarito on February 16, 2010.
11. Richard Alarcón defeated Richard Katz by 29 votes in a heated race for the 20th District State Senate seat. Ironically, Richard Katz was a popular Valley politician who shared common issues of social justice and civil rights with the Latino community and other minorities. The Alarcón victory caused concern in both Latino and Jewish communities. On this, see José Hernández, "Latino, Jewish Rift a Sign of Democratic Dysfunction," *Daily News*, August 5, 1998.
12. Before, other Valley Chicano leaders had run unsuccessfully for public office. José Galván of Sylmar, a reference librarian and longtime active in Valley politics, had run for the Los Angeles Board of Education, the Los Angeles City Council, and the Los Angeles County Board of Supervisors, Mary Louise Longoria of Pacoima, former consultant to the Los Angeles County Human Rights Commission and former teacher and administrator, ran for the Los Angeles Board of Education, and Irene Tovar of Mission Hills, who had been active in community service in the northeast Valley since the 1960s, also ran unsuccessfully for Los Angeles City Council. See *Daily News*, September 1, 1991.
13. Alinsky organizational method is found in Saul Alinsky, *Reveille for Radicals*, op. cit.
14. Other community leaders in attendance at the meeting were Jaime Cruz, Jaime Ayala, Isabel Chacón Estrada, Eduardo Palacios, and Ray Silva. See "Planean formar la organizacion UNO en San Fernando," *The Sun and Breeze* Section in Spanish, December 5, 1984.
15. The members' statements were taken from quotes that appeared in the *Sun and Breeze* Spanish language article cited above.
16. Arturo Chacón of the prominent Chacón family was raised in the barrio where he worked in his father's Chacón Barber Shop on Kalisher Street as a young man until he retired in 2007. Kalisher Street is the heart of the barrio. The namesake of Kalisher Street was Wolf Kalisher (1826-1889), a Jewish immigrant from Poland. He was a businessman and civic leader in Los Angeles. He and his wife Louise were active in the local Jewish community. Louise was the founding president of the Ladies' Hebrew Benevolent Society established in 1878. The local paper could not find any direct connection between the city of San Fernando and Wolf Kalisher. But nevertheless a street in the middle of the Mexican barrio was named after him. *The San Fernando Valley SUN* has a brief history of Wolf Kalisher in its May 10, 1995 issue.
17. Interview with Jess Margarito on April 10, 2010.

CHAPTER 6

The Old Order at Risk

The City of San Fernando became the epicenter in the battle of a shift in cultural and political power in Southern California starting in the earlier 1990s. The San Fernando City Council had its first Latino majority in 1986, consisting of Jess Margarito, Dan Acuña, and Ray Silva. Other council members included James Hansen and Doude Wysbeek, who was appointed to the council in May 1989 replacing Roy Richardson, who had moved out of town. Ray Silva resigned in July 1988 and Evelio Franco was appointed to replace him. The Latino majority did not begin exercising its political clout until after the 1990 city council elections. Then they began taking steps to integrate important city jobs and respond to issues affecting the Latino community. Those efforts strained relations in San Fernando as Whites complained about the city engaging in reverse discrimination. Jess Margarito resigned in August 1990 to work for the city and Salvador Ponce was appointed to replace him, joining Doude Wysbeek, Daniel Acuña, Dr. José Hernández, and James Hansen on the council. In 1992, Rosa Chacón was elected to a full term to fill Jess Margarito's spot on the city council. Ray Ojeda was also elected to the council in 1990 replacing Jim Hansen, joining Dr. José Hernández, Daniel Acuña (mayor), and Doude Wysbeek on the council.

One of the first tasks of the new 1990 council was to search for a city administrator in the spring of 1990. After an extensive outreach, the council hired Mary Strenn after Mayor Jess Margarito and Councilman José Hernández lobbied their colleagues to appoint her as head of the city administrative staff. She was noted as an expert in redevelopment and an advocate for affirmative action. She became San Fernando's first woman city administrator.

San Fernando Splits over City Attorney Replacement

In a June 25, 1993, closed session, a new Latino council majority of council members Major Dan Acuña and Rosa Chacón led by José Hernández moved to replace its legal counsel of 12 years Costa Mesa–based Rutan and Tucker with the Los Angeles Latino firm of Ochoa and Sillas. Councilmen Doude Wysbeek and Ray Ojeda voted against the new law firm. Doude Wysbeek, a Dutch émigré, was the only non-Latino on the council. Ray Ojeda, a local businessman, was his handmaiden. When the decision to replace law firms was announced in the council chambers, tension exploded along racial lines with community leaders of the city's predominantly White old guard. The council chamber was packed to overflowing capacity. Critics of the new law firm questioned whether the new council majority was turning San Fernando "into a migrant town." Others worried that the council only wanted to hire "brown faces." Mayor Acuña was taken aback at the racial rants. Most of them were friends and supporters who refused to accept change. "Latinos don't have a long history of participation in the political process and having the luxury of being in a position of power," he argued. "When we began to assert that power, issues like this take on a new meaning." As the critics became more personal, the mayor had sharp words for his circle of friends: "Put your sheets away—sew up the holes, put them back down on the bed and use them for what they were intended."[1] The scene captured one of the most dramatic events of the evening. After the meeting, the mayor told the reporter of the city's one newspaper that racism was clearly alive and well in San Fernando as he made reference to the "brown faces" and "Mexican" statements.[2] Councilman José Hernández who was upset by the racial remarks made at the meeting didn't believe the majority of the Anglos in San Fernando supported the remarks that were made. He tried to give his view of the developments in San Fernando.[3] He explained: "It's natural for white people who have been the most important in the political lives of their cities to react this way." He added, "But members of the old guard are going to have to learn to share their political influence." A supporter of affirmative action, Hernández believed that the city should create opportunities for minorities in the workplace. He said, "I don't see a reason not to give this minority firm a chance." He felt this development will be happening all through Southern California. At that instance, a *San Fernando Valley Sun* staff writer asked if there were plans to replace City Administrator Mary Strenn with a Latino. The councilman did not know of any plans to replace the city administrator. However, he didn't hesitate to say that there was still injustice in hiring women and Latinos to positions of power and the city had to correct them. Council member Rosa Chacón, also a proponent of affirmative action, agreed that the "city should be doing business with minority firms other than those in construction, but with other professionals as well."[4] Jess Margarito, who served in the council from 1984 to 1990, and the city recreation and social service director, explained that it had only been in recent years that the San Fernando Latino majority had been exercising its clout. "Now we have the political power, and we're using it to address concerns in areas that a lot of people in this town feel have been neglected,"[5] he said. An angry businessman shouted at the council majority, "Watch your back," as he was leaving the council chamber. To paraphrase Councilwoman Rosa Chacón: The protestors were a bunch of angry white, middle-aged businessmen who weren't used to dealing with us; they didn't know how to handle us.

It was interesting to hear the whole argument in this case. The issue was not how qualified Ochoa and Sillas were, but that they were minority owned. Councilman Doude Wysbeek said that the issue was not minority ownership but process. He was concerned that the council majority did not hold a public search before choosing the Latino legal firm to represent the city. Doude Wysbeek, noted for spinning his words to fit his agenda, failed to mention that in 1981 the council in a 3 to 2 vote fired its legal firm for reportedly advising a divided council to vote against a housing project known as Herrick Manor on North Hubbard Avenue. The council majority, made of Mayor Michael Majers and council members Dan Mackin and Perry Harris, voted for the dismissal of the law firm of Richards, Watson, Drefuss and Gershon of Los Angeles which had been representing the city in legal matters since 1977 because they "lost faith in the opinions of the (law firm) City Attorney."[6] Councilmen Pat Modugno and Roy Richardson dissented. About 30 days later the Costa Mesa–based law firm of Rutan and Tucker was hired without a spectacular public display. Councilman Wysbeek knew that in most general law cities, city attorneys as well as city administrators and department heads, unlike civil service employees, are expendable. That is, they are at-will-employees subject to be replaced at the whim of council majorities. Also, some general-law cities do not generally advertise for city attorney positions when they know of a reputable legal firm they wish to hire, saving taxpayers considerable public funds in consultant fees. The salient issue of affirmative action will be the topic of discussion in Chapter XIII. Affirmative Action was a government policy or program designed to increase opportunities for underrepresented groups in education, employment, and government contracts.

The Ochoa and Sillas law firm conflict left some scars and bitterness, especially on Doude Wysbeek and Ray Ojeda who were beholden to the old guard. "Basically, we don't have a choice. They have the votes," Ojeda said. He continued, "I've read about takeover by radical groups. It didn't concern me until last night." Then he issued a warning: "The community should be very concerned. Some of us seem to be knuckling under to radical groups…I don't like the way things are going."[7] This sour note made it clear that the legal snarl was not satisfactorily decided. The fight between the old and new guard was far from over. The ferocity of attacks for the selection of a Latino law firm was a sure sign that the old guard was taking a stand on change.

Jess Margarito Appointed City Recreation and Community Service Director

In August 1990, Jess Margarito resigned his office to take the job as park director of the city recreation and community service department, penetrating the white-controlled lucrative municipal jobs. This was a city milestone. Before, Latinos were excluded from high bureaucratic positions in city government. Jess was the ideal candidate needed for a growing youth community in San Fernando. He grew up at Las Palmas Park playing Little League baseball. After his military duty during the Vietnam War, he was hired by the city as recreation leader. He was highly regarded for having a knack for mobilizing the community when he worked with police and Church leaders clearing the streets of drug dealers. Parents with children welcomed the new recreation and social service head for his high-minded vision of community improvement, envisioning expanded park facilities and activities, lasting programs for senior citizens, and protecting youth from gang activity. The city had abandoned Las Palmas Park and local gangs had moved in as city funds were directed elsewhere. The building janitor was the only city employee assigned to work there. The city council was hard pressed to do something about the parks, long ignored by city administrators who had favored other departments over recreation. (The distribution of public resources is a zero-sum game in the city budget; one group's gain is another's loss.) The park division always came last. In some cases, park directors were either playing golf or attending college during work hours. Jess Margarito was the man who could deliver for the youth and seniors. His understanding of Chicano issues and his obvious problem-solving skills placed him as a top candidate. He knew the community well. However, he lacked heftier management experience in his resume. He had jobs with the U.S. Census Bureau, cable television, and a savings and loan association business. Nevertheless, he became a nimble manager who used his position as an opportunity to change the conditions of the city's neglected families. In 1991, a mother and her three children were caught in a crossfire between two rival gangs as they visited Las Palmas Park. The mother was slightly hurt. The incident prompted the city council to pass a gang injunction banning identifiable gang members from the park despite objections by the American Civil Liberties Union (ACLU). Again Jess Margarito was put to the task as he assisted the police to clean up the park of the unruly gang bangers. As park director he introduced a variety of programs for both youth and young adults, including tennis, boxing, basketball and baseball leagues, and chess classes. The gang injunction expired after six months before the city was taken to court by ACLU attorneys. City staff pressured the hard-core leaders to move out of town. The children got their park back, thanks to the quick action of the police, staff, and city leaders.[8]

Taking On the Bureaucratic Structure

As a start, the new park director got his department budget up from $590,000 to more than $1 million in the 1992-1993 fiscal year, fighting off other department heads for a larger share of the city budget.[9] He pressed the city council to establish its first day-camp program at the parks and started the first after-school program for local school children. One of his major accomplishments as park director was spear-heading the enlargement of Las Palmas Park, including a new building for senior citizens. He steered funds for additional senior meals and expanded social services. He was often at odds with City Administrator Mary Strenn who couldn't control his passion for improving service in his department. He resisted her control. In small cities, city administrators have a firm control over their staff. Jess Margarito felt that he was in a mission with support of the Latino community. In a small town, politics acts when the public pushes its leaders. Here were two forces in a collision course. The city administrator's position was that Jess was moving too fast and should wait a couple of years before he implemented his plans for the parks. Conversely, the restive park director voiced concern that the city had not been doing enough for poor neighborhoods. He was angry and frustrated that the city administrator was stalling improvements in those communities. The tone of his thoughts and action had caused, on some occasions, considerable strife in the workplace. For example, he called to the attention of the police chief two officers who made disparaging remarks about Latino city council members. The city administrator was not amused that a city employee was criticizing other city employees. Also, as park director he reported sexual harassment by a park maintenance employee against a recreation supervisor. He urged the city administrator to act reasonably instead of coddling him, clearly producing a predictably bitter conflict. He was digging a hole for inevitable consequences.[10]

The Tragic Sense of Power

On September 9, 1993, a *Los Angeles Times* article appeared on a front page: "City Official under Investigation by D. A. Office."[11] According to the article, parks director Jess Mar-

---

garito was being accused of falsifying work cards of misdemeanor criminals assigned by the court to do manual work in city parks which they did not perform, and the county district attorney was investigating the allegations. Thus, the council became embroiled in a conflict with political overtones, creating another hostile environment in the city. The public allegations caught council members Rosa Chacón and José Hernández by surprise. They had no idea what was going on. Councilman Hernández was quoted in the local newspaper: "The city administrator did not inform us (in the council) until this thing got out in the public."[12] They wondered who could have turned in the employee to the authorities without the full council's knowledge. This was clearly a break from tradition. In the past, other high-ranking city employees who had committed more serious blunders were treated gentler. They were given either a reprimand or a choice of resignation in closed session, a practice designed to protect the city's image and the employee's future. Chacón and Hernández asked, "Why wasn't the matter settled in-house, when the city was striving to spruce up its image and looking to reinvent itself?" At that time people tended to perceive the city as unsafe and troubled. In the latest incident, the park director was treated differently, igniting a political firestorm. *The Los Angeles Times* staff writer explained, "City Administrator Mary Strenn and other city officials declined to discuss details of the case, which revealed sources. This represented a growing struggle between Latinos and Anglos in a city known for its tiny size and vicious politics."[13] Councilman José Hernández was angry at the city administrator for not having brought the problem to the full council earlier. He reminded her that the council had ultimate powers on such personnel matters of high importance, and that she should have informed the council for official direction. The whole council would have discussed the true interest of the case and the problem might have been better resolved. In the meantime, the case developed a chilled relationship between the council majority and council members Rosa Chacón and José Hernández. The latter sensed a movement afoot against Jess Margarito.

The local *Los Angeles Times*, the *Daily News*, and the city's one newspaper the *San Fernando Valley SUN* described the situation at great length as an ostensibly major criminal problem. The embattled parks director acknowledged that he had not been prudent in following the court's directions. He didn't believe the allegations were serious infractions of the law. The felons had been convicted of petty theft, traffic violations, and other misdemeanor crimes. Jess Margarito admitted signing the release forms of the low-leveled felons. In one case, he signed a time card three days before the work was to have been completed. The parks director also tried to make a reasonable case that he had planned for the court-assigned workers to do their assigned time on weekends. He feared that the manual workers, who held entry-level jobs in Los Angeles, would have lost their jobs if he would have detained them much longer. Obviously, that was not a tenable instance to lean on. As the case unfolded San Fernando residents found the following developments most intriguing. In a closed session in October 1993, the San Fernando City Council appointed City Attorney Julia Sylva of the Ochoa and Sillas law firm to investigate the charges against their city park director. During the initial phase of the investigation, City Administrator Mary Strenn accused the city attorney of unprofessional behavior for interfering with a police officer who was questioning a park employee. Mary Strenn felt that there was a potential conflict of interest due to the city attorney's personal friendship with Jess and the Chicano community. "I have never seen or heard of an unprofessional behavior like this in all the years I have been involved in the community," exclaimed Councilman Doude Wysbeek who had never accepted the council's selection of the new Latino law firm.[14] On November 23, 1993, the city administrator sent a memorandum addressed to Councilman Doude Wysbeek asking him to sign the memorandum directing her to replace the city attorney. The memo was also signed by Councilman Ray Ojeda and Mayor Dan Acuña, a violation of the California Brown Act which governs the meetings of all local legislative bodies in the state.[15] On November 29, 1993, Councilman José Hernández sent a memorandum to the city attorney asking for her opinion whether council members could make formal decisions by correspondence.[16] While Councilman Hernández could not disclose what the city attorney's legal response had been because of its confidential nature, he nevertheless found that the Brown Act "prohibits the use of direct or indirect correspondence … used by a majority of a legislative body to assist in arriving in a decision." The protocol also prohibited "the gathering of a majority of local elected officials to hear, discuss, or deliberate on matters outside the agency's or board's formal meetings."[17] This sparked another bitter fight, pitting the city administrator and the majority against Rosa Chacón and José Hernández. Council members Chacón and Hernández were awakened to the fact that Mary Strenn and Councilman Doude Wysbeek had gone too far on deciding the fate of the director's community standing. They particularly denounced Mary Strenn for her unseemly game of playing politics with key councilmen, a conspicuous problem with city administrators in San Fernando and other small city governments. Chacón and Hernández also questioned whether the council had directed the city's police department to look into the charges against Mr. Margarito. But according to Councilman Doude Wysbeek, the council in a closed session had decided to give the police the lead in the inquiry. Chacón and Hernández blamed Wysbeek for manipulating the council arcane closed session procedures and for making cryptic statements as significant cues to action to frustrate the agendas of his colleagues. As a result, Councilman Hernández requested that all closed sessions be recorded which the council denied.[18]

Tension further escalated as Jess Margarito held a rancorous news conference in front of the city police department building reinforced by activist groups like La Raza Unidad Party and Mexican American Political Association organizations and other supporters. Many had known him since he began his involvement with La Raza Unida Party in 1972. Margarito blasted the city administrator and the council majority for "pitting the city family against one another."[19] He stated clearly that "there is no personal relationship with the city attorney. It's a mendacious ploy manifested by Doude Wysbeek. He should be made accountable. Julia Sylva is basically being held hostage because of her job." Longtime Jess supporter Ruben Rodriguez who helped Jess Margarito in his successful city council campaign in 1984 expressed this point perfectly in his assertion that the "city attorney was forced out of handling the investigation."[20] Julia Sylvia, a partner at the well-established Latino-owned law firm Ochoa & Sillas was also the first and youngest Latina mayor elected in the United States. Ms. Sylvia was elected to the city council, City of Hawaiian Gardens, in 1976, and was elected mayor in 1968 and 1979 (two consecutive terms). She was well respected in San Fernando as the city's first Latina city attorney.

Another politically sophisticated supporter, executive director of Pueblo & Salud, Inc., Xavier Flores, assured the crowd that Margarito was not guilty of any major wrongdoing. He put it this way, "There may have been some inappropriate behavior in his post, but none of us here believe he is corrupt or a criminal."[21] He also stated that the police department was an inappropriate agency to conduct the investigation and that the decision to replace the city attorney with the police should have been made by the proper council rules of conduct. Marjorie Britt praised Jess for his efforts to help all residents of San Fernando.

The upheaval carried an ideological tinge. There were innuendos of "lynching" and "aggressive" police behavior of the investigation with political overtones. Margarito claimed that he was targeted for the probe because of his efforts to bring political change in the city.[22] "We are not going to be intimidated," he said carefully enunciating each word. "We represent political change, and we're not going to back off." He added: "Change is not very popular. We are going to go forward and make the necessary reforms this community deserves."

"It was all about power," replied Lt. Ernest Halcon of the San Fernando Police Department, author of an 82-page report of his investigation of the park director. His conclusion was: "The gain was not financial. He wanted to build a power base."[23] Xavier Flores saw a section of the police report where Halcon had stated that Margarito and a group of associates apparently tried to create a personal political fiefdom within San Fernando city government. "In the apparent quest for political influence … criminal acts have been committed," the report explicitly stated. Commenting on this, Xavier Flores said, "What is really at issue here is (Halcon's opinion) that a city employee is creating this little fiefdom. It may be his perception, but it is not just his. It is also that of the power structure that he represents that is trying to keep intact and has been for the longest."[24]He wished the media focused on this key point and not on the criminal charges. Margarito's attorney Arthur Goldberg agreed. He called the charges "outrageous" and said they were engineered by Margarito's political rivals in San Fernando.[25]

Finally, the former mayor of San Fernando and director of the city parks department pleaded guilty to a felony count of conspiring to submit fraudulent court documents which was reduced to a misdemeanor in August 20, 1996, after Margarito agreed to finish 200 hours of community service time. "Nobody accused him of taking kickbacks or any money, "Goldberg said. "If he got in trouble, it's because he's got a big heart. He was basically doing it because he's a good guy."[26] Xavier Flores also voiced similar views. He noted that the whole process was good in that it proved that Jess did not gain personally from any of his actions, but added that the case should never have gone to court. "We know of many instances where department heads actually pocketed money or had other personal gains, and their cases were handled administratively, as Margarito's case should have been," he said. Councilman Doude Wysbeek, the only emblem of the Republican Party on the council, said, "the assertion that city officials engaged in a witch hunt was untrue."[27]

Summary

In an April 10, 2010, interview, Jess Margarito was in a more reflective mood.[28] As a reformer, he said he wanted to fundamentally do what he thought was right, but found the old establishment conspiring to do him harm. He specifically found fault in the city administrator and Councilman Doude Wysbeek for he thought they shared responsibility in reporting the allegations against him to the county district attorney. He admitted he committed a gaffe, reflecting poor judgment, and learned from it. In hindsight, he explained that he could have helped the court assigned workers just as well by asking them to go back to the Van Nuys volunteer agency responsible for managing the workers hours to reschedule their work time with the city. The agency had a good record, accommodating the workers with the city and would have made reasonable adjustments to the parks director's recommendations. The workers were carpenters by trade and Mr. Margarito had a plan for them to complete their service hours on weekends and evenings to do cabinets and wood shelves for the city parks. However, two of Margarito's steadfast supporters made some revealing criticism of the Chicano leader for defying conventional wisdom. Ruben Rodríguez believed that Jess Margarito made a social blunder as manager of his department. He had lost sight that he was no longer mayor of San Fernando. He also contended that Jess should not have taken on the job as parks director. Logically, he concluded that he was put there by the Anglo political and economic elites to control him.[29] Robert Villafaña was of the opinion that Jess should have resigned the moment the allegations surfaced in public, another interesting case in point coming from a true friend. "Politicians never learn when to quit when they get themselves in difficulties. Once they hold power, they don't want to relinquish it," was his observation.[30]

There is an irony in all of this. Although four of the five council members were Mexican Americans, they could not maximize the power they had since Mayor Dan Acuña and Councilman Ray Ojeda worked closely with Councilman Doude Wysbeek, the only non-Latino on the council. Acuña and Ojeda were front for the old guard. A question was asked why his former ally Mayor Dan Acuña repeatedly turned against him throughout this ordeal, Margarito explained that the mayor wanted to regain the grace of his former business friends whom he had admonished for their racial remarks made in a previous council meeting. Margarito correctly observed that Acuña was looking for a method of being accepted again by his non-Latino friends. He had been in trouble before. He had filed for bankruptcy in 1987 and, after working 20 years as a mail carrier in the area, resigned from the U.S. Postal Service while he was being investigated for not delivering mail.[31] The mail had been found in the trunk of his vehicle when it was repossessed. His business friends had stood behind him. No charges were filed. Nonetheless, in 1991 a recall effort against Councilman Daniel Acuña was initiated by Gabriel Rodríguez and Mary Tuomy, but fell short of the number of signatures needed to put the issue before the voters. They charged Acuña with being unfit for office because of his resignation from his job as a mail carrier and for his personal financial troubles. San Fernando Park and Recreation Director Jess Margarito, Councilmen José Hernández, Salvador Ponce, and Pastor Ullrich of San Rosa Catholic Church stood behind him as they campaigned successfully against the recall. In January 1994, the *Daily News* repeated the charges against Acuña in anticipation of the March San Fernando City Council elections. He lost the election by a wide margin for a third four-year term.

The city administrator adds another ironic twist to this story and a sad one because Mayor Margarito was the one who lobbied the council to hire her as its first woman city administrator. In his view, Mary Strenn determined his fate. It has long been accepted as axiomatic that in politics there are no permanent friends, only permanent interests. In the course of the interview, Jess Margarito said in retrospect that he now realized that power is a process that does not always produce results, but a journey that requires patience and constant work—a condition for social change.[32] As with many reformers, he was a tragic hero. The controversy ended in a predictable way.[33] He was terminated from his job on January 4, 1994, ending his political career.[34] Peter

Sherry, in his perceptive discussion on community resistance to change article "Tolerating Intolerance in American Politics," says, "It is understandable, if regrettable that Latinos encounter resistance today, when they are on the move politically." He also contends that "such excesses are to be expected on the struggle for advancement and power in this diverse and competitive society."[35]

Politics is adversarial, crafty, and painful at times. It's a tough business. Yet it's a noble tradition, especially one of some reward, challenge, complexity, and risk. In a political culture driven by group interest, if people don't get involved, they got nothing—a recurring theme of this study. Many politicians, however, should be admired for their devotion to public service.

Notes

1. "San Fernando Accused of Racial Bias," *Daily News*, June 26, 1993; "San Fernando's Latinos Flex Power, Find Conflict," *Daily News*, July 5, 1993. The authenticity of this section and the following is supported by the fact that the author was serving at the time of the various decisions as a member of the San Fernando City Council. The names of the detractors are withheld to protect their names' sake.
2. "City Council Splits on City Attorney Firing," *San Fernando Valley SUN*, June 23, 1993.
3. *Daily News*, June 26, 1993. In a letter to the *Daily News* Editor (July 15, 1993), Raul Godinez wrote: "The irony is that Rutan & Tucker was selected in much the same manner as Ochoa & Sillas—by word of mouth. Yet no one accused the former all-white City Council of discrimination for hiring a white law firm back then. What I find most troubling is that a great number of those making racist remarks at the City Council meeting on June 25 were members of our business community. More than 80 percent of their sales are attributed to the 'brown faces' of this 'migrant town.' Furthermore, these 'brown-faced' consumers provide 34 percent of the city's general fund through sales tax revenue. Yet, spending city money on a 'brown-faced' law firm offends these people."
4. Ibid.
5. *Daily News*, July 5, 1993.
6. *San Fernando Valley SUN*, August 5, 1981.
7. *San Fernando Valley SUN*, June 23, 1993.
8. *Daily News* staff writer aptly described the incident in "Community Efforts wins Peace in Troubled Park," *Daily News*, December 27, 1992. For more on this, see "ACLU Challenges Law Banning Gangs from San Fernando Park," *Los Angeles Times*, December 18, 1992.
9. *Los Angeles Times*, September 9, 1993.
10. The employee was not reprimanded for lack of sufficient evidence; however, in a subsequent case involving a sexual act in the workplace, he was asked to resign from his well-paying city job by a new city administrator. The public works employee will not be named out of respect for his family.

11. Leslie Berger, "City Official under Investigation by D. A. Office," *Los Angeles Times*, September 9, 1993.
12. *San Fernando Valley SUN*, January 12, 1994.
13. *Los Angeles Times*, September 9, 1993.
14. See "Investigation Ignites Uproar in San Fernando," *Los Angeles Times*, November 12, 1993; "Council Heats Up in Director Investigation," *San Fernando Valley Sun,* November 17, 1993.
15. The Brown Act authored by Assemblyman Ralph M. Brown was passed in 1953 guaranteeing the public's right to know. Actions taken in violation of open meetings unless specifically authorized by the law may be voided. See government code 54950-54962.
16. See "Council Mum on Mysterious Memos," *San Fernando Valley SUN*, December 8, 1993.
17. California government code 54950-54962.
18. *Los Angeles Times*, December 18, 1993.
19. *San Fernando Valley SUN*, November 17, 1993; January 5, 1994.
20. Ibid.
21. Ibid.
22. *Los Angeles Times*, September 9, 1993, op. cit.
23. Paul Hefner, "Files Portray Margarito as Man Seduced by Power," *Daily News*, January 9, 1994.
24. Marianne Barrios, "Parks Director Dismissed," *San Fernando Valley SUN*, January 5, 1994.
25. *Daily News*, January 9, 1994.
26. Ibid.
27. Ibid.
28. Jess Margarito interview.
29. Ruben Rodriguez interview, April 9, 2010.
30. Robert Villafaña interview, April 17, 2010.
31. Councilman Daniel Acuña's personal problems were first made public in an article that appeared in *the Los Angeles Times* on December 16, 1990. See also *El Eco Del Valle*, February 14, 1991, and the *Daily News*, January 14, 1994.
32. For more on this point, see José Amaro Hernández, *Mutual Aid for Survival*, 89-90, op. cit. Also, see letter to Honorable Judge Moreno written by José A. Hernández dated September 11, 1996, appealing to the court for leniency for Jess Margarito. In the letter, Hernández provided the judge with a background surrounding the conflict in San Fernando.
33. See "San Fernando Fires Embattled Parks Director," *Los Angeles Times*, January 5, 1994; "Dismissal of Director Reverberates Through the City," *San Fernando Valley SUN*, January 12, 1994; "Ex-San Fernando Mayor Gets Probation," *Daily News*, September 18, 1996; "Former Mayor Pleads Guilty, Gets Three Years Probation," *San Fernando Valley SUN*, September 25, 1996.
34. Paul Hefner, "Parks Director Says Goodbye," *Daily News*, January 5, 1994.
35. *Los Angeles Times*, July 19, 1998. Peter Sherry, a senior fellow at the Brooking Institution, also teaches political science at Claremont McKenna College, Claremont, California.

CHAPTER 7

Making Government Work for the People

In 1988, the Chicano Roundtable of San Fernando was founded.[1] Initially, it functioned as a Chicano advocacy group as it assisted Professor José Hernández to get elected to the San Fernando City Council.[2] Héctor de Paz, Chicano Roundtable founding member, served as his campaign manager during the election. The campaign was run from the candidate's house garage. Before being elected to the city council, Hernández served on the city planning commission which handles zoning, housing, and other issues relating to land use. The city planning commission and other commissions and boards are appointed by the city council and serve as advisory to that body. The positions are voluntary, but many involved serious policy considerations. They provide an excellent way to make a difference and to learn about city government and the community. The new councilman, a professor of Chicana/o Studies at California State University, Northridge, was a founding member of the university Chicana/o Studies Department. He also served as the university Urban Studies and Planning program coordinator. He was well prepared for the tasks that lay ahead. The most wide-eyed liberal member of the city council on social and cultural issues, he stated during his first month in office that he wanted the city council to "invest in people" in order to help San Fernando overcome poverty and crime, and to provide for the safety of schoolchildren.[3] He also hoped that the council considered helping community service organizations by providing city assistance with their activities. The community non-profit organizations offered a multitude of social services and cultural events to San Fernando residents, services that municipalities should provide. He urged the council to consider lowering income limits for low-income housing rehabilitation loans. He underscored the importance of government action in improving the lives of people. These ideas struck a chord with his conservative friends. A colleague who served with him in the city planning commission fired back at his conviction. "I guess you could classify him (Hernández) as a government employee that believes the government should pay for everything," adding, "I guess one of his biggest traits is he feels that the citizens shouldn't have to pay for services. But we (the city) can't afford to pay. We have to make the citizens pay."[4] Mayor Daniel Acuña assured his constituents that he didn't believe Hernández's lofty ideas would change the council's philosophy.

The Culture of Government Responsibility in San Fernando

Amid the tension over who controlled city government, the city council advanced a vigorous public service agenda. Small city governments generally function properly, providing policy direction and strong financial standing. They are responsible for providing basic community services such as police and fire protection, construction and maintenance of streets and sidewalks, adequate water supply, sewage and waste disposal, operation of parks, libraries, education, public transportation, trauma/emergency service, and the like—vital services the residents pay for. They also provide good-paying jobs with benefits for city employees and their families. Many of these services are paid by the general fund or special assessments. Police and fire protection take over 50 percent of the general fund. Unlike some other small cities, San Fernando has its own police force and water works. It contracts with the City of Los Angeles for fire and emergency services. It also contracts with the City of Los Angeles sewer service for treatment and disposal. The Los Angeles County Library System provides San Fernando with library services. The county also provides the city with water drainage and animal control services. Southern California Edison, Verizon Communications, and Southern California Gas Company also provide other vital services. A private company collects the city's waste and recycling materials. The city also contracted with a private firm for street sweeping service. San Fernando is a member of the Los Angeles Unified School District and the Los Angeles Community College District. San Fernando taxpayers pay for the education of their children.

In small communities, politics is about which neighborhood gets a park upgraded and street improved, and who gets the good city jobs, the name of a street, and public safety. On May 5, 1992, Councilman Dr. José Hernández was appointed mayor of San Fernando. He was chosen as part of a system that rotates the five members of the city council into the office of mayor each year. He had been a city council member since 1990, but had been politically active for many years. On July 1, 1992, the council adopted a $22 million budget for the fiscal year 1992-1993 that helped the city provide a high level of public service despite the state cuts to municipalities. The budget is a political instrument reflecting community needs as worked out by its elected representatives. It clearly reflects the elected leaders' view of the role of government in the community.

New immigrants to the area pumped a new life to local businesses keeping the city healthy economically and on a more positive course of economic development. It was the council's view that political empowerment does not necessarily mean economic empowerment. Economic development affects the entire community. It brings newer shopping opportunities and resources in the form of city revenues and jobs. A city marketing brochure was produced to assist staff in their campaign to attract new business to San Fernando. It had a slogan that read, "City of San Fernando Historic and Visionary." Property values were at an upswing adding tax revenue to the city coffers. Municipal governments generally rely on the property tax, building and business permits, parking meter fees, water and sewage charges, and a host of other permits. California shares with local government state sales and gasoline taxes, and other state fees. In addition, cities get state and federal funds for specific projects. The city hired additional personnel while other cities were reducing their workforce in the dark days of the 1992 recession. The new municipal employees included a police officer and a new code enforcement official. A position for human service specialist was created and filled. The position of assistant to the city administrator was upgraded and filled. Other administrative positions were also upgraded. Trees were trimmed, streets swept, and parks cleaned. Graffiti and crime were at a minimal; however, the proliferation of alcohol sales in San Fernando was a problem. Curbside recycling was introduced in April with a high rate of resident participation in the program. The council put a high priority on police and fire safety as well as youth and social services, and cultural events. A $300,000 communication station was installed in the police department to increase efficiency of police service. Additional parking space was constructed near the city police station on First Street by city employees saving extra taxpayer money. Traffic barriers at railroad crossings were also constructed to ensure public safety and in preparation for the commuter rail service.[5] Yet, many residents were not entirely satisfied with this level of public service. They expected more from government.

The Sylmar/San Fernando Commuter Rail Station

Construction of the commuter rail station on the Hubbard and First Streets site began in March 1993. The Sylmar/San Fernando Metrolink Rail Station started to serve area residents from the east San Fernando Valley in July. The route starts in Santa Clarita and then makes stops in Sylmar/San Fernando, Burbank, Glendale, and Los Angeles. The $1.7 million station project consisted of a canopy, a platform and a 420-space parking lot. The city of Los Angeles contributed two-thirds while the city of San Fernando contributed the remaining cost of the station as part of the project partnership by borrowing funds from the Los Angeles County Transportation Commission.[6] Other improvements to the project included construction of low-income housing next to the station. Another construction addition included an onsite child care facility, one of the first transit facilities in the nation to have child care service on the site. The Sylmar/San Fernando Child Care facility was paid by a state special fund.[7] In 1993, San Fernando also received $999,900 in Proposition C grant funds (state funds) from the Metropolitan Transit Authority to build a bikeway one mile in length along the Sylmar/San Fernando Metrolink railroad right-of-way. The bikeway was completed in 1994. It runs west-east connecting the Metrolink station the city civic center, the San Fernando Middle School, and the César Chávez memorial recreation area. In another project, the council allocated $750,000 of redevelopment money for housing improvement projects in old neighborhoods. This was part of a three-year neighborhood preservation program. Furthermore, four affordable units were constructed on Kewen Street and sold as soon as the properties were put out for bids.[8]

Redevelopment

In 1978, voters passed Proposition 13 which capped annual real estate tax increases, and forced cities to increase their reliance on sales taxes and redevelopment to fund public services. Redevelopment is a clever device for raising local revenues for community improvement. Redevelopment money comes from a special fund created by the California state legislature for municipalities. Under the California Community Redevelopment Law, municipalities declare "blighted area that constitute physical and economic liabilities and required redevelopment in the interest of health, safety, and general welfare of these communities."[9] Municipalities then make out plans for the improvement, rehabilitation, and redevelopment of project areas resulting in increased property values and additional tax revenues to local entities. The "tax increment" as it is called becomes part of the redevelopment fund managed by the Community Redevelopment Agency. In small cities, the city council assumed the role of the community agency. The two bodies are made up of the same people. The agency holds its own meetings apart from the city council agenda. They have separate agendas as well as clearly marked minutes. Agency funds generally are not included as part of the city's general fund. There are strict legal guidelines that separate redevelopment funds from the city general fund. However, the City of San Fernando uses redevelopment money to pay for city staff salaries when the expenditures are related to redevelopment agency services. Twenty percent of redevelopment funds is set aside for low-income housing. Agency members are paid $35 per meeting in San Fernando. Many cities have accumulated enormous sums of redevelopment money used for economic development. They spent these public funds assisting developers to build shopping centers, theatres, Starbucks coffee shops, and the like as a way of creating jobs, sales taxes, and new shopping opportunities. Public land is often given or leased to developers for a nominal sum. (This practice will be discussed in detail in other sections of the study.) In dire need, the governor was able to recover a portion of these funds in order to balance the state budget. In a way, redevelopment funds are state tax dollars allocated to municipal governments for improvement projects. The state legislature allows redevelopment agencies to collect property taxes that would otherwise go to schools. In hard times, the state would save billions by sending the much needed funds back to schools and counties. However, during the 2010 mid-term elections, California voters passed Proposition 23 by a two-thirds vote, barring the state from taking funds from local governments and agencies.

Finally after much community input, the Las Palmas Park Master Plan was completed. It included additional playing fields, tennis and basketball courts, children's playgrounds, and a multipurpose youth and senior center for the community. New youth programs were added in all city parks. Councilman Hernández was at odds with his colleagues and city administrator who sought to protect redevelopment funds for economic development. To him, there had to be a balance between the need of developers—that is, subsidies to developers of strip malls—and the needed recreation facilities and other social responsibilities of the community. He questioned the council inquiring why redevelopment funds have not been used for park improvements. "Public funds for economic development have to spill-over into social programs," he said, adding, "We should not sacrifice social needs."[10] How much government spent for economic development and how much for social programs became a nagging issue in council meetings. Views differ on the use of agency funding. Redevelopment law is not clear on this subject. Fernando city councils have relied on pro-business administrators to decide how redevelopment funds are being used.

Special Funds

In addition to the general fund and a separate redevelopment account, San Fernando has special funds, some of which are listed here: The Street Lighting Fund is a city's voter-approval Landscaped and Lighting Act Assessment to pay for citywide street lighting and landscaping of thruways. Unlike other cities, properties located on street corners pay the same rate as properties in the middle of the block. The Retirement Fund is another voter-approved tax levy designed to pay part of the cost of the city's membership in the Public Employees' Retirement System (PERS). According to city figures, the city's cost has increased significantly due to rising rates in both health and insurance premiums and member contributions to PERS. Employees' contributions to the retirement fund went from 2 percent to 4 percent in FY 2011-2012. The city matched the employees' contribution to the retirement fund.[11] Small cities like San Fernando have run out of options to fund their retirement fund as their leaders continued to bow to labor unions' and police associations' as well as administrators' demands for competitive salary and benefit increases.[12] San Fernando voters will not approve an increase in the city's "retirement tax" rate to cover rising pension costs. Elected officials will have to make tough choices in a struggling economy.

The Quimby Act Fund accounts for receipts from developers, who are required under state law to provide and support park facilities. This fund is indispensable to the housing construction conditions in the city. The Community Development Block Grant (CDBG) sponsored by the U.S. Department of Housing and Urban Development is another important source of revenue in all local governments. These funds are earmarked for local community development activities such as street, sidewalk and infrastructure improvements, housing, and support for code enforcement. This federally aided program has become important especially to small cities that need to revitalize rundown neighborhoods and help low-income residents. The program also provides funding for Meals on Wheels and other programs that benefit seniors. Originally designed to funnel money to large cities in decline, now money is handed out to communities rich and poor. Wealthy cities sell their surplus CDBG funds to other cities at a reduced rate for fear of losing their unused funds to the federal government. The city of San Fernando, for example, has purchased CDBG surplus funds at bargain rates. The exchange rate varied between 49 to 80 cents for every dollar purchased. The exchange rate varies depending upon the amount of surplus funds available. The future of such grants is in limbo as Congress deals with its budget crisis.

Fees paid by residents for water, sewage, and refuse service are held in the city Enterprise Fund. The city has not increased these fees for many years, although cost of government has gone up. The Grant Fund accounts for major grants received citywide from business, state, and federal agencies. City staff brought in $30 million from outside sources from 2005 to 2009. Other special funds include the Street Maintenance Fund, the State Asset Seizure Fund, and the Federal Asset Seizure Fund. Property and money seized in law enforcement raids are distributed to local enforcement agencies and held in these accounts to replenish their department equipment. San Fernando has a Self-Insurance Fund, a self-insured entity that provides for brief legal needs. On some occasions, the City of San Fernando has borrowed to fund major public projects or pay its major obligations.

San Fernando in Forefront of Drive to Honor César Chávez

Immediately after the death of farm labor leader César E. Chávez on April 23, 1993, a number of San Fernando community organizations including the Chicano Roundtable and Pueblo y Salud, Inc., an educational alcohol and tobacco prevention agency, began lobbying the San Fernando City Council to declare a legal holiday honoring the late civil-rights leader. At a good moment, the council on a proposal introduced by Mayor Dr. José Hernández agreed to proclaim March 31, Chávez's birthday, a legal holiday for the city. This was viewed nationally as the first city to recognize the late César Chávez whose long, hard battles against injustices of farm workers brought about major changes in the fields. As a result, the action influenced the State of California and other cities to approve similar actions.[13] Earlier a bid to establish a statewide holiday was vetoed by Republican Governor Pete Wilson. Many families in town identified with Chávez and his struggles to protect farm workers and their families against exploitation. Their parents and grandparents had lived through the problems that affected farm workers and their families. To them, Chávez represented the best in a human being. He stood for the dignity and self-worth of the individual, the right to associate and to organize in the workplace, and practiced nonviolence in citizen protests. Many other San Fernando events commemorating the life and legacy of the famous American hero followed, subsidized extensively by San Fernando taxpayers—namely, La Marcha de Justicia (the March for Justice) inspired by the 1966 historical farm workers march from Delano to Sacramento, the César E. Chávez Social Justice Award that acknowledges community leaders who carry on the César Chávez tradition of service to the community, and the César E. Chávez Memorial, co-funded by the City of San Fernando, the Los Angeles Metropolitan Transportation Authority and the Friends of César E. Chávez Memorial Committee. The Friends of César E. Chávez Memorial Committee were the principal influence for the memorial project providing a leadership role in the planning and funding from start to finish.[14] Business, labor, and non-profit organizations were also major donors to the memorial project.

La Marcha de Justicia Annual Event

In determining to keep César E. Chávez' memory alive, several Chicano leaders planned various events to celebrate the life and legacy of the famous civil-rights and union leader. On César E. Chávez Day March 31, 1994, the first March for Justice was held to commemorate the 1966 historical farm workers march from Delano to Sacramento. Xavier Flores who displayed a certain flair for organizing said it best about the event: "Our goal is to ensure that future generations acknowledge this great leader and carry on in his tradition of struggling for the dignity of the poor."[15] Pueblo y Salud, Inc. under its former executive director has been a key co-sponsor of the event since its inception. The first march began in the evening at two points: at O'Melveny and Workman and Pico and Mission Boulevard (now San Fernando Mission Boulevard) led by the Danzantes (Aztec dancers) and culminating at Las Palmas Park. El Mariachi Los Halcones, and Ballet Folklorico Ollín directed by Virginia Diediker, performed for the large gathering at the park celebration. Joanne Orijel member of the César Chávez Commemorative Committee presented a plaque to Councilman José Hernández in recognition for his drive and initiative to make the City of San Fernando the first in the nation to make César Chávez's birthday a legal holiday.[16] He knew what farm workers went through; he lived their lives.[17]

The annual March for Justice has grown over the years with added youth attractions that include a youth study workshop, a student essay and art contest, a kids' educational corner, and a science fair (Celebra La Ciencia). Colleges such as Pepperdine University, University of California (UCLA), University of Southern California (USC), California State University, Northridge (CSUN), and Mission College alternate each year to assist in the science fair. Local hospitals distribute information on health concerns. Providence Hospital of Mission Hills promotes a Mobile Blood Drive. The youth study workshop discusses issues of importance to students and their families such as preparing for college, college admission procedures, school scholarships and college financial assistance, and other topics of concern to them—that is, immigration, job opportunities, service to others, and respect for others.

The activities for the March for Justice begin at Brand Park across from the San Fernando Mission in Mission Hills. The City of Los Angeles joined the City of San Fernando, Pueblo y Salud, Inc., and the César Chávez Commemorative Committee in sponsoring the activities honoring the late union activist. The César Chávez Commemorative Committee organizes the activities for the popular community event. Participants are united at Brand Park for a fine morning of music and speeches. Elected officials and union organizers address the public. Speakers use the occasion to explain what Chávez stood for. They remind the marchers about the importance of community involvement in their communities, quoting César Chávez's famous refrain, "The End of Education is Service to the Community." Elected officials tell their listeners about bills that are being discussed in their chambers. The music of Los Sencillos directed by Ruben Rodríguez sets the mood for the marchers.[18] The march begins as the young and elderly walk down Brand Boulevard carrying signs with political messages and portraits of their famous hero, chanting Si se Puede (Yes we can), for which César Chávez came to be known. The march led by the Danzantes dance group is about two miles to San Fernando Chávez Park (formerly San Fernando Recreation Park). Mariachi groups welcome the marchers into the park grounds. Schoolchildren are bussed to the event and march as they wave the farm workers union flag. The happy marchers are welcomed by radio and television personalities as well as local elected leaders. The occasion is festive and educational at the César Chávez Park. Work of the winning student participants of the art and essay contest is exhibited. The wild animal exhibit is always popular with children at the science fair. Youth participate in dance and music groups. There is plenty of food and "paletas" (Mexican popsicles). The César E. Chávez Social Justice Award is presented at this time. The annual community event of the March of Justice concludes the following day with an evening Mass at a local Catholic Church.

The César E. Chávez Social Justice Award

On April 13, 1999, the city council presented the first César E. Chávez Social Justice Award to Alex Reza, a longtime teacher at San Fernando High School for teaching youth Chávez's cause (La Causa) for farm workers' justice in the fields as well as highlights of his life of service to others. Each year the recipient of the award is honored during the March for Justice cultural celebration. Mayor Hernández who instituted the award said that the prestigious award is a tribute to those who consistently for at least 10 years have given their time to improve the lives of others. Others who have received the César E. Chávez Social Justice Award in the order presented are Ed Rose, Professor Everto Ruiz, Xavier Flores, Dr. José Hernández, Virginia Diedeker, Soledad Alatorre, Norma Ramirez, José Luis Ramirez, Irene Tovar, Carol Rose, Normal Gallegos, Rodolfo Acuña, and former council member and mayor of San Fernando, Julie Ruelas (posthumously).[19]

In 2009, the City of San Fernando discontinued its sponsorship of the Marcha de Justicia (March for Justice) and the César Chávez Social Justice Award annual events. Currently, the César Chávez Commemorative Committee continues to sponsor the events with support from donations, fund-raisers, Pueblo y Salud, Inc., and the City of Los Angeles. The march begins at Brand Park across from the San Fernando Mission in Mission Hills and ends at Ritchie Valens Park in Pacoima where families enjoy various attractions, good food, and entertainment throughout the afternoon.

The César E. Chávez Memorial

After 11 years of planning, fund-raising, construction, and delays due to its intricate designs, the César E. Chávez Memorial was unveiled on October 22, 2004, to a large crowd on the corner of Truman and Wolfskill Streets in San Fernando. It includes 23,000 square feet of green space, a 6-foot bronze sculpture of the labor leader, a fountain, a 100-foot mural depicting the life and struggles of the farm worker leader, and 10 metal cutout silhouettes of migrant farm workers with a small hoe crouching in the field—a labor of love by Glendale artist Ignácio Gómez.[20]

The occasion of the unveiling was festive and a moment of joy, pride, and appreciation. The main speakers included Max Kennedy, son of the late Robert F. Kennedy, and Paul Chávez, the son of César Chávez, area dignitaries, and many community activists who at one time marched with César Chávez. Ruben Rodríguez, chairman of the Friends of the César E. Chávez Memorial Art Project Committee, served as master of ceremony. The Associated Press reported that the memorial was one of the largest Chávez memorials nationwide.[21] The goal, according to Ignácio Gómez, was "to create a space of hope, inspiration and education," adding "it's personal because I know the hardship of the farm workers and what they went through."[22] Gómez who sculptured the Chávez bronze statue said of the union leader: "He was soft-spoken, but to me he was a giant, and I hope the statue portrays that."[23]

Jesus and Alicía Hurtado of San Fernando were overjoyed at seeing the magnificent display of art which they felt was so fitting for a person who suffered and sacrificed so much for the poor and the humble. "I met him [Chávez] in person along with Dolores Huerta during a grape strike and feel proud of knowing him," explained Alicía Hurtado. She added: "Thanks to God the Memorial was in San Fernando, a great honor for him and all the people."[24] She was happy for San Fernando for building such a positive inspirational monument. Ron Ruiz, assistant to the city administrator observed: "It was well worth it."[25] Dan Labrado city recreation and parks director voiced similar view. Both played key roles in the development of the memorial project. César E. Chávez had long been a hero in the city where more than 90 percent of the population is Latino. Mayor Dr. José Hernández, who conceived of the idea for a memorial to honor the union leader, calls it his proudest moment in politics. He was definitive of the opinion that "César Chávez is an inspiration to all working-class people, domestic laborers—not only to Chicanos and Latinos, but to all. He represents the fight for equality and I am so elated to have this."[26] Andrés Irlando, president of the César E. Chávez Foundation, wrote in a letter to the San Fernando City Council on behalf of the foundation and the entire Chávez family: "We were honored and excited to participate in the dedication of the César E. Chávez Memorial on October

22. Congratulations on creating one of the most important and significant public-art projects on César Chávez in the entire nation."[27]

Following in time, San Fernando Recreation Park located across from the César E. Chávez Memorial was renamed César E. Chávez Park. A section of First Street which parallels César E. Chávez Memorial was renamed Robert F. Kennedy Lane. Robert Kennedy was a chief supporter and friend of the Cesar Chavez family. He worked closely with César Chávez fighting to end the exploitation of workers and get fair wages for working families. The mural painted by artist Ignácio Gómez recreated a favorite photo of Robert F. Kennedy supporting a weakened Chávez during one of his hunger strike. The City of San Fernando maintains this beautiful piece of outdoor art.

In summary, the City of San Fernando was in stable financial condition during the 1990s and thus was able to provide its residents with vital services. Furthermore, the César E. Chávez project represented the city's solidarity with its citizens. It rekindled in people the importance of working together and giving to others as César Chávez had said: "It is my deepest belief that only by giving our lives do we find life." It demonstrated that much can be accomplished when government, business, and community organizations unite to give people a sense of community. The image of San Fernando as a family-oriented community, "historic and visionary," began to improve. Notwithstanding, there were major policy issues that awaited a motivated city council.

Courtesy of Artist Ignácio Gómez and Photographer David Jimenez and the César Chávez March for Justice Committee

Reprinted by permission of Ignacio Gomez (Artist) and David Jimenez (Photographer)

César Chávez receiving Holy Communion with Senator Robert F. Kennedy, César Chávez Memorial, Artist Ignácio Gómez, Photographer David Jiménez

Notes

1. The Chicano Roundtable was organized in 1988. Founding members of the Chicano advocacy group included José de Paz, Héctor de Paz, Everto Ruiz, Ruben Rodriguez, Xavier Flores, and Dr. José Hernández. They hailed from the Chicano Studies Department at San Fernando Valley College (now California State University, Northridge). The Chicano Roundtable is the predecessor of Pueblo y Salud, Inc. of San Fernando.

2. Dr. José Hernández served as Councilman and Mayor of San Fernando during the following periods: 1990-1994, 1997-2009.

3. Quoted in the *Daily News*, April 9, 1990. See city staff memorandums dated December 18, 1992 and July 1, 1994.

4. Ibid.

5. "State of the City of San Fernando," Mayor Report to the Council, December 9, 1992.

6. *Los Angeles Times*, March 23, 1993.

7. Ibid.

8. "State of the City of San Fernando," Mayor Report to the Council, December 9, 1992.

9. Senior city planner Fred Ramirez assisted with this section. For instances of corruption, questionable spending, and poor accountability of many of California's redevelopment agencies, see "Lots of Cash and Little Scrutiny," in *Los Angeles Times*, October 1, 2010. See

also redevelopment and affordable housing issues in *Los Angeles Times*, October 3, 2010.

10. Quoted in *San Fernando Valley SUN*, November 3, 1993. See also Jacqueline Fox, "Balancing Act," *San Fernando Valley Business Journal*, December 8, 2003.

11. This information was presented to city council during the budget workshops.

12. The present writer and other council members felt the need to compensate their city employees and police officers with increased salaries and expanded benefits each year in order to compete for experienced employees with cities of similar size.

13. This popular event was covered by all area newspapers. *Los Angeles Times*, June 14, 1993; *Daily News*, March 28, 1994; *Mexican American Sun*, April 7, 1994.

14. Members of the Friends of César E. Chávez Memorial Committee consisted of Ruben Rodriguez, chairperson; Angel R. Cervantes, teacher, Morningside Elementary; Xavier Flores, executive director, Pueblo y Salud, Inc.; Imelda Gómez, fine artist; Dr. José Hernández, councilman; Nury Martínez, office of Senator Richard Alarcon; Virginia Megerdichian, executive secretary, Pueblo y Salud, Inc., Cynthia Alarcón Negrete, artist; Leonard Negrete, SF Valley Latino Art Council; Alex Reza, retired teacher; and Ed Rose, co-founder of MEND. Chief Engineer Edwin Galvéz and his public works staff were essential members of the project construction team. Other staff members were Recreation Supervisor Helen Collins and Cultural Arts Supervisor Virginia Diediker.

15. Quoted in the *San Fernando Valley SUN*, March 30, 1994. Author's note: On the day after the death of César E. Chávez, the César E. Chávez Commemorative Committee held a vigil celebrating the life of the labor leader. The vigil was held at the Safeway Super Market parking lot on the corner of Mission Boulevard (now San Fernando Mission Boulevard) and Pico Street. With the passing of time, some members of the César Chávez Commemorative Committee had assumed that the vigil held on April 24, 1993, represented the first March for Justice in sharp contrast to other members who felt differently. Those who attended the vigil at the Safeway parking lot were Joan Origel, Virginia Ufano, Virginia Diediker, Francisco Verdín, Everto Ruiz, David and Fran Ramirez, Alex Reza, Rosa Chacón, Jess and Cecilia Margarito, Julian Leon, Ruben and Adriana Rodriguez, Dr José Hernández, Xavier Flores, Ed and Carol Rose, Marjorie Britt, Robert Villafaña, Father David Ulrich, Salvador Ponce, Larry Chacón, María Lozano, Frank Yudico, Eduardo Palacios, Irene Tovar, and others.

16. Ibid.

17. Dr. José Hernández was born and raised in South Texas. He lived for three years what has been called the typical life of an itinerant farm worker, moving in a canvas-covered truck with his brothers and mother and other families under difficult conditions to Minnesota, Indiana, and Illinois to follow the crops. Children were pulled out of school early in May and returned to school late in September. In November 1950 after the beet harvest season, he enlisted in the U.S. Army Air Force in Fargo, North Dakota, and never returned to the low-paying, grueling seasonal work in the fields.

18. The following were the original members of Los Sencillos who initially started providing music associated with the farm workers strike: Ruben R. Rodriguez, Leo R. Salazar, Eliseo Villanueva, Danny Tirado and Arturo Vasquez.

19. Julie Ruelas passed away on December 31, 2011. She was 56.
20. The César E. Chávez Memorial aroused the interest of local and national media. See *Daily News*, October 24, 2004; *San Fernando Valley SUN*, October 28, 2004. See also the *Los Angeles Times*, March 3, 2004; *Daily News*, February 2, 2004. About the project artist, see the Glendale, California *News-Press*, May 2, 2003.
21. Associated Press release, October 27, 2004.
22. *Daily News*, October 24, 2004, op. cit.
23. Ibid.
24. The Spanish-language *La Opinion*, October 24, 2004. The English translation was provided by the author of the study.
25. *Daily News*, October 24, 2004.
26. Ibid.
27. The letter to the city council was dated October 27, 2004.

CHAPTER 8

Public Access to Policymaking in a Small Government

This chapter begins with a brief discussion of what is probably the most important step in self-government, namely, public access to the policymaking process. This is followed by two specific issue areas, which will be examined to show how San Fernando City Council addressed these important issues in the city. Policy makes a big difference in the lives of people. For them, the only way to influence policy was to get involved in politics. Latino victories at the polls gave them access to their elected leaders, pressing them to address their concerns and needs of long standing. As their numbers became large and their voter participation increased, they used their new political clout to demand solutions to the big problems which had loomed in their minds for decades. Thus, the new Latino council majority faced the problem of governance; ignoring their demands risked the wrath of their constituents. Winning elections and governance are vastly different. The appointment of the Mexican American legal firm in 1993 to represent the city's legal matters was the first sign of Chicano empowerment in the 2.4-square-mile city with a population less than 24,000 northeast of downtown Los Angeles.[1] Mayor Daniel Acuña, Mayor Pro-Tem José Hernández, Rosa Chacón, Raymond Ojeda, and Doude Wysbeek formed the 1992 city council. In the past, the crucial hurdle had been getting their issues placed on the agenda of the council and the presence of representatives who were interested to hear about their concerns. But that's not the case anymore.

Agenda Procedures and Order of Business

The agenda is part of the governmental process. Those who control the agenda control the debate and the type of policy formulation and implementation. The city administrator is charged with the implementation of the policy. If the people's issues are not put on the agenda, it's impossible for government to act upon them. In the past, the crucial hurdles for Latinos had been getting their issues placed on councils' agendas for consideration. They lacked adequate representation in this institution to facilitate that step. However, real change came from the grassroots—the ballot.

All municipalities have procedures for the conduct of business at meetings. The procedural manual for the conduct of city council meetings in the City of San Fernando reads as follows: "The order of business of each Council meeting shall be as contained in the Agenda prepared by the City Administrator. The City Council shall follow the order of business as outlined in the prepared Agenda. Items may be taken out of order by the Mayor or by a majority of the Council. The Agenda for all regular meetings, with all background staff report, shall be available to the public at the meeting and 72 hours in advance of the meeting (usually on Wednesday of the prior week) at the City Clerk's office."[2] A council member who wishes to have an item placed on an agenda of the city council meeting "shall provide the City Clerk with an agenda report that provides a general description of the item, the desired action and include any other relevant written materials or information which the member would like to have considered at the meeting. The agenda report and any other supplementary material must be submitted to the City Clerk by 12:00 p.m. the Wednesday preceding the City Council meeting…."[3] Individuals either inside the government structure or with direct access to the council could put items on the agenda as well. The public including advocacy groups were afforded the opportunity to submit their issues on the agenda for discussion and action. The procedural manual required that "Any citizen requesting to place an item on the City Council agenda shall advise the City Clerk or the City Administrator in writing no later than 5:00 p.m. on the Monday preceding the meeting at which he/she wishes the item to be considered. The City Administrator shall make copies of such requests for City Council members prior to the next City council meeting. If the City Administrator concludes that the matter is appropriate for Council consideration, it shall be placed on either of the next two regular City Council agendas."[4]

Approval of the Agenda

The agenda of the meeting includes an item entitled "Approved of Agenda." This occurs immediately after "roll call." During this time, a council member may move to approve the agenda as presented or make a motion to approve the agenda with changes. The next step is the approval of minutes. The council may approve the minutes of the previous council meeting immediately, unless the majority of the council requests a reading of the minutes. The city clerk provides the council with the minutes in a package of the agenda. Finally, the public is invited to address the city council on any item placed on the agenda meetings for discussion, referral, or action. These procedures also applied to city Redevelopment Agency and commission meetings. Public hearings are essential to the growth of a self-governing community.

The Issue of Alcohol Sales Availability and Alcohol-Related Problems

During the early 1990s, the city council faced angry crowds concerned about increasing alcohol-related issues in the city and the failure of elected leaders to deal effectively with the dangers of alcohol abuse. The family-oriented city was known for "people weaving drunkenly through the streets."[5] Councilman José Hernández was central in moving the discussion of the issue forward. On January 1, 1992, he told the public: "If you fear for the lives of your children, read this message carefully."[6] Then he gave an account of the increasing alcohol-related problems of the city and neighboring communities. In December 1991, for example, several convenient stores (a.k.a. liquor stores) in San Fernando were cited for selling beer and wine to minors. Middle school students bragged that it was relatively easy for them to buy beer and wine coolers from San Fernando retail stores. Alcohol was a factor in the tragic death of St. Ferdinand Catholic Church parishioner and Los Angeles police officer Tina Herbrat.[7] Also, a Santa Rosa Catholic Church parishioner was killed in 1991 by a drunk driver at the Glenoaks and Hubbard Streets intersection. These accidents prompted church parish priests to stop providing beer and wine in their annual fiestas. During a discussion period of a council meeting, Xavier Flores, executive director of Pueblo y Salud, Inc., complained regarding the use of alcohol-related advertisements during city-sponsored culture events in the city.

Drunken driving had made the streets the most dangerous in the northeast San Fernando Valley. This section of the valley had the dubious distinction of having one of the highest DUIs (driving under the influence) per capita rate. More than one-third of the drunken driving fatalities occurred in the northeast corner of the Valley.[8] There were 340 accidents alone in the San Fernando area (ZIP code 91340) related to alcohol abuse and 134 were seriously hurt during 1991. According to court referral for drunk driving cases, Latinos accounted for 90 percent of such cases heard in the Los Angeles County Courthouse in San Fernando and 60 percent of those in the Van Nuys Courthouse.[9] Councilman Hernández warned that the problems would get worse if the city did not address the issue of alcohol availability in the city. He felt that liquor store and restaurant owners targeted San Fernando and Pacoima as good places to sell alcoholic beverages because of the growing young immigrant populations.

Questions were raised concerning why Latinos had the largest problem related to alcohol use. Some residents surveyed blamed unemployment, saying that many out-of-work people spent the days drinking. Xavier Flores who worked for Northeast Valley Health Corporation (NEVHC), a government-funded alcohol abuse program, and founder of the Latino Coalition on Alcohol Abuse of the San Fernando Valley, insisted that the "community's drunk-driving problem may not be entirely a cultural one." He said, "I think economics plays a larger role than anything else."[10] José Hernández, chair of the Latino Coalition on Alcohol Abuse of the San Fernando Valley, and professor of urban studies and planning at California State University, Northridge, was of the opinion that newly arrived immigrants to the United States may not have come from places where "laws governing drunk driving were not enforced."[11] (During this period Professor Hernández was on leave with the School of Social and Behavioral Sciences urban studies and planning program.) Others pointed to the overconcentration of liquor-serving establishments in a small areas. Professor Hernández and other Chicano community leaders were not satisfied with the varied opinions of the problem. "We're trying to accumulate data," said José Hernández. "We know Chicanos have the largest problems that are related to alcohol issues. We are trying to find out why."[12] The Northeast Valley Health Corporation took on the task of finding out the roots of the alcohol problem in the northeast Valley communities of San Fernando, Pacoima, Sylmar, and Mission Hills.[13] In May 1988, it hired NuStats, Inc. Research Group to assess some of the more salient alcohol-related problems that affected the northeast Valley. On June 30, 1990, the research was completed. The scientific research found that areas saturated with alcohol sales contributed to environment risks. Environment risks were defined as "environments in which consumption opportunities are greater; environments where consumption levels are higher than average; where controls on drinking-related activities are weak or non-existent; where concern for the consequences of drinking are minimal or suppressed."[14] The study backed an education campaign "to decrease consumption of alcohol in high-risk situations by increasing the capacity of residents to make informed personal, community and public policy decisions regarding the appropriate use of alcohol." It also backed government restrictions of conditional-use alcohol permits on areas impacted by alcohol consumption. Other health experts had arrived at a similar conclusion.[15] They noted that there was a close connection between alcohol-related problems and retail alcohol availability in the community, adding that the problem of alcoholism could not be solved by treating the individual only, but by limiting the presence of alcohol sales as well. These announcements aroused the concern of citizens and community and civic leaders throughout the state.[16] They demanded that elected leaders take a bold stand against alcohol availability in their communities.

In November 1989, the Latino Coalition on Alcohol Abuse of the San Fernando Valley co-sponsored a symposium on alcohol-related issues as they affected the Latino community. Their information became an integral part of the NEVHC research project. On March 4, 1991, Northeast Valley Health Corporation's Community Prevention Recovery Program and the Environmental Alcohol Prevention Task Force of Pacoima and San Fernando sponsored a conference for the prevention of alcohol-related problems through community empowerment.[17] It was assisted by several community-based organizations such as the Chicano Roundtable, Pueblo y Salud, Inc., the Latino Coalition on Alcohol Abuse of the San Fernando Valley, and the Pacoima Coordinating Council who had done extensive study of that community's alcohol prevention programs. Professional and business groups also assisted in the large gathering of interested parties. Xavier Flores, director of the Community Prevention Recovery Program of NEVHC, was the principal organizer of the conference. The conference focused on four goals of its prevention activities: "to inform the public of local alcohol-related problems and their relation to alcohol availability; to develop prevention action plans to be institutionalized in the community' agencies and organizations; to develop policies for managing the community's own alcohol environment; and to formulate a broad-based coalition to implement prevention action plans."[18] The conference was well attended. The plenary session presenters were Dr. Friedner Wittman, director of the Institute for Study of Social Change, University of California, Berkeley, and author of a community manual for prevention of problems related to alcohol availability; Dr. Juana Mora, associate professor of Chicano Studies at California State University, Northridge, and investigator for a funded research project, "Alcohol Use Patterns Among Mexican-American Women"; and Dr. Carlos Arce, former researcher at the Institute for Social Research of the University of Michigan, and noted authority on data about Hispanics and in the acquisition, analysis and interpretation of population statistics. A series of workshops important to the conference were offered. Workshops facilitators included Xavier Flores, longtime activist and organizer in the battle against drug and alcohol abuse; Ruben Rodríguez, chairman of MAPA (Mexican American Political Association); Irwin Rosenberg, president of the San Fernando Chamber of Commerce; Irene Tovar, longtime community activist and organizer; Marianne Haver-Hill, executive director of MEND (Meet Each Need with Dignity) and president of the Pacoima Coordinating Council; Rev. Arthur Broadous, executive director of the Pacoima Community Youth Culture Center; and Dr. José Hernández, chair of the Urban Studies Program at California State University, Northridge, chair of the Latino Coalition on Alcohol Issues of the San Fernando Valley, and council member of the City of San Fernando—to name just a few. The conference was tremendously successful at the end of the day. Now the people had substantial statistical evidence to press their elected officials in Los Angeles, San Fernando, Palmdale, and Lancaster to pass legislation restricting retail sales of alcohol in their communities. These cities began taking steps to draft plans to control alcohol permits in their communities. Similarly, San Fernando City Council directed the planning commission on June 19, 1991, to develop guidelines for evaluating conditional-use applications for off-sale alcohol beverages but was not able to complete them. Defenders of the status opposed them.

San Fernando Liquor Ordinance No. 1428

Police statistics on alcohol-related problems in San Fernando painted a telling picture. The critical need for an ordinance to protect the citizens was evident. On June 10, 1992, José Hernández, now mayor of San Fernando, wrote in the local press:

> It's now apparent more than ever that we need an ordinance with standards limiting the proliferation of alcohol sales in San Fernando. Without a city ordinance the council will continue to face angry crowds and a confused business community. Indeed, I will ask the City Council to consider drafting a conditional-use permit ordinance requiring clear standards for deciding whether and how new on-sale and off-sale liquor establishments will operate in the city…. State law allows local governments to set zoning guidelines for locations under which businesses may or may not sell alcohol beverages. …Community support for action is there, and we will act.[19]

Under city zoning procedures, the planning commission considered applications to sell alcohol beverages on a case-by-case basis. Some applicants were approved, others were denied. City staff and businesses were confused with this practice.

On July 8, 1992, a long line of angry residents formed to present their views to city council regarding their granting a liquor permit to a restaurant owner on a 3 to 2 vote that upgraded a conditional-use beer and wine permit to hard liquor while other requests were denied.[20] Mayor Hernández and council members Rosa Chacón and Dan Acuña voted in favor of staff recommendation to upgrade the liquor permits on conditions set by the city. Councilmen Wysbeek and Ojeda voted to oppose the permit. The council majority was accused of catering to the restaurant owner who was considered influential in local politics. The planning commission had refused to grant the owner of the restaurant a permit to upgrade the restaurant permit. The owner appealed the decision to city council because the planning commission had approved earlier an alcohol permit for a supermarket next to his restaurant and he wanted to see more consistency in the granting of conditional-use permits to sell alcohol in the city. The city had no clear policy for granting permits for restaurants and bars, and considered applications instead on a case-by-case basis. This case sparked a debate whether to adopt stricter guidelines or a formal ordinance as city policy designed to regulate the issuance of liquor permits in San Fernando. During the June 19, 1993, council meeting, Mayor Hernández made a motion seconded by council member Rosa Chacón to adopt a formal ordinance for both on-and-off sale liquor establishments that would limit alcohol sales in San Fernando. One is a carryout, the other is an on-the-premise consumption permit. The motion was defeated. Councilmen Wysbeek and Ojeda voted it down. Subsequently, Wysbeek made a substitute motion to adopt new guidelines with standards that would give flexibility for future uses. The motion passed on a 3 to 2 vote with Mayor Hernández and Chacón voting it down. Many VOICE (Valley Organized in Community Efforts) and Pueblo y Salud, Inc. supporters at the meeting were upset at Doude Wysbeek whom they did not trust, including City Attorney Bob Bower who offered justifications for a resolution supporting guidelines to regulate liquor permits. The city attorney said: "Change as in an ordinance is very costly; change in a resolution is not that difficulty."[21] The city attorney who lived in affluent Costa Mesa did not understand the people of San Fernando. VOICE leaders rallied their church constituents for the race for a tougher ordinance that would curve the spread of liquor establishments in the city.

The 2.4-square-mile city with less than 24,000 residents had 32 stores that sold carryout liquor and 23 restaurants and bars that sold it on premise. Combined, this was about one for every 428 residents considered by the state as "an undue concentration" of spirits in a location and subjected to a host of cases including domestic violence, teenage drinking, auto accidents, and drinking in public. Sister Carmel Somers, RSC, a member of Sisters of Charity and a former lead organizer for VOICE, said that the city should have had no more than one liquor outlet for every 1,000 residents matching the average across the Los Angeles County. Xavier Flores, an advocate for environmental justice, considered it an unlawful threat to environment justice (i.e., that minority and low-income communities deserve to have the same consideration as everyone else when decisions impacting the environment and public health are made). VOICE leaders intensified their demands to limit liquor outlets through a zoning ordinance.[22] Raul Godinez, a VOICE spokesperson and Los Angeles civil engineer, said he opposed the proposed council guidelines because they did not go nearly far enough to control the problem and could easily be changed by city administrators.

The VOICE campaign against the guidelines was too much. Bowing to community pressure, the council issued an emergency moratorium on new alcohol sales permits to give city staff time to work out the details of an ordinance. It held three workshops bringing in health experts in community medicine, and community and business groups to help the planning commission decide how the city could limit the number of businesses selling alcohol in San Fernando. With the workshops, the city allowed the community the opportunity to assist city staff as to what form and shape the ordinance could take. The VOICE and Pueblo y Salud, Inc. organizations were key players in the discussions throughout, helping to mold the final draft of the zoning ordinance. Mayor Hernández and VOICE initially demanded that an ordinance be developed by both community and city staff that would address both concerns and be enforced by the city. VOICE trained families how to address the city council on basic parliamentary procedures and debate pointers. VOICE was the community political voice, energizing the community to act on alcohol and other community issues. Pueblo y Salud, Inc., as well, was vocal in all workshops, planning commission and council meetings, videotaping them and masterfully using information generated by several years of research to make its case for a special city ordinance. Pueblo y Salud, Inc. provided the intellectual support essential in crafting a policy that endures in time. Finally after three years of frustration, the grassroots campaign of families and groups of community activists ended on Monday, April 5, 1993, when the council members voted unanimously to adopt the stringent ordinance for the issuance of liquor permits. After the vote, Mayor Hernández said: "I'm glad this is over. I haven't slept in a year."[23] Michael Lehron, VOICE activists referred to it as a "landmark night." He explained how this grassroots effort began. He related the death of Daniel Miramonte who was killed by a drunk driver, leaving a pregnant wife and now a child without a father.[24] Mayor Hernández commended many members of VOICE for their dedication to make the city a better place, particularly for familiarizing residents with the legislative process and understanding how to approach government with their concerns and legally achieving their goals. It showed people how to exert power. The mayor also recognized Xavier Flores, executive director of Pueblo y Salud, Inc., for bringing the importance of this alcohol issue to the city and for spearheading the thought that it was the availability of liquor beverages that generated many of the problems in the Latino community. Then he handed the gavel over to the new mayor. Hernández looked at Acuña and said, "This is my last day as Mayor of this great city." Acuña responded as he walked to the center seat as the new mayor: "Mayor Hernández, you are going out in a blaze of glory."[25] He guided the efforts in drafting the liquor ordinance as mayor until the council approved it. He was joined by cheers and a chant long familiar among progressive elements "People united, will not be divided." The victory served as a clear example of how a community when mobilized can influence an outcome of a policy. Latinos recognized that they had to vote to have a voice in the policies that affected them following their Spanish slogan "Su Voto es Su Voz" ("Your Vote is your Voice").

Main Features of Liquor Ordinance No. 1428

Liquor Ordinance 1428 outlined procedures for conditional-use permits (CUPs) for offsite and onsite sales of alcohol beverages.[26] Offsite sales referred to the sale of alcohol off the site from which it was sold, such as liquor outlets and supermarkets. The term onsite sales referred to restaurants and bars where liquor was consumed on the premises. The new ordinance changed the ratio of offsite alcohol permits to one for every 1,000 residents. At that time, there were 33 outlets in San Fernando, or one for every 745 residents. Based on these figures the city was prohibited from issuing another CUP outlet until the city population reached 33,000. Ordinance 1428 also stated that offsite and onsite locations should be at least 600 feet from public schools, churches, parks, and playgrounds. It also established distance requirements between offsite and onsite and set specifications for adequate parking, lighting, trash receptacles, and hours of operation. There was an exception of not less than 100 feet for major retail shopping centers of more than 175,000 square feet. This was added to the ordinance in last-minute changes. No dancing and video games were allowed in restaurants and bars. Under the original ordinance, offsite and onsite CUPs automatically expired after five years and business owners had to re-apply to the city for a new permit. This provision was later removed from the ordinance because it violated state statutes. Businesses were required to have both a state license and a city-issued CUP to sell alcohol. The state controlled the sale and taxing of alcohol sales, the city governed the locations and conditions of operation. The State Board of Alcohol Beverages Control encourages local jurisdictions to limit alcohol sales through the CUP process. Under state law, CUPS are issued on the property, and not to the owner of the site. The CUP stays with the property when it is sold.

The new liquor policy squared with the principle of environmental justice, which the business community could not understand. The vice president of the San Fernando Chamber of Commerce immediately denounced the city council's new CUP ordinance in a position paper rejecting the onsite and offsite sale of liquor within the city commercial district. "New, quality full service restaurants ...," he claimed, "will not be able to find a location area where they can serve beer, wine or mixed drinks if the location is close to schools, parks, and churches."[27] An owner of a restaurant prohibited from applying for a permit hosted a dinner to raise money to challenge the ordinance in court, to no avail. The restaurant was located within the 600-foot distance requirement from an elementary school for a restaurant to sell alcohol drinks. Mayor Hernández said the council was aware the ordinance would have an impact on businesses, but he reiterated: "I see this as a community trying to protect their families, and their neighborhoods." His anti-liquor stance to community development would come back to haunt him in later years. Nonetheless, the new city alcohol ordinance was hailed by organizers fighting alcohol and teen drinking, including Mothers against Drunk Driving (MADD) and the Marin Institute on Alcohol Research as well as labor groups and the Los Angeles County Board of Supervisors. In a light moment, the council voted unanimously to ban liquor beverages in public parks and recreation areas, and alcohol advertisements during city-sponsored cultural events. It also banned smoking in city parks and in playgrounds in an effort to safeguard the public from secondhand smoke.

ARTIST: Anthony Juarez, 18 yrs. old.

© Anthony Juarez. Reprinted by permission.

The Quest for Equal Opportunity in the Workplace

Demand for better and more efficient public service became another critical issue during this period. A united front of residents complained that city administrative officials were not relating well to the problems of their modest neighborhoods. They had ignored their demands for additional school stop signs, traffic lights on troubled intersections, affordable senior housing, expansion of social, recreational and cultural programs that enrich the lives of children, recruitment of major businesses which produce significant tax resources and jobs—to name a few. Underscoring that, they further alleged that area men and women had been denied city job positions while outsiders with no knowledge of the city's history and its resident cultural experiences were given lucrative and important jobs. The newfound success at the polls sparked in Latinos a new interest on the status of affirmative action in San Fernando. They began to negotiate on this issue, and on others that were important to them. The issue of equal opportunity in the public workplace was endemic throughout the Los Angeles region while the Latino population had surged and White population numbers dwindled. Councilman José Hernández quickly got behind the issue of Equal Opportunity or Affirmative Action as the controversial government mandate became known. His colleague, Councilman Doude Wysbeek, falsely treated affirmative action as preferential treatment of unqualified minorities. Nonetheless, as an initial consideration, Councilman Hernández challenged the seminal city hiring practice and the testing and promotional exams that limited opportunities for minorities and women. He boldly advocated changing the city hiring methods, and asked the city administrator to look for ways to reach out to qualified women and minorities as job openings become available to the White coveted management positions. To him, the city testing procedures had no demonstrated relationship to job performance. It was a matter of relating to the needs of a unique community. The practice discriminated against candidates that bring other traits that enhance the quality of employee performance of their duties. The councilman was critical of the city hiring practice for relying heavily on standardized tests and on oral interview procedure conducted by people who had no knowledge of the city's conditions and cultural importance. He recommended that candidates for supervisory and top management positions not only have the level of administrative experience but also a level of cultural competency. There were people in the job market who had both skills. He also suggested that women and minorities should help develop hiring practices. It was the educator-turned politician view that if women and minorities participate fully in personnel selection procedures, there would be no need for government positive action in addressing diversity in the public workplace.[28] Affirmative Action policy grew as part of the Civil Rights Act of 1964 passed under President Lyndon Johnson when institutions could not integrate management and employee structures with people of color and women. The U.S. civil rights legislation required institutions to make sure that diversity in the workplace was achieved. It required development of specific goals and time tables for the "prompt of full and equal employment opportunities."[29] Councilman Hernández requested to the city administrator to provide a report to the council on the status of the city's affirmative action plan and on what the city had done (or not done) in this important area. In the meantime, Councilman Hernández visited several cities in the Los Angeles area to observe their plans. He returned home highly impressed with the cities' improvements in addressing employment opportunities for Latinos, women, and other disadvantaged groups. Conversely, the staff report of the San Fernando Affirmation Action Plan was not as complimentary. On February 1, 1993, the interim personnel director submitted an outdated city employment outreach plan that showed that previous city councils had failed to initiate appropriate remedial actions to promote diversity.[30] It was one thing to set goals in the city record; it was quite another thing to make sure the goals were achieved. The complete lack of enforcement led the council to direct City Administrator Mary Strenn to prepare a new analysis of the city job force and to bring back a report with city employment goals that would boast diversity at their departments.

City Administrator Mary Strenn had a small talk with Councilman Hernández voicing her concern about his insistence that the administration put the city on a more vigorous course in affirmative action. She asked him to take a more nuanced view on the issue. "You are pushing too hard," she cautioned, noting that "it was not the right time for affirmative action in San Fernando."[31]

"If it's not now, how much longer do we have to wait?" He asked, "Another generation? Now is the time for remedy." Hernández with his liberal bent refused to shy away from the principle of affirmative action to end discrimination in the public workplace. While Mary Strenn was under pressure from employee groups to delay any government positive action to fill city job vacancies with Latinos, Hernández became the betê noire for some conservatives—that is, the person most disliked in the council for his progressive and expansive approach to city government. His critics found him caustic and inflexible.[32] He defended his work in a local paper:[33]

> It's a mistake to pretend that the needs and wants of Hispanic and Anglo American residents are always identical…Elected officials should not be afraid to discuss them openly without intimidation. Only then will we be able to resolve differences as we work together to form a truly unified community of caring citizens….The city senior management is composed mainly of white males, but only of one Hispanic (a woman) and one Asian

American. Yet, the city's population is 83% Hispanic.... Our area young Latinos are graduating in greater number from high school and college. Those who qualified should be given an equal opportunity to compete for city jobs....Why should I create ill-will in the community when I argued for a change in the city's hiring practice ....? San Fernando is not what it used to be 20 years ago .... We have reached the point when we must acknowledge the changing trend in San Fernando and work with it. Other cities in Southern California have done so, why not in San Fernando?

The Revised City Outreach Plan

A public workshop on employment-related procedures and a review of the revised city affirmative action plan was held on September 27, 1994.[34] According to the latest assessment, the city had met or exceeded its minority hiring goals in all departments. But former councilman José Hernández (he was not reelected in the March 1994 council elections) objected to the improper placement of several job classifications and whether they were appropriately allocated.[35] Specifically, he noted that the positions of community preservation officer, police lieutenant, and assistant to the city administrator were classified to the job category of "Officials/Administrators." They were grouped on the same level with the city administrator, police chief, and other members of the city's senior management team. According to Hernández, community preservation officers did routine code enforcement tasks. They had been listed as general employees under the revised salary plan effective June 26, 1993. Also Hernández argued that police lieutenants were professionals and should have been classified accordingly. The assistant to the city administrator supervised the city block grant program and other routine administrative assignments and should not have been classified in the same level as the city administrator and department heads. Furthermore, the former councilman objected that part-time school crossing guards were put in the same category as law enforcement officers. Another concern was that the plan made no distinction between full-time employees and part-time seasonal workers. In 1994, the senior management team was made mostly of White males, one Latino, and one Asian American department head. By including two minorities in the management team, three Latino code enforcement officers, two Latino police lieutenants in the police department, and one Latina administrative assistant, and combining full-time employees and mostly Latino part-time workers together as the city workforce, it could be shown on paper that the city was seriously engaged in providing equal employment opportunity to all groups. To respond to concerns expressed by community members as well as council members regarding the city's outreach plan, the council invited the affirmative action officer for the County of Orange, California, Ben Alvillar, to evaluate the report and determine if the city had complied with the Equal Employment Opportunity Commission (EEOC) guidelines.[36] He oversaw all EEOC programs for Orange County for proper procedures and government direction. He was also professor on the subject at California State University, Long Beach. After examining the plan, the consultant said the plan was not "perfect, but made a significant progress."[37] He concluded that the assistant to the city administration and the police lieutenants were properly allocated to "Officials/Administrators." They were doing considerable administrative work. However, he cited the community preservation officer position as inappropriately allocated to the "Officials/Administrators" category. Instead, it should have been designated as either protective service worker or service maintenance worker depending on the work they do. Similarly, crossing school guards should have been classified as paraprofessional workers rather than law enforcement. Further, he suggested that the city affirmative action plan should make a distinction between full-time employees and part-time workers. In fact, he questioned whether or not city part-time employees should be included in the city employment outreach plan. He rationalized: "If part-time positions lead to regular full-time employment, they definitely should be included." He advised the council: "In particular the City should pay attention to the Officials/Administrators category and attempt to fill those positions with people who support the plan, therefore, making it more probable that the plan will be successfully implemented."[38]

Others raised the question regarding the proper parity to be used in the employment outreach plan. City staff recommended parity based on a combination of the demographics of Los Angeles County and the demographics of the City of San Fernando. The consultant agreed with city officials that the parity procedure "enhanced statistics for unrepresented groups as well as allowing for a wider recruitment area." He added that he supported a workforce that would reflect the local constituency. Finally, he recommended that the council conduct annual assessments in attaining yearly goals. On February 3, 1995, the personnel director presented to council a final detailed description of Ben Alvillar's report on the city's employment outreach (affirmative action) plan.[39] The San Fernando City Council accepted the changes and immediately approved the new plan.

In 1995, affirmative action became a statewide hot issue when minorities and women began to compete with White middle-class men in the job market. Proposition 209 became the Republican platform during the March 1996 primary elections. Governor Pete Wilson, who was facing a tough reelection battle, campaigned to kill affirmative action policies alleging that minorities and women had been the beneficiary of preference hiring and admission in higher education. The salient issues of affirmative action fed with racism, xenophobia, and anti-immigrant sentiment won easily on statewide elections, dismantling affirmative action and other anti-immigration measures. Notwithstanding, after working seamlessly on the issue, the San Fernando City Council laid the groundwork to a workplace that reflected the city's overall population.

On January 17, 1994, a horrible earthquake hit Northridge and the surrounding area. The earthquake measured 6.9 magnitude on the Richter scale, damaging more than 65,000 homes and businesses, killing 57 people, and injuring another 900. California State University, Northridge classrooms and office buildings were damaged or destroyed. Classes were resumed on the university grounds. Several students died in their dormitories at 4:31 a.m. when the earthquake struck. Collapsed freeway overpasses closed the area freeway system. The City of San Fernando also suffered substantial damage. Many of its residents were put in tents throughout city parks. This was the second time in two decades that the city fell victim to a devastating earthquake. The 6.5-magnitude San Fernando–Sylmar earthquake of 1971 was still on the minds of area residents. Emergency assistance arrived immediately from California and all parts of the world. Henry Cisneros, secretary of Housing and Urban Development (HUD), and a team of FEMA (Federal Emergency Management Agency) staff arrived early in the morning with emergency aid to the ailing cities hurt by the tremor. Secretary Cisneros visited San Fernando parks and talked with families, personally encouraging them to stay strong. The devastated communities of San Fernando Valley pulled together as before with pride and resolved to rebuild their homes and businesses.

Notes

1. See Carmen Chandler, "San Fernando's Latinos Flex Power, Find Conflict," *Daily News*, July 5, 1993, op. cit.
2. Procedural Manual for the Conduct of City Council Meetings in the City of San Fernando adopted by Resolution No. 6434 on July 3, 1995. The manual was later amended by Ordinance No. 1543 on July 21, 2003.
3. Ibid.
4. Ibid.
5. On this, see the turn of events over the city anti-liquor controversy in Loiederman, Roberto, "Anti-Semitism Charge Colors Liquor License Fight in City of San Fernando," *Jewish Journal of Greater Los Angeles*, April 8, 2008.
6. Quoted in the *San Fernando Valley SUN*, January 1, 1992.
7. Letter to Councilman José Hernández from Rev. Scott Hill, O.M.I., Pastor of Saint Ferdinand's Catholic Church, San Fernando dated March 13, 1991.

8. A good assessment of this case is found in the *San Fernando Valley SUN*, January 1, 1992. See also "Northeast Valley Unites to Fight Against Alcohol Abuse Problems," *Los Angeles Times*, April 23, 1989.

9. Ibid.

10. Ibid.

11. Ibid.

12. Ibid.

13. See "The Environmental Alcohol Prevention Task Force of Pacoima and San Fernando: A Conference for the Prevention of Alcohol-Related Problems Through Community Empowerment," March 4, 1996.

14. Ibid.

15. Health experts advanced a strong case against alcohol availability in the Surgeon General's Workshop on Drunk Driving, Background Papers, U.S. Department of Health and Human Services, Washington, DC, December 14-16, 1988.

16. Reported in the General Telephone and Electric of California (GTE) 1990 Community Issues and Priority Survey: How Community Leaders View Priority Community Needs, Spring of 1990.

17. See the Northeast Valley Health Corporation Final Conference Report on objectives and conclusions, March 4, 1991.

18. The data is from the San Fernando Police Department for crimes (19 major offenses) committed during 1992 in each reporting district within the city. See Memoranda to San Fernando Council and Planning Commission dated January 26, 1993.

19. Quoted in the *San Fernando Valley View*, June 10, 1992. *San Fernando Valley View* is part of the *San Fernando Valley SUN* network of local newspapers.

20. Sister Carmel Somers, RSC made a fine point in "Alcohol Vote Turn the Table on Constituents," *San Fernando Valley View*, June 17, 1992. See also "Alcohol License Issue Heat Council Meeting," *San Fernando Valley View,* July 8, 1992, and "San Fernando to Withhold Permits for Liquor Sales," *Los Angeles Times*, July 7, 1992.

21. Quoted in "Frustration Marks Council Meeting," *San Fernando Valley View*, June 20, 1993.

22. VOICE or Valley Organized in Community Efforts was part of a network of community organizations that acted as an educational agent for members and as a pressured group committed to social change. It worked closely with Community Organized for Public Services (COPS) of San Antonio, Texas and United Neighborhood Organization (UNO) of East Los Angeles. These groups were part of the Industrial Areas Foundation of professional community organization that helped to set up each of the three groups. The foundation was founded by the late Saul D. Alinsky, a social reformer and labor organizer. His philosophy was: "Pick battles you can win." Other members of the San Fernando VOICE group were Joe and Virginia Barragán, Michael Lehron, Linda Jauron, John Becker, attorney Lenor Ramirez, Cindy Olmsted, Sister Una Connelly RSC of the Sisters of Charity, José Hernández, Neal Keller (group leader, San Fernando United Methodist Church), Father Paul Waldie, OMI (group leader, pastor of St. Ferdinand Catholic Church in San Fernando), and Father David Ullrich, OMI (group leader, pastor of Santa Rosa Catholic Church in San Fernando). Mayor José Hernández was a founding member of Valley Organized in Community Efforts.

23. Quoted in "Council Praises Ordinance; Group Claim Victory," *San Fernando Valley SUN*, April 7, 1993. See also "San Fernando Endorses Law Limiting Number of Liquor Stores, *Los Angeles Times*, April 7, 1993.

24. Quotes in *San Fernando Valley SUN*, April 7, 1993.

25. Ibid.

26. Copies of Ordinance No. 1428 are available at the City Clerk's Office, City of San Fernando, California. Also available on file is "Report on Existing Liquor Outlets and City Regulations" addressed to Mayor Nury Martínez and council members by City Administrator José E. Pulido dated April 17, 2006.

27. Copies of the San Fernando Chamber of Commerce position paper were mailed to the mayor and council members of the City of San Fernando.

28. For this position, see "Minorities Should Help Develop Hiring Methods," *SUNDIAL* California State University, Northridge student paper, March 2, 1995. See *Los Angeles Times* Editorial "Testing on a Level Field," *Los Angeles Times*, October 3, 1996. The editorial quoted the watchdog National Center for Fair and Open Testing, based in Cambridge, Massachusetts, that "Test scores and grades alone are not enough. Merit comes in many forms and should be measured by many methods."

29. Title VII of the U.S. Civil Rights Act of 1994.

30. William Hamilton, Interim Personnel Director, "Employment Outreach Plan for the City of San Fernando," February 1, 1993.

31. These were in their words.

32. See *San Fernando Valley View*, April 20, 1994. See also Letters to the Editor, *Daily News*, October 1 and October 4, 1996. See also Carmen Ramos Chandler, "Selling Out a Street Tradition," *Daily News*, June 5, 1991 and Richard Lee Colvin, "Carts Caught in Culture Clash," *Los Angeles Times*, June 5, 1991.

33. "Dr. Hernández Defends his Work as San Fernando Councilman," *San Fernando Valley View*, April 27, 1994.

34. A review of the issues discussed in the community workshop is found in "Employee Outreach Plan is Making Significant Progress," *San Fernando Valley SUN*, October 5, 1994.

35. These views were recorded earlier in a preliminary analysis of the new plan in a memo to the mayor and council members: "Proper Identification and Classification for Affirmative Action Plan," dated April 21, 1994.

36. Orange County Affirmative Action Officer Ben Alvillar's analysis of the latest affirmative action plan became part of a written report presentation to the city council until February 3, 1995. He had been busy in his work at Orange County. He had provided this service as a professional courtesy.

37. Ibid.

38. Ibid.

39. "Ben Alvillar's Report on the City Employee Outreach Plan," was included in a memo to the mayor and council members by Christine Manriquez Lissik, city personnel director, dated February 3, 1995.

CHAPTER 9

The City in Distress

The Crucible of Social Change

In the March 1994 city council elections, Mayor Daniel Acuña, 53, and Councilman José Hernández, 63, lost their bid for reelection. Acuña was running for his third consecutive four-year term. They were replaced by Raul Godinez II, 32, a VOICE (Valley Organized in Community Efforts) leader and an engineer for the Los Angeles Department of Public Works, and Joanne Baltierrez, 37, a single parent and social worker for a non-profit organization. Doude Wysbeek, the only White non-Hispanic on the council, was reelected to a second four-year term. In this election, the old-guard establishment reclaimed control of city politics as Joanne Baltierrez, the darling of San Fernando Republicans, formed a majority on the council with members Doude Wysbeek and Raymond Ojeda. This development is a stark reminder of the difficulty of sustaining a well-functioning power base—a severe test of social change.

Political Malpractice

On April 5, 1995, a year after she was elected to the city council, Baltierrez broke protocol and voted herself mayor of San Fernando in a controversial 3 to 2 vote. The next person in line, according to council protocol, was Mayor Pro Tem Rosa Chaccón who had been a council member for three years. Baltierrez followed the rule of poli-

---

tics: make big decisions when you have leverage on your side. Power changes and so do priorities.[1] "People were calling me to accept the responsibility and I have," she explained.[2] In an interview with the *Daily News*, the new mayor promised transparency, openness, and bringing the community together. She wanted "to make sure that everyone who dealt with City Hall was treated equally."[3] She believed there was a perception that people were not being treated equally, and she needed to find out if there was any truth to it. She also said she would work to avoid making race an issue in council's decision making. While she made an important point here, it was worth noting that there are racial implications to practically every decision councils make in multiethnic communities of Southern California. She bowed to bring people together, but her decision to break tradition threw the council into disorder. Rosa Chacón was a strong advocate for women and Latino/a issues. Anticipating a power ploy, a collective voice of many citizens of San Fernando, including the San Fernando business and professional women, the chairwoman of the San Fernando Residents Council, a former mayor, and a former councilwoman, requested that the council appoint Rosa Chacón mayor. They warned the council that the selection of Baltierrez as mayor could exacerbate tension among city leaders. They also feared that the council decision to break with tradition would set a troubling precedent in appointing qualified persons to the position. A lady in the audience made a fine point when she said the issue shouldn't have occurred in the first place. She hastened to add that "those in power are afraid of appointing Rosa. They think that they will be giving up power. People don't trust anymore."[4] Instead of being preoccupied with the issue of power, the audience urged the council to move on and focus on resolving community concerns. During that time, the community of Las Palmas Park was being threatened by gang warfare. Parents kept their children away from the park for their safety. Guns were heard more frequently in the middle of the night on the south side of town. People were frightened when they heard gun shots in their neighborhoods. The council didn't seem to take these incidents seriously. Finally, the new mayor promised to institute a series of town hall meetings to hear what residents and businesses needed.

Parking Issue in San Fernando

Councilman Wysbeek pressed city administration of the need to enforce all new developers in San Fernando to include adequate parking with their facilities. The total number of parking spaces in a construction project is determined by the type, use, and size of the development. In certain situations, developers could waive their parking space requirement by paying an "in lieu of" fee for parking they could not provide. The fee at that time was $8,000 per space. He objected that certain developers received unnecessary waivers or other exceptions to the parking requirement exacerbating the city parking problem. As a businessman, Mr. Wysbeek knew that parking enforcement had always been an issue in the city and difficult to resolve. He owned an electric motors and sales repair shop in town for many years before he retired.

Citizens Reclaimed City Property

Several vocal citizens, particularly former council members Carmilla Noltemeyer and José Hernández, and community activist Beverly Di Tomaso grew suspicious about San Fernando Community Hospital (SFCH) Board of Directors' dealings with the city.[5] They were concerned about the city losing to special interest a hospital property valued over $5 million. A previous council had sold a large portion of San Fernando Recreation Park land to an industrial complex at a ridiculous low price. That's another story. Now the details of the hospital property will be reviewed quickly, for the sake of context.[6] In 1976, the city served as a conduit in support of a tax-exempt bond sale to finance the purchase of the San Fernando Community Hospital, located on Mott and Chatsworth Drive. In exchange the hospital board of directors signed a trust agreement giving the city full title to the hospital property in March 2000 when the bonds were to be paid in full. Few in government were aware of the hospital trust agreement with the city. The hospital issue had been discussed during a civic association luncheon while a city council member was present. Further, in 1992 the San Fernando Community Hospital Board purchased the Panorama Community Hospital with a loan based on a lien on the San Fernando hospital property. In 1994, former councilman José Hernández questioned the SFCH board's indebtedness and motives for the purchase of the Panorama Community Hospital which merged with the San Fernando Community Hospital.[7] He also feared that the board would not meet its obligation with the financial institutions, thus jeopardizing city assets. He warned that hospital lobbies were secretly sending messages to certain council members for support to release the city of "certain reversionary rights" held by the city on real property. That drew the ire of San Fernando Community Hospital Board Chairperson Jean Olin-Nelson. She made it emphatically clear: "There is no quid pro quo, no deal. When the bonds are paid, the city takes the property."[8] Councilman Doude Wysbeek felt that the citizen's concerns were an unimportant matter. Noltemeyer and Di Tomaso were struck by the quote from Doude Wysbeek: "The real issue is whether the hospital or land was an asset to the city."[9] His full statement deserves attention. He had received a $15,000 campaign contribution from a principal partner of a firm that was managing the operation for the two hospitals. Councilman Ray Ojeda received a $500 campaign contribution as well. However, the city attorney declared that they were legal contributions. Finally, the hospital board met all its financial obligations and the city recovered full title to the property. The hospital board chairwoman said that the board had all the confidence that it would honor the trust agreement. City Attorney Julia Sylva was a key figure in assisting the city to reclaim its rightful property. She studied the main provisions of the trust agreement carefully and advised the council accordingly. From all that has been said it ought to be clear that citizens must be engaged in their government if taxpayer dollars are to be protected.

Feeling at Home

Councilman Ray Ojeda was not a friend of immigrants. On September 16, 1996, an article appeared in a local media extolling the virtues of the City of San Fernando.[10] Notwithstanding, Ray Ojeda spoiled the tone of the fine article as he insinuated that immigrant shoppers, mostly Mexicans and Latinos, were creating a "Little Tijuana" slum conditions in a popular retail center area bordering Pacoima. (Tijuana is a Mexican border town south of San Diego with some extreme poverty.) The business center attracted a large number of shoppers looking for bargains as well as push-cart vendors. The misanthropic commentary was an insult to the Mexican American community, especially when slum conditions were not viewed simply in terms of demographic trends. Government policy has had the effect of encouraging, even forcing the pace of neighborhood decline by allowing the concentration of retail centers in selective areas that attract large numbers of shoppers with little or no planning. Furthermore, he should have known better than to bash immigrant consumers. They contributed greatly to the economic health of San Fernando, created jobs, paid taxes, and helped to pay for public service. Because they were accustomed to being maligned, it was unclear whether his flagrant remarks would hurt him in his reelection bid for a second term in office.

Council Supports Affirmative Action

On October 7, 1996, the council passed a resolution on a 3 to 2 vote opposing Proposition 209. The statewide statue called for the elimination of affirmative action. Council members Ray Ojeda and Doude Wysbeek voted in the minority.[11] Ray Ojeda lacked real leadership in advocating for the people who put him in office. He and Doude Wysbeek voted against the interest of San Fernando residents who were, for the most part, minorities and women. Their opposition to the council resolution was focused on preference. Both insisted that a qualified minority or woman would be discredited when they obtained a position due to preference and not solely on the basis of their qualification.[12] The irony of this scenario was that the two officials claimed to be acting in the best interest of minorities. Ojeda wasn't speaking for Latinos. He never earned the right to speak for them. However, on rare occasions, Councilwoman Joanne Baltierrez broke rank with her friends and voted with Mayor Rosa Chacón and Councilman Raul Godinez in opposing Proposition 209. Mayor Chacón feared that the dismantling of affirmative action would have a devastating impact to qualified minorities or women who aspired to excel in higher education or at a high position of employment. Affirmative action programs in education, employment, and government contracting would be eliminated. To Councilman Godinez, affirmative action was about equal opportunity which could be achieved only through government action. The voters of California had the last voice. They voted to end affirmative action as practiced that time.

Doude Wysbeek vs. the City Treasurer

Councilman Doude Wysbeek was difficult to work with. Liberals considered him sly, showing no remorse for playing with peoples' lives as an elected official. It seemed as if he took pleasure in making incendiary statements that aroused people unnecessarily. His full statement below deserves attention: During a council meeting held on October 21, 1996, he made a comment that there were "improprieties" on how the city treasurer was being compensated. He would take the matter to the state attorney general if the council failed to correct them.[13] While he did not explain what the improprieties were and who he would take to the state attorney general, he left to the public the impression that he was referring to the long-term city treasurer's (Elvira Orozco) job performance. Stalwart supporters of the city treasurer were outraged that Wysbeek was questioning the treasurer's integrity after she had held that office for 26 years. About 80 of them held a candlelight vigil in front of city hall in response to his wild remarks.[14] City Attorney Michael Estrada later explained that Wysbeek was referring to a confusion surrounding the treasurer's job description and the method in which she was being paid, not to her job performance. According to Treasurer Elvira Orozco, a past council had put the treasurer in the financial technician civil service position as a method of paying the part-time elected treasurer to work full time. That arrangement had worked fine over 36 years. She complained that a recent audit of the treasury department was inaccurate and incomplete. Some at the aroused crowd questioned the motives of Councilman Wysbeek for bringing up the issue during that time after serving more than 10 years on the council, and giving that the pay structure of the city treasurer had been in placed well before Elvira Orozco took office

26 years ago. Could it be because she was up for reelection the following year? Others expressed concern that the councilman had plans to merge the office of city treasurer with the finance department, eliminating the position of city treasurer.[15] The people of San Fernando had fought over the years to keep an independent city treasurer. At the end of the discussion, the treasurer's job description remained unchanged.[16] Other small cities across the state had adopted similar practices.

Conservative Direction Interrupted

Council members Joanne Baltierrez and Doude Wysbeek's attempt to lead San Fernando in a conservative direction was brief, as the city's progressive movement scored a big win during San Fernando municipal elections on March 4, 1997. Dr. José Hernández was elected to a second term. He previously served as a city councilman from 1990-1994, and was mayor of San Fernando in 1993. Councilman Raymond Ojeda and Mayor Rosa Chacón chose not to run for reelection. There were six council hopefuls who vied for two vacancies in the council: a banker, a businessman (the only White non-Hispanic), an anti-alcohol crusader, a nurse, a professor, and a social worker.[17] Two of the six candidates were women. One, a native of Nicaragua, had become a U.S. citizen in 1977. Two of the six candidates were registered Republicans. Silverio Robledo, a vice president of a Los Angeles bank, won the second seat. He and his wife moved into San Fernando from Dinuba, a farming community in Central California. After the 1997 municipal elections, he joined Hernández and Raul Godinez to form a majority in the council, carrying out extensive changes in San Fernando city government. It appointed Raul Godinez mayor of San Fernando. It fired the city attorney, replaced Councilman Doude Wysbeek as the city representative at the Metropolitan Water District, merged the personnel and finance departments, and streamlined the budgetary process. As the reader has seen before, every council election in San Fernando is followed by an immediate change in direction.

Mayor Raul Godinez II, Transformative Leader

In one of its first actions, the new majority council fired the law firm of Richards, Watson & Gershon and hired the legal firm, Beltrán, Leal, and Medina. Councilwoman Joanne Baltierrez who voted against the change accused the council majority of firing a qualified law firm in favor of a less experienced staff of Latino attorneys. She charged: "Ethnicity has been an issue for certain council members."[18] This has come up before. Joanne Baltierrez, who courted the religious right, was never comfortable representing the concerns of the Latino community. Mayor Godinez stated that race didn't factor into the decision. "We have one Latino replacing another," he said, noting that Arnoldo Beltrán, who is Latino, replaced Michael Estrada, another Latino, who represented the Richards, Watson & Gershon legal firm in San Fernando since 1995.[19] Councilman Robledo also defended his decision adding, "We're moving San Fernando to a more positive future, a more voter responsive direction."[20] Mr. Beltrán came to San Fernando with the good name of one of the most successful Latino law firms in municipal government. Further, Councilman Hernández was impressed with his educational background. He was a graduate of Stanford University and the Stanford University Law School. At Stanford, he was part of the editorial staff of the Stanford Law Review. He was a fine role model for local school children.

Other Major Developments

The council also appoints representatives to serve on commissions, advisory committees, and other government agencies. At the meeting on May 5, 1997, members appointed Sergio Rascón, business manager of Laborers' Local 300 of Los Angeles, to represent the city at the 52-member Metropolitan Water District Board, replacing long-time Councilman Doude Wysbeek who was in his eleventh year as a liaison to MWD.[21] The water district supplied water to the San Fernando water system and other member cities. The replacement of Mr. Wysbeek was in no way a reflection of his fine work in the agency. "We have to make opportunities for others to gain leadership experience," said Mayor Godinez. Councilwoman Joanne Baltierrez and City Administrator Mary Strenn were disappointed at the change, for Councilman Wysbeek had served the city well in important water agency committees that benefited the city. However, it was the position of the council majority that MWD issued millions of dollars in construction projects and that Mr. Rascón was in a position the help the working class city get a share of the construction jobs. He was a member of the Los Angeles Building Trades Council, State Building Trades Council, the Labor Council for Latin American Advancement, Los Angeles County Federation of Labor, and the State Federation of Labor.

City Administrator Mary Strenn Resigns

On July 18, 1997, during a closed session, the council accepted the resignation of City Administrator Mary Strenn and negotiated a settlement, with Robledo, Hernández, and Mayor Godinez voting in favor and council members Baltierrez and Wysbeek voting against. "I think it was a lousy deal, an orchestrated forced resignation," said Councilman Doude Wysbeek. "They are systematically disassembling city government and the citizens had better keep their hands on their pocketbooks."[22] Mary Strenn had been chief administrative officer for seven years, about the time most city administrators leave San Fernando for bigger challenges. She was making $101,296 a year, plus $20,259 for benefits and $4,200 for car allowance. This was a modest annual income considering that San Fernando was a small city. She later found employment with the city of El Segundo, a major industrial center next to the Los Angeles International Airport (LAX). City officials were looking for a chief administrator strong in economic development and found her, assisted by Councilman Hernández's recommendation.

The FY 1997-1998 Budget Debate

Another major change occurred when the new council majority halted approval of the FY 1997-1998 budget that city administration had prepared for acceptance by the previous council. City staff had recommended a 7.8 percent increase in sewer (and water) rates and other fees that would have made a dent in taxpayers' pockets. During a budget study session the council majority appointed Councilmen Silverio Robledo and José Hernández to serve on the Ad Hoc Committee on Budget to study ways to make savings and provide efficiency in government service. Councilman Doude Wysbeek opposed the Ad Hoc Committee because he sensed that the new council had plans to reorganize city government. After three study sessions, consultations with the city administration and finance director, the committee researched data on comparable cities. Ideas for action were submitted by employees throughout the city workforce and addressed to the council. The Ad Hoc Committee on Budget made its recommendations to the council in a memorandum dated July 16, 1997.[23] Specifically, the committee recommended that the position of assistant to the city administrator be eliminated and the name of the finance department be changed to "Administrative Services Department," a practice that was becoming popular in small governments. The committee also recommended that the entire personnel functions be taken over by the "Administrative Service Department Director" and the position of personnel director be eliminated. The committee assured the council that the current finance director possessed experience managing a major municipal office responsible for finance and personnel functions. The research findings indicated that this arrangement was necessary in small cities if they were to achieve greater efficiency in the delivery of services. In a 3 to 2 vote, the council approved on July 21, 1997, the committee recommendations that saved the city money and provided added services to the people of San Fernando. A full-time building inspector, three school crossing guards, who were needed, two new police patrol officers, and a youth recreational specialist for Las Palmas Park were added. The department was made more accountable and efficient.[24] The council also added new educational and sport programs for the youth so that they may live better. It opposed water and sewer rate increases in response to the needs of senior citizens who lived on fixed incomes. Police supervisors were ordered not to take staff cars to their homes or drive them for private use, and they refused to fill a lieutenant position that had been vacated for several years. For the first time, the council equipped police patrol cars with high-powered, semiautomatic rifles. The current assistant to the city administrator was reassigned as a senior accountant in the new government structure, while the personnel director was released from her job. The case sparked strong emotions from her supporters. She had been hospitalized for cancer in an Orange County hospital. Unfortunately, she lost the battle against the terrible disease. She had been aware of the impending consolidation of the departments, and it was known that she was looking for another job. The merger of both departments and the subsequent elimination of her position happened before she was diagnosed with liver cancer. Her husband filed a wrongful termination suit against the city for $175,000, but later agreed to settle for $33,000. In addition, the entire council agreed to facilitate the family in obtaining other financial benefits, including life insurance and retirement benefits. The vote in the settlement was unanimous. Letters in a vindictive tone and dire predictions came attacking the council majority.[25] It became an audacious crusade to demean the character of Mexican American civic leaders.

The Wysbeek Parody

At one point during the July 21, 1997, Redevelopment Agency meeting, Agency Member Doude Wysbeek addressed the chairperson (without any explanation) and said in a condescending tone pointing the finger at Agency Members Hernández and Robledo: "As you can see, I look in the mirror every morning and I shave and I do look different than most of them."[26] In the council meeting that immediately followed, he warned the city employees present that "tomorrow morning, when you take a bath and look at the mirror to comb your hair, take a good look at yourselves, and see if they fit the image of the council majority, and if you feel it does not, then you should go to the next classified page and look for employment because that is the handwriting on the wall."[27] This scene captured one of the most dramatic events of the council during that day. If that wasn't enough, Wysbeek turned the American flag upside down during the Pledge of Allegiance ceremony with an angry voice shouting that the "city was in distress."[28] He gave the appearance of a desperate man losing control of "his" government. But the acts were offensive and racist to many in the audience.

People become sensitive when a public official makes offensive remarks, especially statements with underlying messages that are not difficult to discern. According to the American Flag Code, an upside down flag indicates an international signal of the nation in distress. To Latinos, Wysbeek's statement perpetuated the myth of a "Mexican invasion" of San Fernando. This was not the first highly public flap he found himself, but now he crossed the line. A master of subtleties, he stepped up his inflammable rhetoric by pandering to the irrational fear of the White audience. His action was self-inflicted, self-destructive, possibly facing the consequences in the following council election. It was clear to many well-informed citizens that the city wasn't in danger, but that this was a political ploy to discredit the Mexican American officials. It ignited a public firestorm of aroused citizens. War veterans considered the display to be a desecration of the American flag. Former Mayor Rosa Chacón wrote, "This was an agonizing experience for many of us in the audience, especially my husband who was wounded in the Vietnam War. Our enemies have burned our flag or stomped Old Glory for ideological reasons. Councilman Wsybeek sought to put down our flag for his political gain."[29] Others believe Wysbeek committed a federal offense and urged the council to censure him. Others suggested that he resign his office. Very few of his supporters cheered him.

Concern of the Old Guard

Defenders of the status quo worried that many changes had been occurring in the city and felt they were disruptive for its citizens. A lady who lived in San Fernando since the 1950s did not like what was happening in her city. She paused to ask, "Why is the environment different? There were many Latinos living in the city back then… People spoke English… They want to take everything over…?"[30] However, a businessman seasoned in politics didn't believe race or ethnicity played any significant role in San Fernando politics. Michael Majers, former councilman and mayor of San Fernando from the late 1970s, rightly observed, "Whenever there is some change occurring, there will be people opposing it for different reasons. Some are honest reasons, others are based on fear, and others may be for some animosity."[31]

"Paradigm Shift"

In a brilliant expression, Mayor Godinez summed up the changes in city government since the March city council elections: "We've had a paradigm shift."[32] Speaking at a November 5, 1997, chamber of commerce meeting, he explained: "A paradigm is a pattern or model." He added: "The changes caused a lot of grief for people in city government, business and community residents because there's a lot of comfort in the status quo." However, the mayor logically issued a warning, "You shouldn't get comfortable with any one paradigm."

A Final Note on the Budgetary Process

While all the infighting was going on, the council approved the city's $32 million spending plan; the general fund represented $12.3 million. It set aside a hefty reserve for unexpected expenditures, a smart decision in fiscal responsibility. It also approved $18,000 for a proposed weekend farmer's market, $4,800 for a Mexican heritage celebration, and $30,000 for improvements at the Las Palmas Park facilities. The council also approved spending $780,000 from a county bond issue to pay for a building addition to Las Palmas Park. In another matter, the council unanimously approved $110,000 to develop a specific plan for the city's downtown business section, with guidelines for future mixed-use development. In a delightful moment, the entire council adapted a zoning law in the city specific plan of development, requiring developers to set aside 15 to 20 percent of their units for modest- and low-income families. The money came from a $1 million grant from the Federal Economic Development Agency.

This was a case when the council majority immediately took charge of the budgetary process, refusing to rubber stamp the 1997-1998 budget cycle submitted by the city administration for approval. They asked pointed questions which should have been asked by staff (i.e., how can we do better than we did last year?). They made important changes in the budget as a result of input from community workshops. In short, the budgetary process in San Fernando was no longer the same. Councils that followed began to take a more active role at the onset in preparing the budget document, questioning every line item of staff reports. Mayor Godinez began a tradition in recognizing the small businesses located in the city that demonstrated qualities of good entrepreneurship that others could emulate.

Council Cracks Down on Preferential

Councilwoman Joanne Baltierrez, who campaigned on transparency, openness, and equal treatment of residents who dealt with city hall, found herself in a difficult and embarrassing situation over preferential treatment. On October 6, 1997, an irate resident approached the city council complaining that the councilwoman was receiving preferential treatment over payments of delinquent water bills and wanted an investigation of city policy on collecting a backlog of water charges.[33] The resident produced a document showing that Baltierrez's water meter had not been shut off while she was six months behind in payment of her water bill. She denied that she had been given special treatment, for the city had made similar exception for other city employees and residents. "It's obviously a ploy to try to discredit me," she reiterated.[34] Faced with council chambers full of angry citizens, the council instructed the city attorney to investigate the matter. In a future council meeting when the city attorney submitted his report on the water bill allegations, an intense discussion ensued.[35] The report stated that the city water code allowed only one 30-day extension annually and that the city business office had practiced more leniency with Baltierrez and others than was allowed. The report also assumed that the source of the document on Baltierrez's delinquent water bill was a city employee. Baltierrez tried to rationalize that she was having a hard time paying her bills and that the public should understand that some people go through difficult times. She also explained that as a single parent of three children she had made many sacrifices in service to the city. Both Baltierrez and her council ally insisted that there was no preferential treatment; instead, they focused on the actions of a city employee who divulged the information. The city attorney argued that it was difficult to discipline the person releasing the information under First Amendment rights. Moreover, he emphasized that residents' utility bills were public record that could be released upon request. After a spirited debate and personal exchanges, the council voted 3 to 2 to formally censure Council Member Joanne Baltierrez in the form of an admonishment for allowing city staff to keep her water turned on in spite of the overdue water bills. Mayor Raul Godinez, Mayor Pro Tem José Hernández, and Councilman Silverio Robledo voted in favor and Council Members Joanne Baltierrez and Doude Wysbeek voted against it. In addition, the council adopted an amendment to the water code that provided hardship extensions to needy families, excluding all city employees and elected officials from receiving such breaks. It instructed the city administrator to arrange a training program for department heads regarding security measures to protect public records.[36]

Redevelopment Agency Stepped Up Community Improvement Agenda

In 1998, the city council began a smart campaign of community rebuilding using Redevelopment Agency taxpayer funds. The agency joined partnerships with property and business owners, using its funds to restore and replace buildings destroyed during the 1994 earthquake. It became a major partner with Pueblo Construction Company, owned by Martha and Sev Aszkenazy, as they broke ground on Library

Plaza, a mixed-use development which included a 8,500-square-foot library and 9,000-square-foot retail space with a coffeeshop, a barber shop, a commercial delivery service, and food court. The city Redevelopment Agency also assisted an aerospace manufacturer in moving to San Fernando to a renovated building. In May 1998, it was estimated that there were about 125 manufacturing plants and about 410 retail stores in the 2.4-square-mile city. Indeed, the city was well on track on its economic expansion plans.[37]

The 1999 City Council Elections

There were five candidates for three council seats in the March 3, 1999, city council elections, representing a cross section of the city.[38] Council Members Joanne Baltierrez and Raymond Ojeda decided not to seek a second term. Baltierrez was not able to survive the furor over her water bill, and Ojeda was not accepted in the Mexican American community. The candidates were John Becker, 47, a service representative of the Auto Club of Southern California; Beverly Di Tomaso, 65, a receptionist at the Guided Dogs of America of Sylmar; Cindy Montañez, 25, student at the University of California, Los Angeles (UCLA); Richard Ramos, 30, San Fernando third-grade teacher; and incumbent Doude Wysbeek, 67, owner of an electric motor repair business. They all voiced strong support for the city's redevelopment plan to revitalize the downtown business corridor, economic development, increased public safety, and recreational and education programs for youth and senior citizens. Cindy Montañez, the more liberal candidate, supported city employment for local residents, hiring of the mostly Latino working-class residents during Redevelopment Agency construction projects, and attracting businesses that provide well-paying jobs. She also was in favor of women center organizations and programs affecting women and their families such as family planning, day care, parenting and domestic violence classes. At UCLA, she fought for the establishment of a Chicano Studies Department.

Voters Backed Youth and Gender

Cindy Montañez, Richard Ramos, and Beverly Di Tomaso came out winners for the three city council seats in the March 3, 1999, city elections. Incumbent Doude Wysbeek who lost his bid for a fourth term was outvoted by a college student, a local elementary teacher, and an office receptionist.[39] The hard-fought race involved a mailer accusing Wysbeek of being unprofessional and unethical.[40] The mailer sent by the San Fernando Valley Mexican American Political Association (MAPA) chapter a few days away from the city council elections also accused him of opposing affirmative action, a claim that Wysbeek said was false. He described the information in the mailer as untruthful and distasteful. While he was a Republican, he explained that he opposed Proposition 209 and that he was not a racist as the mailer implied. MAPA chapter president Xavier Flores was convinced "this man [Wysbeek] has done some pretty ugly things and it's time that he was held accountable."[41] Another angry Chicano resident had enough of Wysbeek for "taking unilateral actions affecting the city without Council approval."[42] Chicano activists loathed his motivations. Nevertheless, Wysbeek had some supporters in the Mexican American community. One reader wrote to the local press: "Yes, Doude is a Republican, but I'm a Democrat and he crossed (party) lines and tried to work with me."[43] Another wrote, "I cannot see why and how MAPA would send out a mailer describing him [Wysbeek] as an insolent and pernicious man. He is a man that gave so much to our community... I guess you have to expect the worst in us."[44] Nonetheless, Wysbeek had been under mounting pressure during the election to defend his troubling comments about race. Notwithstanding his combative and crafty style, he was one of the most knowledgeable and experienced politician in San Fernando municipal government.

Notes

1. The appointment of the first Latina mayor made headlines in the local press. On this, see the *San Fernando Valley SUN*, April 5, 1995, *Los Angeles Times*, April 5, 1995, *Valley News*, April 19, 1995, and *Daily News*, April 23, 1995.
2. Quoted in the *Daily News*, April 23, 1995.
3. Quoted in *Valley News*, April 19, 1995.
4. Quoted in the *Los Angeles Times*, April 5, 1995.
5. See the *Los Angeles Times,* December 14, 1995.
6. San Fernando City Council Minutes, July 19, 1995.
7. For the different views of this issue, the reader is referred to the *San Fernando Valley SUN*, June 29, 1994 and October 12, 1994.
8. Quoted in the *Los Angeles Times*, December 14, 1994, and the *San Fernando Valley SUN*, June 29, 1994.
9. Quoted in the *San Fernando Valley SUN*, October 12, 1994.
10. See "Feeling Fine at Home," *Daily News*, September 16, 1996.
11. San Fernando City Council Minutes, October 7, 1996.
12. A strong letter campaign attacking Ojeda and Wysbeek regarding their opposition to the resolution appeared in Letters to the Editor, *Valley View*, October 10, 1996.
13. San Fernando City Council Minutes, October 21, 1996; see also *Valley View*, October 30, 1996.
14. Many residents wrote letters to the Editor offering support for the City Treasurer. See the *Valley View* issue of October 30, 1996.

15. San Fernando City Council Minutes, September 16, 1996.

16. San Fernando City Council Minutes, March 7, 1997.

17. A resume of candidates for office is found in Luz Villarreal, "6 Council Hopefuls Vie to Shape San Fernando," *Daily News*, January 20, 1997, and Carmen Pinto, "Six Candidates; Two Seats," *ME Magazine*, March 6, 1997.

18. Quoted in Luz Villarreal, "Small City Sees Change in Tone; New Guard Worries Old," *Daily News,* April 28, 1997.

19. Ibid.

20. Ibid.

21. San Fernando City Council Minutes, May 5, 1997. This story also appeared in the *San Fernando Valley SUN*, May 7, 1997.

22. Quoted in the *San Fernando Valley SUN*, July 23, 1997.

23. Memorandum of AD Hoc Committee addressed to Mayor Raul Godinez, July 16, 1997.

24. San Fernando City Council Minutes, July 21, 1997, and personal notes of Councilman Jose Hernandez.

25. Letters to the Editor were sent to the following issues of the *San Fernando Valley SUN;* April 4, 23, 30, 1997; June 11, 1997; July 16, 23, 1997; August 4, 6, 1997; and October 14, 1998.

26. San Fernando City Council Minutes, July 21, 1997. Wysbeek's remarks were also covered in the *San Fernando Valley SUN*, August 6, and 13 1997.

27. Ibid.

28. Ibid.

29. Rosa Chacon was also a member of Veterans of Foreign Wars (VFW) and American Legion Women Auxiliaries. She was quoted in the *San Fernando Valley SUN*, August 6, 1997.

30. Comments of an entrenched group of city residents who feared change were recorded in the *Daily News*, April 28, 1997. The reader is also referred to the *Daily News* issue of April 4, 1997.

31. Quoted in the *Daily News*, April 28, 1997.

32. The present writer was also in attendance at the November 5, 1997, chamber of commerce luncheon. Matthew Crain, staff writer of the *San Fernando Valley SUN*, was also present to record the mayor's statements which appeared in the *SUN* November 12, 1997, issue.

33. Juana Mojica, a former candidate to the city council, brought the charges before the city council. See San Fernando City Council Minutes, October 6, 1997.

34. Quoted in Yvette Cabrera, "Review Set in San Fernando Water Flap," *Daily News*, October 5, 1997. Other accounts of this episode are found in the *Los Angeles Times*, December 17, 1997; *San Fernando Valley SUN*, December 17, 1997; *Daily News*, December 20, 1997; and the *Los Angeles Times*, December 25, 1997.

35. San Fernando City Council Minutes, December 15, 1997.

36. Ibid.

37. This section is based on the present writer's direct involvement with the Agency joint partnership with business owners' projects and on notes from Pat Kramer, "Original

Mission City Strive to Spruce Up Its Image," *San Fernando Valley Business Journal,* May 18, 1998.

38. A resume of the five candidates for public office is found in "1999 San Fernando City Council Candidates Survey," *San Fernando Valley SUN*, February 24, 1999.

39. See Yvette Cabrera, "Incumbent Wysbeek Voted Out," *Daily News*, March 3, 1999.

40. Yvette Cabrera, "Campaign Mailer Alleged Violation of State Law," *Daily News*, February 27, 1999.

41. Quoted in the *Daily News*, February 27, 1999.

42. Vietnam veteran Robert S. Villafaña is quoted on page 3 of the *San Fernando Valley SUN*, August 13, 1997.

43. Former councilwoman and mayor Joanne Baltierrez is quoted in the *Daily News*, February 27, 1999.

44. San Fernando resident Alban C. Calsada in quoted on page 2 of the *San Fernando Valley SUN*, March 31, 1999, which the present writer herewith modified for clarity.

CHAPTER 10

Conflict in Changing Times

At the March 16, 1999, city council meeting, the council appointed Councilman José Hernández, 69, mayor of San Fernando. During this meeting, the mayor in his opening remarks urged his colleagues to "stay on course" in support of the radical changes that had benefited the city.[1] He also stated that his priorities included extending children's programs and recreational facilities, new housing projects, and city image enhancement. He stressed the importance of extending economic development and putting an emphasis on the ongoing core redevelopment economic area 12-year plan. A key element of the plan was to identify retail/entertainment opportunities for the residents of the community. It was also important for the council to promote what the city had in the existing business community. The mayor also insisted that the council hire a full-time grant writer to pursue grants from federal, state, and local government agencies, and private funding sources to finance its infrastructure and streetscapes improvement plans. On April 7, 1999, the council hired City Administrator John A. Ornelas who brought with him an excellent background in economic and city management. Former mayor of San Fernando Raul Godinez had some thoughts about the new mayor's challenges. He observed that getting a majority of council members to work together was his biggest challenge. He said, "He has three new folks. It's going to be a little raucous for the first eight or nine months. His challenge is to build the same type of team we had."[2] There was a great deal of truth in his judgment as the following discussion will show.

The Theater Fiasco

On April 5, 1999, the San Fernando Redevelopment Agency voted in closed session to negotiate exclusively with Burbank-based V. G. Industrial/Commercial Real Estate, who had proposed a $20 million, 20-screen theater multiplex and a furniture superstore in the downtown business core area. The exclusive agreement provided protection to the developer that the city would not negotiate with anyone else; however, the city had the prerogative to rescind the agreement anytime. Mayor Hernández and council members Ramos, Robledo, and Di Tomaso voted in support of the negotiated agreement. Councilwoman Cindy Montañez cast the dissenting vote. She criticized the Redevelopment Agency for moving quickly into exclusive negotiation with the developer while there were many questions that needed answers.[3] The Agency's decision also caused some concern among existing business owners, and many residents who felt that there was little community discussion of the retail development. The local small-business merchants were concerned about being displaced by the new retail tenants. Other residents criticized the Agency's action made in closed session. Many were not familiar with the Agency's planned overhaul of the downtown business area and needed more time to learn about the city's plans for redevelopment. Under pressure, the council rescinded the exclusive agreement with V. G. Industrial in a 3 to 2 vote and reopened the bidding process to other developers. Chairman José Hernández, and Agency members Cindy Montañez and Richard Ramos voted in favor of the decision, while Agency members Silverio Robledo and Beverly Di Tomaso voted against. Also, the new council majority (Ramos, Robledo, and Di Tomaso) voted in favor of changing law firms.[4] They were not satisfied with the legal advice of the attorney assigned to the council/Agency by the Beltrán, Leal, and Medina legal firm. The current legal firm was replaced by Richard, Watson, & Gershon, the legal firm that the council released on April 3, 1997, in order to hire Beltrán, Leal, & Medina. Mayor José Hernández and Councilwoman Cindy Montañez stood firm in support of Beltrán, Leal, & Medina law firm. What happened was intense.

The League of California Cities' Workshops on Redevelopment

The League of California Cities sponsored various conferences and workshops on city governmental affairs, including workshops on redevelopment. San Fernando City Council encouraged its members as well as the administrative staff to attend these important meetings. City officials in redevelopment, finance, the planning commission and the council took advantage of the League's programs in preparation for the city's revitalization effort. The city bore the cost for these and other valuable educational experiences.

The City Opens New Bids for the Big Retail Project

The city started the bidding for the theater project anew. A proposal other than V. G. Industrial was submitted by San Fernando–based Pueblo Construction and Pacific Development Partners (Maya Cinema). This proposal included a 10- to 15-screen complex with restaurants and coffeeshops. In preparing for this task, the council mapped out a strategy for getting educated on how to best develop their multimillion-dollar theater project, a major step in the city's plan to revitalize its downtown core area. The training included council's tours of theater projects of the towns in nearby Los Angeles communities. The purpose of the tours was to show council members the inside detail of each theater, parking setups, food areas, and traffic control. There was a workshop to teach council members financial and legal requirements and how development was put together. Another workshop focused specifically on retail and theater development. The public was invited to participate in every step of the redevelopment process. Finally, on October 4, 1999, the city council, acting as the Redevelopment Agency, held a public hearing to hear presentations of two proposals.[5] Then, the council expected to decide on a developer whom the city would enter into an exclusive right to negotiate to build the cinema and retail complex. The meeting was held at Recreation Park to accommodate a large crowd that had expressed an interest in participating in the discussion at the meeting advertised as "probably the most important decision in local government."[6] Many had read the San Fernando Central Core Redevelopment Plan Market Analysis prepared by an independent consultant that was available at the local library. The developers' presentations were very professional and well prepared with colorful maps and diagrams. Competing developer Victor Georgino, owner of V. G Industrial/Commercial Real Estate of Burbank, explained that his $20–30 million, 20-screen project was bound by Celis, Coronel, Mission, and Maclay. However, he did not elaborate who would purchase that stretch of land of downtown. Developer Georgino had a proven record of building elegant movie theaters in California and Arizona. Conversely, Severyn (a.k.a. Sev) Aszkenazy, vice president of Pueblo Construction Company's project named Old Town would be located where the old Sears building on Celis Street was. This was adjacent to the historic San Fernando Post Office. His company owned 61 percent of the land needed for the mega movie and retail complex, an added value to Aszkenazy's proposal.

Developer Victor Georgino hired consultant James Acevedo, a local politico, to lobby for his project. Acevedo promised the audience that the V. G. Industrial project would "bring in national tenants that have a reputation of attracting people in town." The Old Town project called for a $20–30 million, 10- to 15-screen theater operated by a new Latino chain, Maya Cinema. According to owner Moctesuma Esparaza, his company would set aside one of the screens for foreign films, especially Mexican and Latin American films. The well-known, award-winning filmmaker also suggested that the screen could be used for community events as well. In addition, Mr. Esparaza said he would donate 10 cents of each ticket of the theater for college student scholarships. The multimillion-dollar project included a theme restaurant, fitness center, utility payment center, and retail center. The Old Town proposal appealed to the vast majority of those in attendance. A few speakers, however, objected over the use of a Spanish-speaking screen for fear that the theater might not attract Anglo American moviegoers to the theater/retail complex. This led to a heated exchange of words. The evening was long and people started to leave the room. Some didn't care who would be selected to construct the project as long as it was a first-class movie and shopping mall. They said they were tired of eating and shopping out of town. Dr. José Hernández, the Redevelopment Agency chair, failed to get a motion to decide on a developer who would negotiate the contract to build the cinema complex. He adjourned the meeting. The following morning, Victor Georgino called City Administrator John Ornelas and informed him that he was opting out of the competition for the exclusive agreement to negotiate the construction of the theater complex.

San Fernando Redevelopment Plan to Revitalize Downtown Put on Hold

During the October 4, 1999, San Fernando Redevelopment Agency meeting, the Agency on a split 3 to 2 vote, rejected the Old Town/Maya Cinema proposal for an exclusive right to negotiate the construction of a large movie theater and commercial center downtown, in spite of strong public eagerness for a much needed entertainment complex.[7] The Pueblo Construction Company's proposal was the only one on the agenda for consideration since Burbank-based V. G. Industrial had withdrawn its bid to compete for the project. During the Agency's new business, Vice-Chair Silverio Robledo had motioned to reject the Old Town proposal and to issue a new request for proposals, inviting any interested developer to bid for an exclusive agreement to negotiate with the city to build the downtown theater/retail complex. The motion was seconded by Agency member Beverly Di Tomaso. Robledo's motion to reject the proposal was based on four reasons: (1) the developer's lack of economic development experience; (2) the developer's lack of theater development and track record; (3) the developer's inability to complete its first commercial project (i.e., the library plaza); and (4) the developer's inability to obtain a federal finance package to construct the commercial project (i.e., again, the library plaza). Before a vote was taken, a public hearing was held,[8] where 38 people spoke, with 26 in favor of the Old Town proposal, 6 opposed, and 8 undecided. Additionally, the city clerk received 79 letters supporting the Pueblo Construction Company's Old Town proposal. After the public hearing, Agency members debated the merits of the proposal and a vote was taken. Agency members Ramos, Robledo, and Di Tomaso voted in support of the motion to deny Sev and Martha Aszhenazy, owners of Pueblo Construction Company, the exclusive right to negotiate with the city on the economic expansion plans. Agency members Hernández and Montañez cast the descending votes. The decision utterly angered the large crowd who were supporting the San Fernando–based company's plan to modernize the downtown center. Thus, the plans to build a theater complex in San Fernando were put on hold, after no other developer showed an interest in competing for the city's entertaining and commercial plan. In the aftermath, businessman Sev Aszkenazy emerged as a major player in the city's economic and political life. Meanwhile, the Redevelopment Agency in a split 3 to 2 vote approved a $125,000 grant in city assistance that attracted Starbucks Coffee Company to San Fernando. Mayor Hernández and Councilwoman Montañez both voted against the subsidy. Montañez thought that the taxpayers' subsidy was an outrageous amount for a business conglomerate that didn't need the money. Mayor Hernández opposed the Starbucks grant in retaliation for the Agency denying him $100,000 in redevelopment funds for the city's youth and senior programs. The city administrator defended using the redevelopment funds as an investment to help attract other national retailers to San Fernando.

The City Stepped Up Its Cultural Activities

Ballet Folklorico dancers and youth Mariachi bands performed on weekends on city parks as families congregated to enjoy a relaxed evening. The city offered free classes in music and dance. On September 16, San Fernando celebrated Mexico's Independence Day. People from the neighborhoods turned out in numbers to celebrate and honor their heroes. Once, the city council was assailed by a small, but vocal segment of the city population disapproving of their hard-earned tax money going to sponsorship of Mexico's Independence Day. The group also criticized the council for allowing the display of the Mexican flag alongside the American flag, and for hosting the patriotic annual event at the footsteps of San Fernando City Hall. The criticism was myopic, by and large, from religious right gadflies, who were effusive in their hostility towards Mayor Hernández for promoting the observance of Mexican independence. One postcard mailed to Mayor Hernández read:

> What rights and liberties did Mexico secure? Keep in mind that those of you celebrating Mexican independence here are not only insulting the United States of America (the nation that won and secured the rights

and liberties which you are not enjoying in Mexico), but you are also insulting Jesus, whose land you're living in... Don't forget that you are living in the Lord's land, enjoying the rights and blessings that were secured in His name... You should be placing much more emphasis on July 4th rather than on some obscure independence celebration which represents nothing but revolution and instability in your own homeland....[9] Sincerely, Concerned Christian in the Lord's Land

Another wrote:

You must be a terrorist ... to equate Mexico with America... God help your children for they will turn against you. God help your students for they will learn to hate this country as you do....[10]

It was obvious that the estranged protestors were not well versed in American history. Further, they ignored the social reality of San Fernando, as they tried to deny the 90 percent of the city's population (who also paid taxes) a sense of community. They also forgot the fact that Mexican Americans/Latinos celebrate the Fourth of July with equal fervor, praising those who fought for freedom and setting high standards for others to emulate—love of country, respect for the American flag, and defending freedom. Many Latinos died in battlefields defending these values. During the Mexican Independence civic celebration, local leaders paid tribute to the heroic deeds and sacrifice of men and women who fought valiantly for the independence and freedom of New Spain, including the independence of San Fernando which was part of the Mexican territory under Spanish colonial rule. The commemoration of this important event was held in front of city hall to acquaint the people with the center of their government. The exhibition of the Mexican flag during the ceremony had nothing to do with nationalism; rather, it had to do with people demonstrating pride in their forefathers' long struggles to gain national independence, and pride in the challenges that continue. Still, both Whites and Latinos enjoyed an evening of celebration with fine food, dancing, music, and sharing of common values.

The Mayor's Menudo Cook-Off Day

Another community event, the Mayor's Menudo Cook-Off, was first held on November 21, 1999, with approximately 8,000 people attending. Menudo is a Mexican soup made from chunks of tripe (the lining of the cow's stomach), pigs' feet, and hominy. It's also made up with chili powder and garlic and served with chopped onions and fresh cilantro.[11] Menudo is a Sunday favorite in Mexican restaurants. It is enjoyed in the morning after church services and throughout the weekend. The Mayor's Menudo Cook-Off was the central event of the colorful weekend fiesta that offered carnival rides, games, food booths, cultural art exhibits, and a great line of entertainment. The Mayor's Cook-Off competition was held on Sunday and prizes were awarded in different categories. The judges of the contest were, at different times, elected officials, news network/entertainment celebrities, Menudo aficionados, and food critics. San Fernando restaurant Tortilleria La Talpense had won First Prize for several years, including the statewide Mayor's Menudo Cook Off. Mayor Hernández, who dreamed up the Mayor's Menudo Cook-Off idea, said the event was another way of bringing people together and enjoying a weekend of family fun, and promoting the city's history and culture. At one time, the Menudo event attracted approximately 30,000 people during the statewide Mayor's Menudo Cook-Off competition. San Fernando fiestas, noted for their family-oriented character, date back to the days of Spanish colonial rule.

An Anglo American newcomer to the city, a 42-year-old studio production electrician, said that he and his wife were very happy living in San Fernando.[12] They had bought a 16,000-square-foot property with a circular driveway, guest house, and a large garden, after living in a mobile home with their children. They couldn't believe they were living so peacefully in their new community. Originally, they had some trepidation about buying in San Fernando, believing it was a city overrun with gangs. A Latina 59-year resident and longtime teacher who raised five children, aptly said, "San Fernando is very family-oriented, and we always watch out for each other's children." She added, "I've always felt like I know everybody in town."[13] A Latino fashion designer, who designed clothes for Spanish-language television programs and produced lines of children's clothes for a clothing manufacturer, said that he bought his house in San Fernando because he was attracted to the city's small-town atmosphere He also liked the family-character of his neighborhoods. "I can walk everywhere," he said. "The people are friendly. My next-door neighbor is the Mayor."[14] The mood of the residents was uplifting.

Council Splits on Use of Funding Sources

As part of their goal to extend the city cultural and image enhancement, council members Cindy Montañez and José Hernández invited Espresso Mi Cultura, a Hollywood trendy café, bookstore and performance theater, to locate in San Fernando. Its store in Hollywood was well known among Latinos. It offered old and new books with Mexican/Latino themes, book signings, poetry readings, plays, an art gallery, and musical performances. People stopped by to read their favorite book, exchange stories, while sipping a cup of espresso or cappuccino. In order to move to San Fernando, the owners of Mi Cultura asked the council for a $170,000 grant to build the culture center next to city hall. Many people showed up at several council and redevelopment agency meetings to speak in favor of the cultural project. At the July 5, 2000, council meeting, the council on a split 3 to 2 vote denied Mi Cultura the full $170,000 grant requested with members Cindy Montañez and José Hernández voting in the minority.[15] Mayor Silverio Robledo, and members Richard Ramos and Beverly Di Tomaso refused to award Mi Cultura what it sought. "We're not in the business of building start-ups (businesses)," said Mayor Robledo.[16] Yet, a month earlier, the trio without question supported the multibillion-dollar Starbucks Corporation with a $125,000 gift to open a Starbucks Coffee shop at the Truman Shopping Center. Specifically, 10 speakers got up during the meeting to argue for the Mi Cultura project.[17] They explained that Mi Cultura was more than a business venture; rather they said that it was also about a much needed cultural center in the area for people who craved more arts and for a sense of place and community. These could not be measured completely in dollars and cents. They were disappointed at the council majority's decision, for on a previous occasion they had defeated the Maya multiplex theater project as well.[18] Both projects would have contributed positively to the cultural environment of San Fernando. The trio—Robledo, Ramos, and Di Tomaso—had put themselves on an uncertain position in the coming 2001 city elections. In a subsequent decision, they rejected a motion that would have used $75,000 of redevelopment agency funds for improvement of park restrooms and a concession stand.[19] They based their decision on their belief that the improvements did not meet the agency's criteria to combat blight. It was the opinion of Mayor Robledo that redevelopment funds should be used only on projects that generate tax revenue. Chicano progressive leaders were troubled at their changed attitude towards advancing the recreational and cultural needs of the city youths as well as the needs of small businesses. It was clear to them that they couldn't trust the three politicians in any future leadership roles for the community. Sev Aszkenazy, an influential businessman who exercised a leadership role in the local economic and political scene, was also upset at Robledo and his council majority for their anti-redevelopment positions. These and others were bound to have a say in the next city council elections. The council's controversial decisions became test battles for the 2001 city elections.

The Fallout of the Theater Project—

March 6, 2001, City Elections

During the March 6, 2001, city council elections, four candidates vied for two council seats. They were incumbents Silverio Robledo and José Hernández, who were seeking a second and third term, respectively. The other two candidates were businesswoman Maribel de la Torre and Los Angeles Unified School District administrator María Elena Tostado. Both Robledo and Tostado received heavy campaign contributions from out-of-town sources who wanted to influence the 2001 race. Martha and Sev Aszkenazy, the new players in city politics, raised $8,000 in a fund-raiser for Hernández's campaign.[20] The three-month election campaign was relatively quiet. The major downtown redevelopment plan took center stage in the campaign debates. Other minor issues involved a dispute over stolen campaign lawn signs, and rumors of a possibility that "machine" politics could come to the city. A malicious mailer ("hit piece," to use the preferred political lingo) was sent to voters' households as a political ploy to discredit incumbent Robledo. It was nasty, unfair, and hard on the candidate's family. No one claimed responsibility for the mailer.

Election Results

Incumbent José Hernández, the 70-year-old CSUN professor, and University of California, Berkeley graduate Maribel de la Torre, a sister of Councilwoman Cindy Montañez, came out top winners. Maribel de la Torre and Cindy Montañez were the first two sisters to serve on a city council in California. De la Torre became part of a new council majority, joining Hernández and Montañez, the latter who was unanimously elected by the council to serve as new mayor. Outgoing Mayor Robledo, who was defeated in the municipal elections, attended his last council meeting and thanked the people of San Fernando for giving him the opportunity to serve them. He was a classic person, for seldom do defeated council members return to their last council meetings to thank the public for giving them the opportunity to serve. City council members Richard Ramos and Beverly Di Tomaso remained on the five-member council until 2003 when their terms expired. They did not seek reelection. Elvira Orozco, who ran unopposed for the eighth time as city treasurer, was reelected to that post.

City Administrators Stepped Down

Three top city administrators—longtime Police Chief Dominck Rivetti, Economic Development Manager Sarah Magaña-Withers, and City Administrator John Ornelas—resigned their offices after the March municipal elections. It was the opinion of Councilman Richard Ramos that they were forced out by the new council majority.[21] However, no one was forced out. Council members Montañez and Hernández tried unsuccessfully to dissuade Chief Rivetti from leaving San Fernando after he announced his plans to retire in 2000. He agonized for a time after the March elections about retiring after 32 years of service to the citizens of San Fernando. Finally, he took steps to retire in May after he was offered a wonderful opportunity to work in the Los Angeles District

Attorney's Office. It was not uncommon for police officers to retire in their early 50s with generous retirement benefits, and then seek other jobs in police work. Economic Development Manager Sarah Withers left the city to start her own consultant firm. She resigned her job even though she enjoyed the security of civil service. City Administrator John Ornelas resigned on September 1, 2001, after serving three years as chief administrator. He offered no explanation to the press for his resignation. Community Development Director Howard H. Miura succeeded Ornelas on an interim basis.

Notes

1. A brief summary of the mayor's goals appeared in a memoranda address to the council, dated March 16, 1999. It also appeared in the *Los Angeles Times*, March 19, 1999 and March 22, 1999, and in the *City of San Fernando Visions: Historic* & *Visionary Bulletin*, 1 (Spring 1999).
2. Quoted in the *Los Angeles Times*, March 22, 1999
3. There were many people from San Fernando and the northeastern part of the San Fernando Valley keenly interested in the upcoming, high-grade theater plans. See the *Daily News*, April 12, 1999; the *San Fernando Valley Business Journal*, May 17, 1999 and May 31, 1999; and the *San Fernando Valley SUN*, May 12, 1999.
4. See the *Daily News*, May 7, 1999; the *Los Angeles Times*, May 8, 1999; *San Fernando Valley View*, May 12, 1999.
5. See Minutes of the San Fernando Redevelopment Agency, October 4, 1999. Audio cassette tapes of actual council and Redevelopment Agency's minutes are available for listening in the city clerk's office.
6. In a letter to the editor, Mayor Hernández invited the public to attend the meeting and participate in the decision to bring a theater to town. See the *San Fernando Valley SUN*, September 29, 1999.
7. See Minutes of the San Fernando Redevelopment Agency, August 16, 1999 and October 4, 1999. Minutes of the Redevelopment Agency during this period are found in Book 8, April 2, 1996, to December 6, 1999, available in the City Clerk's Archives.
8. Ibid.
9. Letters and postcards were mailed to Mayor José Hernández at his office at the California State University, Northridge, with dire predictions for promoting the city-sponsored event. Two are cited here as examples of the group's religious beliefs.
10. Ibid.
11. Stories of the city's culinary delights appeared on the *Los Angeles Times*, November 20, 1999; the *San Fernando Valley SUN*, December 1, 1999; and the *San Diego Tribune*, November 3, 1999. See also http://www.uniontrib.com/news/uniontrib/sun/news//news_1n-5menudo.htm1.
12. For personal views of San Fernando residents, see Diane Wedner, "Family Ties at Home," *Los Angeles Times*, February 13, 2000.

13. Quoted in "Family Ties," *Los Angeles Times*, February 13, 2000.
14. Ibid.
15. Minutes of San Fernando City Council, July 5, 2000.
16. Ibid.
17. Ibid.
18. See the discussion of the issue in the *Daily News*, June 8, 2000; the *Los Angeles Times*, June 8 and August 13, 2000; and the *San Fernando Valley SUN*, July 5, July 12, and July 26, 2000.
19. Minutes of the Redevelopment Agency meeting, February 7, 2000, Book 9, City Clerk's Archives.
20. Financial reports of Candidates are filed in the City Clerk's Office.
21. See the *Los Angeles Times,* August 7, 2001.

CHAPTER 11

New Council Challenges

It was evident from the foregoing episodes that Mexican American civic leaders were of several minds. For the most part, they were seriously committed to their constituents. But they also felt vulnerable to the pressures of special interests and/or self-interest. As a result of the current hostile mood of voters, it had been difficult to get a 5-0 vote consensus on certain issues. A split 3-2 vote became a fact of life in San Fernando, even amongst Mexican American elected officials who share common backgrounds. They ran for public office on different agendas. Yet, the previous council (Ramos, Robledo, Di Tomaso, Hernández, Montañez) fully agreed on several issues of importance to the community. For example, it adopted a resolution that banned smoking from the parks, citing reasons of health, especially for the children, Ordinance No. 1503 restricting the advertising and promotion of alcoholic beverages to minors, and Ordinance No. 1504 restricting the advertising and promotion of tobacco products to minors. Also, it adopted Living Wage Ordinance No. 1514 ensuring that every employee who by city contract had a decent wage, and it adopted a resolution for Las Palmas Park expansion. It approved several awards of construction contracts for street renovations, including $170,000 for the North Maclay Streetscape Master Plan. Maclay is a major north/south access street and one of the major entrances to the city. The plan consisted of an attractive streetscape design with welcome signs, finger planters in each block, decorative lanterns, and bus stop shelters. The council recommended the hiring of local residents on city contracts from the local labor pool if possible. The busy council members hired an environmental expert to make sure that San Fernando's underground water system was cleared of chromium and that it met all federal and state guidelines. They sent letters of support for the Children's Museum at Hansen Dam (Pacoima) to Los Angeles City Council and to the Children's Museum Executive Board. There was full consensus in support of "Día de Los Muertos" (All Souls Day), a community event honoring the dead with ceremonial alters in display, an old tradition held each November. People celebrate life by remembering the dead in a festive way. The public, and particularly children, enjoyed the parade of masqueraded "living souls." Families also enjoyed the art exhibits and music performance.[1]

There were many other decisions made by the previous council that are worth mentioning here. For instance, it converted the old Mission Community Hospital to an educational and training campus in cooperation with Panorama City Hospital and the University of California, Los Angeles (UCLA). The facility also included a diabetic center and offices that housed several medical service foundations. The council also reopened the San Fernando Health Clinic at San Fernando Mission and Celis Street in partnership with the county health department. The San Fernando Redevelopment Agency Board, acting as city council, provided financial assistance to auto dealers, Starbucks' Development Associates, Bernard Brothers Investment Company, San Fernando Farmers Market and Family Festival, and other businesses. It introduced the First Time Homebuyers Program with low down payments.

Library Plaza Project

On May 15, 1998, the San Fernando Redevelopment Agency Board appropriated financial assistance to Pueblo Contracting Services for construction of a library plaza commercial center in the form of a fully amortized loan of $751,000 at forgiving interest rates. The loan included $69,000 for the purchase of a 7,125-square-foot vacant lot at 226 Hager Street. The developer, Sev Aszkenazy, noted that the lot acquisition fulfilled the city's parking requirement for the project. The deal was contingent upon a decision by Los Angeles County to approve of the library expansion funding and the developer's own funding sources. In return for the city's funding contribution, the community gained an expanded library facility and added revenues from the commercial tenants. The library served as an anchor for the plaza center, thus helping to move the project forward. The construction took several years to complete as the developer had difficulty in negotiating with the county its share of funding as well as with the developer's own financial investors. In July 2, 2001, a ribbon-cutting ceremony was held during the Library Grand Opening Gala. The open-air center included a barbershop, a flower shop, coffeehouse, and the branch county library.

O'Melveny & Meyers Law Firm Scholar

On May 15, 2000, Patsy Amaya Orozco was introduced during the council meeting as the new civil engineer employee. This is another wonderful story that needs to be told about the youth of San Fernando. While a student at O'Melveny Elementary School, she and other students were challenged by the distinguished O'Melveny & Meyers Law firm to stay in school and excel in their schoolwork. If they met the challenge, they would be rewarded with a four-year scholarship to any major university. Patsy met the challenge. During her San Fernando High School senior year, she received the Warren Christopher Scholarship established by the law firm to honor its former chairman and former U.S. secretary of state, the preeminent secretary who served in President Bill Clinton's administration. Patsy went on to attend California State University, Northridge, where she graduated with a bachelor's degree in civil engineering. The O'Melveny & Meyers Scholarship Program has contributed millions of dollars throughout the United States and the world for first-generation college students. The international law firm has offices in major U.S. cities and abroad. The O'Melveny & Meyers scholarship assistance program is a good example of how the private sector can help to pave the way to a fulfilling career for deserving public school students.

Esteemed Notables Visited Local School

On March 23, 2001, city leaders and school officials welcomed First Lady Laura Bush and Mexican President Vicente Fox who were visiting with students at Morningside Elementary School. The honored guests talked with the students and mingled with them during a reception.

San Fernando City Council Appoint New City Administrator

On September 4, 2001, the new city council appointed José Pulido as its new city administrator. He was highly recommended by Mayor Cindy Montañez. Mr. Pulido came from the City of Montebello, California, where he was head of the city redevelopment agency. A graduate of the University of California, Berkeley, and the University of California, Los Angeles (UCLA), he was well received by the town people. He grew up in San Fernando, attended local public schools, and worked his way through college with the assistance of academic scholarships and summer jobs. His parents still resided in San Fernando.

The Politics of Redistricting

At the September 4, 2001, meeting, the San Fernando City Council unanimously voted to go on record in opposition of proposed boundaries of two Valley congressional districts that would have impacted its residents.[2] Every 10 years the state legislature was charged with redistricting the electoral state and congressional district lines to reflect the population shifts in the state. In 2001, the state Senate Redistricting Committee plan recommended that approximately 250,000 Latinos be moved out of Representative Howard L. Berman's 26th Congressional District to Representative Brad Sherman's 24th Congressional District in exchange for an equal number of White voters.[3] Specifically, the Senate plan had recommended that the largely Latino neighborhoods of San Fernando, Sylmar, Pacoima, and Arleta merge with many White communities of Sherman Oaks, Studio City, Toluca Lake, and Burbank. The City of San Fernando with a population of 90 percent Latino did not share a community interest with the mostly White West Valley communities.[4] The redistricting plan supported by Howard Berman would have reduced the Latino population in his district from 65 percent to 41 percent. This, according to the Chicano community activists, was a deliberate act of Latino voter disenfranchisement and voter dilution. To their amazement, the plan had the backing of Valley Chicano state legislatures and other Democrats who had cut a backroom deal with Republicans to protect incumbents. Frank del Olmo, associate editor of the *Los Angeles Times*, felt disgusted with Latino politicians and fired back at the blatant gerrymandering scheme when he wrote: "These politicians, including many Latinos, were willing to allow their own people to be treated as political pawns as long as they remained safe in Latino districts."[5] The Pacoima native hoped that "when citizen electoral reforms take place, we will see fewer hacks with Spanish surnames elected to office and more honest, courageous officeholders like Vargas, Correa, and Reyes."[6] State Senators Lou Correa and Sarah Reyes voted against the gerrymandered plan. Senator Juan Vargas abstained rather than vote for it. This kind of politicking over district lines drew the ire of the California electorate. In 2008, it led California voters to take redistricting out of the hands of state legislatures and give it over to a Citizens Redistricting Commission. Proponents of the new redistricting process hoped that new districts would be more competitive when reapportionment maps of the 2010 census are being planned.

Cano v. Davis Lawsuit

A case filed by María Cano of San Fernando and others (*Cano v. Davis*, Case no CV 01-08477 MMM-RCX), and brought by the Mexican American Legal Defense and Educational Fund (MALDEF), charged that the district lines in the San Fernando Valley, the southern part of Los Angeles County, and parts of San Diego County were the work of self-interest incumbents who were eager to keep their seats, thus preventing Latinos from electing candidates of their choosing.[7] A panel of three federal judges rejected MALDEF's claim on the grounds that Latinos had made some political progress in non-Latino districts. MALDEF did not appeal the lower court decision to the U.S. Supreme Court. Finally, after a strong appeal for Congressman Berman's support, the city council succeeded in getting the City of San Fernando back in the 28th Congressional District. This also worked fine for Representative Brad Sherman. He had felt that the Senate Redistricting Committee plan to move additional Latino voters from the 28th Congressional District to his districts would pose a threat to his congressional district seat. However, under the new map of the 2011 citizen's redistricting plan, U.S. Representatives Howard Berman and Brad Sherman ended up in the same San Fernando Valley District, as a new congressional district in the East Valley was created. In effect, the proposed 29th Congressional District would replace the current 28th District, long the safe district of Representative Howard Berman. The new boundary changes raised the Latino population from 57.5 percent in the old district to approximately 69 percent in the new one. Latinos now had the first opportunity to send a person of their choice to Congress.

Valley Elect the first Latino to Congress

Tony Cárdenas was elected in the November 6, 2012, elections as the first Latino to represent the San Fernando Valley in Congress. A graduate of San Fernando High School and University of California, Sana Barbara, he replaced veteran Democratic Representative Howard Berman in the new 29th Congressional District. This change reflects the group's growing political influence in the Valley.

Community Clean-Up Day

On October 27, 2001, the Council arranged for the Kiwanis Club and Wells Fargo Bank to co-sponsor a neighborhood clean-up day. Fifty-three bins collected 170 tons of debris with the assistance of city council members and staff volunteers.

A New Chief of Police Appointed

On May 20, 2002, Anthony Alba was sworn in as chief of police by the city council, a landmark decision in that Alba became the first Mexican American police administrator. A 31-year veteran and retired lieutenant from the Los Angeles Police Department, Alba replaced Chief Dominick Rivetti. On November 2, 2002, José Hernández was appointed mayor of San Fernando when Mayor Cindy Montañez was elected to the 39th Assembly District.

Council Opposed Valley Succession

At the August 19, 2002, meeting, the council passed a resolution opposing the break-up of the San Fernando Valley from the City of Los Angeles.[8] The West Valley leaders of the succession movement held data that showed that a smaller government would be more efficient, less costly, and more accountable in the new city. The progressive city of San Fernando saw it differently. Although it was not part of Los Angeles, the council feared that succession would have negatively impacted its citizens and the Valley's predominately Latino communities. San Fernando contracted services from the Los Angeles Fire Department. Its sewer lines were connected with Los Angeles sewer system. The council was afraid that these long-standing arrangements with Los Angeles would be affected. Many local residents attended the council meeting to voice their concerns to those who were behind the separation. They questioned their motives for supporting a separate city.[9] They said that the Valley had not fared well in advancing the education of minority students.[10] The West Valley was the home of the English-only movement which eventually served as a springboard for dismantling bilingual education in the state. In 1990, Homeowners Associations of San Fernando Valley opposed a city redistricting plan that would have added Latino representation to the Los Angeles Unified School District Board. In 1994, the West Valley vastly supported the failed school district breakup and the school voucher movement. It joined forces in support of Proposition 187, a state initiative that would have put children of undocumented families on the street. A large part of West Valley residents were advocates of Proposition 227 which passed in 1998 posing limits on bilingual education in the classroom. Others in the audience were concerned that working people would lose vital social services available to them through the City of Los Angeles, possible elimination of rent control and living wages under a Republican-controlled new city. However, there were a few Latinos who were for succession. They felt that Valley residents in mainly Latino, low-income neighborhoods were not receiving needed services from downtown politicians, and thus, supported the smaller city that was more caring.[11] The plan to break up the City of Los Angeles into a Valley city of 1.5 million inhabitants eventually did not work out well. The voters rejected it.

Nobel Peace Prize Laureate Visited San Fernando

Nobel Peace Prize Laureate Rigoberta Menchú Tum visited San Fernando on November 15, 2002. She was invited by Mayor Cindy Montañez to address the city council about her work for world peace, and to address the students at the San Fernando Middle School about her experience as a youth growing up in her country.[12] A Guatemalan leader internationally known for her work in the promotion of the defense of human rights, peace and indigenous peoples' rights, the Nobel Laureate made a fine impression as she addressed the council. She received the Nobel Peace Award in 1992 as the first indigenous and the youngest person to receive that prestigious honor. She was recognized for fighting against the injustice, misery, and discrimination suffered by indigenous people of Guatemala. Members of her family were tortured and assassinated by the military that protected the ruling elite of the country. Death threats forced her to go into exile to Mexico in 1980. Middle school students were impressed when she spoke to them in the school auditorium about the children of Guatemala and other parts of the world. The girls liked her colorful, traditional Indian dress, and the manner she addressed them. The Nobel Peace Laureate spent the whole afternoon at the school as she spoke to them about her experience working for peace. In the evening, the City of San Fernando and the Northeast San Fernando Valley Chamber of Commerce sponsored a dinner where she gave another of her lively discussions of world events. The luncheon was well attended by local dignitaries, teachers, students, and community organization leaders. Nobel Peace Prize Laureate Rigoberta Menchú Tum's visit to San Fernando was a great honor to the people of San Fernando and to its business community. She told Mayor Montañez that she had never been received with so much love as in the City of San Fernando.

On December 27, 2002, the council created the Aquatic Planning Committee chaired by Councilwoman Maribel de la Torre to provide input and recommendations to the council during the initial planning phase of the new state-of-the-art swimming pool that was under consideration.

The San Fernando Head Start Controversy

In the latter part of 2002, a controversy made the local news over a series of issues between Latin American Civic Association (LACA) Head Start Executive Director Irene Tovar and a teachers' union and some parents. The teachers' union alleged that teachers were overworked and classrooms overcrowded. The union also said that teachers had to buy their own classroom materials because school supplies were not adequately provided. Some teachers claimed that they were verbally mistreated by administrative employees, and that some Head Start schools were unsafe. They accused the chief administrator of mismanagement. There were several employees who complained that they were wrongly terminated from their job with LACA Head Start. The LACA Head Start Program assistant director was one of the employees terminated earlier from her position by LACA Board of Directors. The local union president stated that LACA Head Start Executive Director Irene Tovar had broken the union contract because she had refused to meet with the union representatives to discuss the issues. Then there were some parents who claimed that they were asked to falsify admission forms by office employees, and that children were not getting the necessary health service. But first, a quick look back.

The federally funded educational agency had been in existence since 1965 when it opened its first class in San Fernando (see Chapter III). The San Fernando LACA Head Start was considered the most successful and ambitious educational program in Southern California, providing Head Start training to low-income children in the San Fernando Valley and Santa Clarita. The program provided children of needy families with free lunches, and it provided the children and their parents with medicine, health, and mental health services. Parent involvement was required through both volunteer and employment as Head Start staff. In 1963, LACA Head Start went through some setbacks that prompted the LACA Advisory Board to reorganize its administrative staff. As a result, longtime community activist Irene Tovar was appointed LACA executive director, replacing the previous chief administrator. Since then, Irene Tovar was credited for turning the agency around. In 2003, there were 24 school sites throughout the Valley and Santa Clarita with about 300 employees that worked with students ages 3 to 5.

In the latest dispute, the disaffected teachers and parents who were mostly Latinos went to extremes by going to the *San Fernando Valley Sun* to vent their grievances against Head Start Administrator Irene Tovar.[13] The newspaper, now owned by local developers Martha and Sev Aszkenazy, provided a public platform for selected teachers and parents who publicly aired their personal problems.[14] This put Irene Tovar at a terrible disadvantage in the public eye. She faced great difficulties defending herself and her staff in a public forum. The law prohibited them from divulging personal matters. Hence, Tovar refused to talk with the editor of the paper who had insisted on hearing Irene's position on the allegations. The newspaper made a spectacular case against Irene, who had a fine reputation for protecting the rights of working families and unions. Irene faults Aszkenazy's newspaper for being one-sided and for seeking to avenge LACA's rejection of Aszkenazy's proposal to do construction work for the association. It was clear in her mind that Sev Aszkenazy was using his newspaper in revenge to bully her. Friends of LACA Head Start Children, a coalition of teachers, students, parents, and community leaders, held a support rally on January 14, 2003, in front of the Head Start headquarters.[15] Speakers spoke before a rapt crowd waving signs that reflected their support for Irene and Head Start Children. One placard read: "NO YELLOW SUN JOURNALISM." (Yellow journalism refers to a practice that involves sensationalism and distortion of stories to fit the publisher's particular agenda.) The speakers questioned the newspaper's "journalistic credentials and integrity" for statements that were not investigated for accuracy, attacking the publishers for exploiting the issues to create sensation. CSUN Professor Rodolfo Acuña, otherwise known as Rudy Acuña, spoke passionately on behalf of Irene Tovar. He was quoted as saying, "I read most of the articles in the *Sun* and I found them very irresponsible. Being a historian you have an obligation to deal with documents and documents are what will tell you if something if true or not."[16] He had known Irene for over 40 years as an honest person. A counter rally of some teachers and parents was held waving signs that read: "WE DO NOT SUPPORT IRENE'S JOB PERFORMANCE," "SUPPORT THE UNION OF THE TEACHERS."[17] Finally, the Los Angeles County Office of Education (LACOE) that oversees the non-profit Latin American Civic Association Head Start program, intervened and began an investigation of the charges against the LACA Head Start administrator. On January 21, 2003, the county released a summary report of its findings of the investigation.[18] First, the report made it clear that there was no evidence to substantiate that LACA funds and resources were used inappropriately. Secondly, it did not find violations with issues of teachers not receiving enough educational materials and supplies. However, the report found several discrepancies. One employee out of 35 who had been terminated was found to be wrongly terminated in violation of federal personnel procedures. The investigation also found evidence that LACA volunteers had recommended that some parents falsify documents. Irene Tovar was found to have participated in a community anti-secession rally during her office working hours. In the final analysis, the investigation team recommended that LACOE provide training and technical assistance to all LACA management, staff, and volunteers. Further, it recommended that the agency must have sufficient funding to be able to implement and manage the agency's mental health program as required by law. However, the bickering continued.

There Were No Winners

As the quarrel between union and management continued, LACA Head Start funding was discontinued. According to former LACA Head Start director Irene Tovar, its operation was divided into two or three different organizations. Once the funding shifted to other organizations, many LACA Head Start teachers and volunteer staff were replaced with the new organizations' staff. The teachers' union was dissolved. Many of the city's Head Start students were scattered and, most notably, the community lost an important source of income.

A New City Council Introduced in 2003—All Had College Degrees

In the March 2003 city elections, Councilman Richard Ramos and Councilwoman Beverly Di Tomaso chose not to run for a second term. Mission College Professor Julie Ruelas, California State University, Northridge; Professor Emeritus of Chicana/o Studies José Hernández, California State University, Northridge; graduate Nury Martinez; and University of California, Los Angeles (UCLA) graduate student Steve Veres were elected to the San Fernando City Council. For the first time in the city's history, all council members were not only Mexican Americans, they all had college degrees. Dr. Hernández, who was serving his third term on the city council, was reappointed mayor while Maribel de la Torre was reappointed mayor pro tem.

One of the first acts of the new council was to attempt to improve the educational level of students in local public schools. According to U.S. Census information, 53 percent of San Fernando residents 25 years and over had at least a high school education, and 8 percent had a bachelor of arts degree or higher. The local educational achievement level was far below the City of Los Angles student average levels of 80.1 and 29.4.[19] These numbers inspired Mayor José Hernández, Mayor Pro Tem Maribel de la Torre, and City Administrator José Pulido to pursue higher educational goals for local youths. They became involved in assisting the Los Angeles Unified School District Board (LAUSD) in acquiring a 17-acre site in November 18, 2002, for a new high school in San Fernando. In light of the difficulties involved in undertaking such an endeavor over school site procurements in Los Angeles, school officials agreed with San Fernando leaders' request that the new school be college prep. Implicit in their demand was that the school be made into three academies: Academy of Mathematics, Science, and Technology; Academy of Performing Arts; and Academy of Social Justice. On March 14, 2003, Hernández and de la Torre addressed the school board demanding participation in the construction, school design, and curriculum of the school. Both spoke passionately in front of the LAUSD Board about the need for the school district to provide students of the Northeast Valley with the same academic opportunities and support that other students enjoyed in the school district.[20] Dr. Hernández demanded that the school architecture reflect the history and culture of San Fernando. He also asked the school board to consider hiring local union workers in the construction of the school project. Superintendent of Schools Roy Romer warned the board against setting a precedent in making exceptions for individual cases. But board members, impressed by the speakers having made the unusual trip downtown to make their case, vowed to work with the city. Board member Julie Kornstein, representing the Northeast Valley Region, made a strong pitch for the need of the new Valley school. The school district held several community meetings throughout the construction phase with architects, construction superintendents, and school curriculum coordinators. Many of the community suggestions were well received. The new school site, part of the San Fernando Swap Meet on Glenoaks Boulevard and Arroyo Avenue, opened in the fall of 2011. A fourth teacher preparation academy was added. The world-class high school that specializes in technology, social justice, performing arts, and education will relieve the pressure on overcrowded Kennedy High School (Granada Hills), San Fernando High School, and Sylmar High School. On October 13, 2011, the School Board Naming Committee, composed of community, teachers, students, and civic leaders, met to discuss the naming of the school. At this meeting, City Council Member Maribel de la Torre and Mayor Pro Tem Brenda Esqueda urged the committee not to name the school after a Spanish-surnamed person because it would lower city property values. This, of course, was a ridiculous statement to the usual negative images about Mexicans from people who still haven't learned about their historical and cultural importance.[21] This was not the first time that Maribel de la Torre balked at anything Mexican. It happened before with alarming frequency. This issue will come up again in the chapter that follows. Nonetheless, students overwhelmingly voted to name the new school César E. Chávez Learning Academies after the civil rights and labor leader who devoted his life to improving working and living conditions of farm workers in California. President Bill Clinton posthumously awarded César E. Chávez the Presidential Medal of Freedom, the highest award a civilian can receive for service to the nation. Chávez passed away on April 23, 1993. The City of San Fernando is home to the largest and most creative monument recognizing the life of this American hero.

On November 2, 2011, the community joined school officials, teachers, students, and other notables to celebrate the ribbon-cutting of the new Valley school. The community was recognized for its tradition of citizen participation. Individuals were acknowledged for their role in the school development, including Councilwoman Maribel de la Torre, former city administrator José Pulido, and former mayor and councilman José Hernández for laying the groundwork of the school project. Through the efforts of Pulido, de la Torre, and Hernández, they were able to negotiate with the school district for the academy-style of school curriculum. They also succeeded in the use of the community to share the multipurpose room, playing fields, basketball courts, and practice gymnasiums at the school.

Council Takes a Bold Stand on the War on Iraq

In a display of unity, the council approved a resolution in 2003 opposing U.S. military action against Iraq.[22] The resolution blamed the Bush administration for failing to present convincing evidence that Iraq posed a military threat to U.S. security. Council members asked, "Why Iraq when there are other countries in the Middle East that have weapons of mass destruction?" The council urged President Bush to actively join the United Nations' efforts to support and encourage diplomacy as a mean of dealing with world problems. The resolution was sent to the White House.

San Fernando Senior Housing Project

The State of California mandates cities and counties to provide affordable housing to low and moderate income residents, including senior citizens based on a formula for each individual local entity. It also permits redevelopment agencies to curve out blighted neighborhoods for improvements through partnerships with private developers, giving them the power of eminent domain to obtain properties or to lease. The City of San Fernando complied with the state unfunded mandate, using redevelopment tax increment funds in partnership with private capital to construct senior housing in the city. On September 15, 2003, the San Fernando Redevelopment Agency Board approved Aszkenazy Development, Inc, of San Fernando as the developer for its proposed senior housing project.[23] The board authorized the Agency Executive Director José Pulido to negotiate a disposition and development agreement (DDA) with Aszkenazy Development, Inc. (the "Developer"). During that time, the council, acting as the Redevelopment Agency, did not see the need to issue a report for proposals (RFP) for the potential development of the housing project. The developer had a proven record of apartment construction in the city, and owned several parcels that could be used in the building sites of the proposed senior housing. The proposed agreement was between the Redevelopment Agency and Aszkenaszy Development, Inc. for the construction of a 98-unit affordable housing project for very-low-income and low-income senior citizens. It was to be located on three sites in the city. First, on March 15, 2004, the Agency/council entered into a ground lease with the developer or 55 years with an annual rent of $1 for each of the nine city-owned parcels on site 1 with 21 senior housing units located at 333 Kalisher Street and site 2 with 25 senior housing units located at 499 Kalisher Street. At the end of 55 years, the developer had the option to renew the lease for 44 years or sell the properties. Then, on June 21, 2004, the developer came back to the Agency requesting a change in the initial ground lease from 55 years (plus 44 years renewal) to 57 years (plus 42 years lease) pursuant to the initial approved lease. The request was approved unanimously after the developer agreed to contribute $300,000 for relocating tenants in the affected parcels. The city attorney advised the Agency that the extension was reasonable (still 99-year term lease) and because the loans were unlikely to be paid in 57 years, 75 years was necessary in order to assure Internal Revenue Service tax credits. Moreover, during the December 6, 2004, Redevelopment Agency meeting, Developer Severyn Aszkenazy, also known as Sev Aszkenazy, approached the Agency Board again insisting for a second change in the ground lease agreement. He also asked for an additional 2,466 square feet of public real estate for proposed site 3 with 52 senior housing units located at Park Avenue and First Street. In the sequence of events, the Developer specifically asked the lease of land change to 75 years instead of 57 years pursuant to the previous approved lease. The overall term of 99 years remained the same. On response to questions, Sev Aszkenaszy explained that the agreement was a complicated deal with much work involved.

The change sparked discomfort among residents attending the meeting. It certainly appeared to them that the ground lease was an excessive giveaway of city property. They blamed the council for allowing the developer to dictate the terms of the deal. Others lamented at the council's self-imposed predicament for not requiring competing biddings for the senior housing project. Both Agency board members Julie Ruelas and José Hernández agonized at the price the city had to pay in order to bring senior housing to San Fernando. They were troubled at the increasing demands of the developer and torn over whether or not they should continue supporting the project. A representative of Aszkenazy Development, Inc. reported that the total cost of the project, not including the land was $12.4 million. Out of that amount, the city was contributing $293,000 in grant money while it retained ownership to the land. Agency board member Nury Martínez urged her colleagues to move the project forward. She believed subsidized senior housing was long overdue in the community, and that the Agency/council had done its best in coming up with a balance between bringing in a good project and making sure that the city was holding on to its fair share of the cost. The Agency/council voted 4 to 1 (Julie Ruelas) to approve (a) to change the initial ground lease term to the San Fernando Senior Housing Project to be up 75 years instead of 57 years; the overall term of the 99-year lease would remain the same, (b) the conveyance of additional 2,466 square feet of city-owned land to the Agency, and lease to the developer pursuant to the previously approved lease, (c) the annual rent during the extended lease term to be $10 for each of the city's parcels (now 10), and (d) the developer pay all costs of relocating and removing the improvements from the additional area. Julie Ruelas, the fiscal conservative of the council, steadfastly opposed the builder's request for additional city subsidies based on a sound principle, but one that could carry political risk. She figured the project was getting too costly for the city and its citizens. The last 52 senior housing units were completed on February 2007. The total cost of the senior housing projected was $12,233,876. The developer provided financing for construction of the project through various financial and government instruments. The City of San Fernando contributed approximately 40 percent of the total necessary to develop the three apartment sites. City subsidies took the form of a million-dollar loan from the California Housing Finance Authority at 3 percent interest ($300,000), cost of relocating prior residents of land acquired, cost of demolition of acquired property, a $293,542 San Fernando Redevelopment Agency grant to the developer, and sale of city-owned property. This raised the ante (city's stake) to $4,458,087, a marriage with a windfall for the developer.[24] In a way, using redevelopment tax subsidies was an egregious form of corporate welfare; it was the city's attempt to compensate for the shortcomings of the free enterprise system. The city made an extensive investment to significantly increase the supply of housing affordable to very-low- and low-income seniors. It fulfilled the state mandate on affordable housing. The senior housing project was also consistent with redevelopment efforts to improve neighborhood conditions.

The Fallacy of Public-Private Partnership of Senior Housing

Ironically, many barrio (Mexican neighborhood) senior citizens could not qualify for living quarters at their neighborhood senior housing sites on an $800 Social Security check unless they received additional government assistance or support from their children. The minimum Social Security check was not sufficient to pay the rent and other basic needs. The San Fernando senior housing was not designed for the extremely poor. The city senior housing apartments were developed by a private firm, and they were privately owned and operated for profit. The minimum rent for a single room unit was $600. Rent was set according to the U.S. Department of Housing and Urban Development guidelines. A county agency monitored the rent schedules. The city was not in a position to consider requests for assistance to individual renters due to both legal and fiscal constraints. The Aszkenazy Development, Inc. senior housing project turned out to be expensive to build.[25] It had been difficult involving private capital on social programs unless governments provided attractive incentives for their participation. Sev Aszkenazy maintained that most developers were not interested in doing business in San Fernando because they saw few opportunities to profit. Hence, he felt obligated to assist the city in its revitalization efforts.[26] However, people complained that the local developer was not building for the area's poor; rather instead, he was forcing gentrification upon the city.[27]

The term "gentrification" is often referred to as the restoration or rebuilding of old working-class neighborhoods in order to accommodate the interests and tastes of middle and upper classes. The battle over gentrification in the United States and elsewhere is a long war between the poor and those who want to replace them. Gentrification advocates treat gentrification as a purely positive trend and a remedy for the environmental and tax-based crisis of declining minority communities. Under this form of redevelopment, proponents of gentrification want to elevate these communities by providing upscaled housing for young professionals and amenities for those who yearn for trendy restaurants, 30-screen theaters with ample parking, and stores other than J.C. Penney and Sears outlets. In most cases, gentrification results in the displacement of the original working-class occupiers. Poor residents and small-business owners are the first to be forced out. It also means that there will be less family-style housing. To do this, developers first need to put people in public office who do not have reservations about unreasonable cost of redevelopment and who support eminent domain for private use.

On the surface, gentrification can be appealing. Who doesn't like converted lofts, cool bars, dinning alfresco, live music space, faddist clothing stores, and the good life? It's easy to be seduced by city perks like spacious lofts and first-class restaurants. But sometimes these can come at a high price. Gentrification is usually buttressed by public funds. Developer Sev Aszkenazy, who made frequent use of public-private partnerships, had already received thousands of dollars in tax subsidies with the support of the city council in revitalizing efforts. In a conversation with City Administrator José Pulido over the senior housing project, Councilman José Hernández, who had approved many of Mr. Aszkenazy's projects, admonished the developer for being too greedy and for returning to the Redevelopment Agency three times making unreasonable demands. This statement brought the long-servicing council member serious problems in a splitting, all–Mexican American city council. The reader will observe this in the following chapter.

The Public Economic Development Program Comes to an End

On December 2011, the California Supreme Court threw hundreds of redevelopment agencies out of business. In a unanimous decision, the court ruled in favor of a state law passed in the summer of 2011 that abolished redevelopment agencies at the request of California Governor Jerry Brown to help solve the state's fiscal crisis. The ruling guarantees billions of dollars for education and public safety. Furthermore, developers will no longer take advantage of this fine pool of public funds; instead, they may be forced to market forces for their investments. After the court ruling, a state assemblyman said, "Redevelopment has become a cash cow for developers ... who have been on the public dole for a long time."[28] A critic of redevelopment, Los Angeles Board of Supervisor Chairman Zev Yaroslavsky, said, "Redevelopment over the years evolved into a honey pot that was tapped to underwrite billions of dollar worth of commercial and other for-profits." He added, "The redevelopment projects had nothing to do with reversing blight, but everything to do with subsidizing private real estate ventures that otherwise made no economic sense."[29] Later, during a luncheon speech attended by lawyers representing redevelopment interests, the supervisor was correct in saying that it was "only a matter of time" before redevelopment activities prompted a backlash. "You had a good thing going for a long time," he said, "and you got greedy."[30] Advocates for the agencies agreed the state supreme court ruling will benefit state budget coffers but hamper local economic development and housing programs. In San Fernando, Sey Aszkenazy argued that partnerships have been formed with the city to create developments (including senior housing). He said that it takes architecture, investments, and a lot of hard work, and that's not called "special treatment." He believed that there is misinformation (about redevelopment partnerships) in the community.[31]

The Dismantling of the City Redevelopment Agency Program

During the February 6, 2012, special meeting, the San Fernando City Council began the process of dismantling the city Redevelopment Agency ordered by the governor and legislature. First, the council passed a resolution creating the Successor Agency to the Redevelopment Agency, authorizing the Successor Agency to adopt an enforceable obligation payment schedule of all debts owed by the Redevelopment Agency. Secondly, the council passed another resolution requiring Redevelopment Agency remaining moneys to be put in the Local Agency Investment Fund of the State of California for state allocations. Finally, the council passed a third resolution to reimburse the city for Successor Agency to the San Fernando Redevelopment Agency expenses. The council will decide at a later date how all future tax increments from the prior city redevelopment project areas will be distributed.

Notes

1. For a summary of actions taken by the city council during this period, see City Clerks Archives, Book 44, City Council Meetings, April 20, 1998 to April 16, 2001. The City Clerk has records of Council and Redevelopment Agency minutes, including tape recordings of the minutes.

2. See Book 45, May 7, 2001 to December 29, 2003.

3. This brazen gerrymander of California redistricting plan caught the interest of national media. See the *Washington Post*, October 31, 2001; *the Los Angeles Times*, September 7, 8, 11, and October 7, 2001; the *Los Angeles Times*, June 12, 13, 14, 2002; and the *Daily News*, September 9, 11, 2001.

4. Based on 2000 U.S. Census, Latinos made up 91 percent of the city's population.

5. Frank del Olmo, "Getting Away with a Blatant Gerrymander," *Los Angeles Times*, June 16, 2002. See also Frank Sotomayor and Magdalena Beltran del Olmo, *Frank del Olmo: Commentaries of his Times*. Los Angeles: A Los Angeles Times Book, 2004.

6. Ibid.

7. Cano Retainer Agreement. Appeal, WPD addressed to plaintiff José Hernández.

8. Book 45, City Council Meeting, August 19, 20002.

9. Opponents of city succession alleged that Republicans, including car dealers, realtors, apartment owners, homeowners associations, and key affluent people were behind the efforts to break up Los Angeles and found a new Valley city. See also the *Daily News*, June 5, 2002.

10. See Irma Lemus, "Do Latinos Support Succession?" *San Fernando Valley SUN*, August 22, 2002.

11. Ibid.

12. Book 45, City Council Meeting, November 15, 2002.

13. The *San Fernando SUN* (formerly *San Fernando Valley SUN*) was purchased by Severyn Aszkenazy and his wife Martha Diaz-Aszkenzy, owners of Pueblo Contracting Services, Inc., from Publisher and Editor Thelma Barrios, circa February 7, 2001. The paper was later renamed *San Fernando Valley SUN* to be inclusive of Valley news. The paper is free and tossed in neighborhood lawns every week.

14. A series of articles regarding the Head Start controversy appeared in the *San Fernando SUN*, December 5, 12, 19, 2002.

15. A letter of support for Irene by the Friends of LACA Head Start was sent to Sev and Martha Aszkenazy dated December 20, 2002. It appeared in the *San Fernando SUN* in January 2, 2003, signed by California State Assemblywoman Cindy Montañez, City of San Fernando Mayor Dr. José Hernández, former San Fernando High School teachers Alex and María Reza, CSUN Professor Everto Ruiz, Mission College Professors Ed Raskin, Andrés Torres, Joe Flores, and José Luis Ramirez, teachers Diane and Sergio Hernández, Olivia Robledo, and community activists Paula Rangel, Norma Ramirez, Baltazar Martínez, Alma Martínez, Yolanda Fuentes, and Xavier Flores as well as Artist Otto Sturke.

16. See "Tovar Supporters Hold Rally; Union Says Rally Political Game," *San Fernando SUN*, January 16, 2003.

17. Ibid.

18. Findings of the report appeared in the *San Fernando SUN*, January 23, 2003.

19. U.S. Census estimates, American Community Survey, 2005-2009.

20. See Helen Gao, "San Fernando Moves to Improve Its Schools," *Daily News*, March 16, 2003.

21. This statement was given to the present writer by Margarita López, Mission College student, and Arlene Irlando, representative of Los Angeles Unified School District Board Member Nury Martínez, who served as members of the committee to name the new school.
22. City Clerk Archives, Book 45, May 7, 2001 to December 29, 2003.
23. The reader is referred to the Summary Report on Disposition and Development Agreement by and between the San Fernando Redevelopment Agency, City of San Fernando, and Aszkenazy Development, Inc., March 1, 2004 and the Memorandum sent to Chairwoman Maribel de la Torre and Agency members dated December 9, 2004 from City Administrator José Pulido.
24. See Memorandum to Mayor Julie Ruelas and council mMembers dated August 20, 2007, from City Administrator José Pulido. Also, the present writer is much obliged to current Community Development Department Director Fred Ramirez for his assistance regarding the senior housing project.
25. Ibid.
26. The reader is also referred to Rachael Uranga, "Builder Stirs San Fernando Ambitious Draws Mixed Reaction," *Daily News*, November 28, 2005.
27. Ibid.
28. Quoted in the *Los Angeles Times*, December 30, 2011.
29. Ibid.
30. Quoted in the *Los Angeles Times*, January 12, 2012.
31. Sev Aszkenazy's statement was made during a city council discussion. See Minutes of City Council Meeting, March 21, 2005.

CHAPTER 12

End of an Era

Beware the Ides of March

In 2005, Los Angeles and neighboring communities were getting ready for the coming spring elections. In anticipation of the elections, Xavier Flores, president of Mexican American Political Association (MAPA), San Fernando Valley Chapter, sent a memo to the group membership reminding them about the elections.[1] In the memo, Flores issued a dire warning that the elections could have the potential to create a great deal of division within the communities. In San Fernando, people were already seeing a great divide among members of the council. There was a widely held perception that Councilwoman Maribel de la Torre and Councilman Steve Veres were gearing up to take out Councilman José Hernández during the upcoming elections scheduled for March. (Hernández and de la Torre were up for reelection.) In his view, Flores wrote, "One has to ask what role State Assemblywoman Cindy Montañez is playing in all of this, and it could be hard to imagine that her local chief of staff Veres and her sister would be acting without her knowledge. The other question is why?" Logically, Flores concluded, "The answer, of course, is pure unadulterated power."[2] The dispute was one of power. In the past, Hernández and Maribel had enjoyed a good working relationship on the council until Hernández refused her suggestion to join her, her sister, and Steve Veres on a coalition to control city government. Ruben Rodríguez, a seasoned Chicano activist, described her past behavior pattern as vindictive, restive, and reckless, exposing the city to some liability. He stated, "She doesn't know when to stop, and one day she could pay dearly as a result."[3]

Maribel de la Torre and José Hernández won their election campaigns handily. Hernández won his fourth, four-year term in office, De la Torre her second, four-year term. Not surprisingly, Flores's impending fears became real. After the election, the council became adversarial and disruptive, especially when Maribel teamed up with Steve Veres and City Administrator José Pulido in blaming Dr. José Hernández for their own shortcomings. There was a deliberate effort to cast him as anti-Semitic, clearly a political ploy to hurt him. In politics, perception matters. This issue will come up again in a later section. During the years 2005 to 2009, the city council was composed of Maribel de la Torre, José Hernández, Nury Martínez, Julie Ruelas, and Steve Veres. The division was evident when the council approved Councilman José Hernández's proposal to limit travel by council members. The change, approved by a 3 to 2 vote by members José Hernández, Julie Ruelas, and Nury Martínez, limited travel to only two conferences a year. Members Steve Veres and Maribel de la Torre opposed the travel restrictions because it limited elected officials from access to valuable information that could be used to benefit the city. The council majority agreed with the proposal to limit travel because of the budget crunch the city was experiencing. Also, the council majority in another 3 to 2 vote restricted council members' use of the city credit card.

The Council Got Things Done

The council, nonetheless, got things done. The drive for community improvement did not stop with the Library Plaza and the senior housing projects. The council continued reshaping the future of the city. It completed Heritage Park, a place for respite on Fourth and Hubbard Streets, with a $2,063,596 state grant obtained by State Assemblywoman Cindy Montañez.[4] Other improvements included pedestrian and bike paths, and a trolley transportation system. Federal funds for the trolley cars were obtained by Congressman Howard Berman for San Fernando. Within a period of eight years, San Fernando received $35 million in grants from state and federal sources. The city had been great in getting grants from these and other sources. City leaders renamed First Street from Jessie Street south to the cul-de-sac to Robert F. Kennedy Lane. San Fernando Recreation Park was renamed after the famous farm labor leader César E. Chávez. Cultural arts programs multiplied. The city's community development department assisted homeowners with home refurbishments, façade improvements, and new residential and commercial investments.

The City Corridor Specific Plan

The city council gave approval to the City Corridor Specific Plan for Maclay, Downtown, and Truman/San Fernando commercial districts.[5] This project involved mixed-use residential, retail, office, and neighborhood commercial development. A "restaurant row" was created within the downtown retail center with defined boundaries allowing for the sale of alcoholic drinks. The idea for this decision was to lessen the restrictions of the highly controversial city liquor ordinance. The goal of the Specific Plan was to create a vibrant business center and promote opportunities for investments in the city. It included an inclusive zoning law requiring builders to set aside 15 to 20 percent of development for low and median family income. Staff held six workshops for business and residents' input. Many of the participants' recommendations were incorporated into the Corridor Specific Plan.

Builders Agreement

The council worked out a watershed labor agreement with the Builders and Construction and Trade Council of Los Angeles and Orange Counties to use their workforce on major city projects.[6] The Builders group agreed to put forward an apprentice job program for local workers that would bring good careers for area residents. The council also adopted a living-wage ordinance that called for businesses and unions not only to offer decent pay and benefits on city jobs but also to ensure that the work came from local communities.

Employees' Retirement Benefit Tax

The council fixed a new tax rate to comply with the city's obligation to the California Public Employees' Retirement System (PERS). The tax was fixed at $0.28 per $100 of assessed valuation of all taxable property in the city. The tax tied to the property tax was estimated to raise $3,073,800 million for the fiscal year 2007-2008.[7] San Fernando was among only 13 cities in the state allowed access to this tax. In 1946, San Fernando voters approved fixing the tax rate to the property tax. Concerning taxpayers' anti-government stand, any future employees' benefit tax increase will be in doubt.

Employees' Harassment

On the July 17, 2006, council meeting, the council chamber was packed with community leaders appealing to the city administrator and the council to respect city employees who were being disrespected and who claimed harassment by their department heads. The employees sensed favoritism and preferential treatment of a department head by the chief administrator who had refused to assist them in their workplace problem. During the meeting, representatives from the local Mexican American Political Association (MAPA) and the League of United Latin American Council local chapter spoke on behalf of the workers asking that the harassment stop. The workers had sought relief from these organizations because they could not count on the city administrator to intervene on their behalf. A MAPA representative said that the grievance procedures had not been implemented in a consistent and unbiased manner, and spoke about an "inappropriate intervention by a Council member" on the personal issue.[8] A Recreation and Community Services Department employee also reported that she personally had experienced much adversity and distress due to the issue at hand. She stated that a "Council member was abusing her power and asked the Mayor to look into that matter, too."[9] The council majority—Mayor Nury Martínez and members Julie Ruelas and José Hernández—were upset that the problem occurred under the city administrator's watch. They pressed him to do his job and settle the issue, but the city administrator was tepid to the idea of safeguarding the employees' right to a quality working environment. He felt that there were procedures/protocols set up to deal with personal problems. But the general employees' union, the Service Employee International Union (SEIU) Local 721, was placed on an unusual position. It represented the employees and the city's top administrators. The council was helpless in doing anything, too. It could not micromanage city staff activities; hence, the council majority opted instead to order an employee evaluation of their supervisors and top management. This did not sit well with the top manager.[10] The action resulted in a tiff between the council majority and the city administrator, deepening a divide between the two. The employees' harassment problem was eventually resolved when the controversial director moved to a job in another city.

Momentous Council Decisions

The Battle for Alcohol Returns

At the March 10, 2005, meeting, Councilman José Hernández asked the council to waive the fee requirement to appeal a city planning commission decision allowing a local businessman to sell alcohol in a proposed business establishment. The planning commission decision endorsed by the city's community development director was made on March 1, 2005, to grant a conditional-use permit (CUP) for onsite and consumption of alcoholic beverages for a proposed steakhouse restaurant on 1245 San Fernando Road. The director had advised commissioners that the applicants,

Sev and Martha Aszkenazy, had met all the CUP requirements. Immediately, Councilman Steve Veres denounced Hernández for his opposition to a much-needed, upscale restaurant in the city. However, more liquor in the area was the last thing the neighborhood needed as it tried to overcome a negative image caused from years of violence related to an overconcentration of alcohol sales.[11] Councilwoman Nury Martínez said that she was concerned about the "over proliferation" of alcohol licenses in the area and about the message being sent to the people who lived there and who had to endure any negative impact. Other residents expressed similar fears about the problem that additional liquor would bring. After the public debate, a motion was taken to waive the fees to appeal planning commission CUP (2005-01) decision on a 3 to 2 vote, with Steve Veres and Maribel de la Torre voting in opposition. The city attorney and city administrator assured the council that staff would comply with noticing requirements and that the item to overthrow the planning commission decision would be brought back to a council meeting when they meet again.

More Limits on Alcohol Sales Backed

During the March 21, 2005, council meeting, the motion to overthrow the planning commission CUP to sell alcohol on 1245 San Fernando Road was approved on a 3 to 2 vote, with members Nury Martínez, Julie Ruelas, and José Hernández voting in the affirmative. Members Steve Veres and Maribel de la Torre voted in opposition to the motion under the veil that the city needed more liquor. Only 3 people favored the applicant's proposed liquor restaurant during the public hearing, compared with 13 residents who stood behind the council majority's rejection of the CUP. Hernández reiterated his position that he would support the steakhouse restaurant CUP if it would be located in the downtown business district "restaurant row." Nury Martínez reiterated her concern that the overconcentration of liquor licenses in that area was detrimental to the health of the neighborhood. She added that there was no point in serving the community if "we are not going to listen to it." Using state criteria, in 2005 the Los Angeles County's ratio for allocating licenses that sell alcohol on the premise was 1 license per 1,185 residents.[12] Using that guide, only 6 licenses would have been allocated on San Fernando Census Tract 3203 where the steakhouse was being proposed. In 2005, there were 13 existing liquor licenses in Census Tract 3203, which had a population of 7,200 residents as noted earlier in this book. Even the city's community development director acknowledged that there were 13 onsite alcohol outlets (one for every 554 residents) within Census Tract No. 3203. He also acknowledged the area as having undue concentration of offsite (carryout) retail alcohol licenses. There were 14 offsite alcohol outlets (one offsite alcohol outlet for every 514 residents) within Census Tract 3203, which exceeded Los Angeles County ratio of one offsite alcohol outlet license for every 1,568 residents. Thus, per state criteria Census Tract No. 3203 had an overconcentration of establishments selling alcohol. The state used data that confirmed that liquor licenses left uncontrolled potentially lead to a variety of problems, including drunk driving, alcohol use among youth, and other crimes related to alcohol abuse. Efforts aimed at reducing alcohol use among youth through education and behavior modification had mixed results. The link between unchecked alcohol consumption and violence was well established. Recently, Robert Nash Parker, professor of Sociology and Co-Director of the University of California, Riverside Presley Center for Crime and Justice Studies, led a research effort on how to reduce violence in neighborhoods and found that the density of liquor availability had a measurable effect on crime."[13] The state legislature gave municipalities the power to determine the location where beer, wine, and liquor can be served. This empowered communities to reduce access to and limit sales of alcohol, leading to lower crime rates and improved public health and safety. Nevertheless, the attorney for the Aszkenazys was not satisfied at the council's decision, saying that the denial of the conditional-use permit was a violation of due process and state law, and a violation of the applicants' civil rights, to which he immediately added, "They are prepared to sue the city."[14]

San Fernando Station, LLC v. City of Sam Fernando, et al.

Martha and Severyn (Sev) Aszkenazy (plaintiff) filed a lawsuit July 15, 2005, in Superior Court of the State of California County of Los Angeles on behalf of San Fernando Station, LLC seeking to overthrow the council decision that had denied the plaintiff a conditional-use permit (CUP) for sale and consumption of alcohol beverages on a proposed site for a high-end restaurant.[15] The lawsuit took aim at the city, Councilman Dr. José Hernández, and Councilwoman Julie Ruelas for violating the plaintiff's right to due process. The city faced additional difficulties and expense when members Maribel de la Torre and Steve Veres joined the city administrator on court depositions to cast Dr. Hernández as anti-Semitic, giving the plaintiff another reason for adding charges alleging that Dr. Hernández had opposed the CUP because the developer was Jewish.[16] Their statements raised the plaintiff's stakes, costing the city money. His anti-liquor approach to community development finally came back to haunt him during his fourth term in office. The case with a gaudy allegation was offbase because Hernández had voted before on numerous times (20, to be exact) in favor of the plaintiff's projects over his long tenure in public office.[17] He voted against the plaintiff's proposals only once, the subject of the San Fernando Station lawsuit. His glaring and most critical failure was that he stopped defending the plaintiff's proposals in the city.

The Los Angeles County Superior Court Reversed the Council Decision

On February 8, 2007, the court granted the plaintiff's writ on the basis of a legal technicality which arose when the council failed to use the proper form in noticing the appeal of the planning commission's decision. This was a mistake on the part of the city administrator who oversees the preparation of the council's agenda.[18] During the council meeting when an appeal of the planning commission decision was passed, the city attorney and city administrator had assured the council that staff would comply with noticing requirements when the planning commission decision would be brought to a council meeting.[19] Also, because the evidence of discrimination was so scant, the court on October 30, 2007, entered a summary judgment in favor of Dr. Hernández on the plaintiff's cause of action for denial of equal protection.[20] Most developers would grasp the CUP and start running with it. Sev Aszkenazy didn't do that. Despite the court rulings, he persisted to espouse the anti-religion charge as a red herring lengthening the trial that was costly for both parties.

Friends of José Hernández Voiced their Support for the Councilman

Although Los Angeles County superior judges did not detect any nuance of anti-Semitism in their courts, the specious accusation against Hernández triggered a flood of support for the embattled councilman. Teachers, old acquaintances, Jewish educational colleagues, and civil rights activists, who valued him as a friend and crusader for social justice and racial equality, came to council meetings to denounce the outrageous characterization of him.[21] *The Jewish Journal of Greater Los Angeles* recognized him as a strong proponent of interfaith dialogue with Jews.[22] Hernández also received letters of support. In one letter, a Jewish colleague and professor wrote: "To those who use prejudice as a weapon to gain their personal objective, I…remind them that this sword cuts two ways."[23] A letter from another Jewish professor expressed "outrage [because] when such charges…are used to increase personal wealth or power…it denigrates all those who legitimately fight anti-Semitism."[24]

During one of the council meetings, a woman exploited in a brief but angry voice as she shouted at City Administrator José Pulido: "You betrayed the man you work for."[25] Chicano activist Xavier Flores, Hernández's most stalwart supporter, told the council that he had read all of the court depositions related to the court filed against the city, Julie Ruelas, and Dr. José Hernández, and found that among those responsible for causing the lawsuit were members Maribel de la Torre and Steve Veres.[26] The latter, a master of Byzantine politics, made it easy to make spurious charges. The depositions shed light on who were the plaintiff's friends in the case. What was so incredible, in a sense, was that they didn't care how the city would be affected. The council was so divided that it made it difficult to fight and win the case in court.

A Settlement Agreement

On February 19, 2008, parties in the San Fernando Station case agreed to the terms of a settlement made as a result of a mediator's recommendation.[27] Under the terms, the city agreed to reinstate the plaintiff's CUP and its entitlements, and to extend until March 21, 2010, the construction of the San Fernando Station project. The plaintiff agreed to dismiss its petition against the city and members Dr. José Hernández and Julie Ruelas. In addition, the parties agreed that the "Compromise did not constitute an admission of liability or of the truth of any contention of any Party."[28] Finally, the City of San Fernando was told to pay the aggregate sum of $750,000 to the San Fernando Station. However, according to the city attorney, the city saw the $750,000 as a better deal, compared to the $2 million the plaintiff wanted.[29] Each party was to bear its own attorney fees and costs. The city's attorney fees came to about $800,000. Things would have been better for both parties had the plaintiff dropped the tawdry, religious allegations that added to attorneys' fees.

A Resort-like Aquatic Center

At the July 6, 2006, council meeting, a motion to approve $2,188,700 as the first step in a plan to replace the city's ailing swimming pool was approved unanimously. Throughout the construction planning, bids kept soaring because the council couldn't decide on the structural design of the aquatic facility, nor the funding sources. Finally, an the July 6, 2007, meeting, the council approved a final bid for $9,542,538 for an elaborate aquatic center, and an additional $508,200 for design services, project management service, and unforeseen work. This was a difficult project for elected officials and staff. The construction project dragged on for six years causing the public to find fault with their elected representatives.[30] Then the cost of the building and swimming pool facilities went up to $14.5 million. City staff blamed world demand for cement and steel products, including rising fuel prices. The increase was also attributed to the delay with the negotiation for additional state support. The council voted to pay for the aquatic facility with federal community development block grants, state grants, a $500,000 Los Angeles County contribution, and a bond issue to be paid with redevelopment funds set aside before a state law abolished redevelopment agencies. The bond obligation is due on September 2020.

The premier aquatic center composed of a Craftsman-style, two-story clubhouse, an Olympic-size swimming pool, a two-story water slide with adjoining splashes, and recreational pools for all ages was finally completed in 2008. Many people expressed concern that the project was too extravagant for a community that had an annual budget of approximately $30 million and 26 percent of families living below the poverty level (Los Angeles County families poverty level, 15.7 percent, state, 13.7 percent).[31] San Fernando medium household income was $39,909 compared to the county medium household income of $55,476.[32] But Councilwoman Maribel de la Torre, who sparked the construction of the resort-like aquatic center, had urged her colleagues to act under the banner that the working-class community of San Fernando deserved the best. The entire council agreed; however, the facility which was supposed to be open yearround was closed for a year for lack of money for operational cost, fueling a crisis in the community. Lack of council oversight worsened the crisis.[33] Other communities in the Valley were having problems opening their swimming pools for lack of resources in hard times. In 2011, the city hired a full-time pool manager and the aquatic center is now open yearround.

San Fernando Mixed-Use Parking Lots Development

On September 16, 2004, the city council and Redevelopment Agency issued a request for proposals (RFP) for all city-owned parking lots on the downtown business district to access developer, business, and non-profit interest in a mixed-use development of these city properties. The objective of the parking lots project was to encourage commercial and residential development as part of one or more mixed-use projects on underutilized city parking lots. The future mixed-use projects were intended to increase the city's sales tax revenue generated by new retail sales and increase property tax from the reassessed value of new commercial and residential land and buildings. The Agency Board received three proposals by the specified parking lots RFP deadline. A proposal by Aszkenazy Development, Inc., owned by Sev and Martha Aszkenazy, was eliminated from consideration by the project review committee because it was deemed incomplete. Sev Aszkenazy, an aggressive advocate at city hall for his business, had been actively engaged in major construction projects in San Fernando.

After three years of public hearings, three community workshops, and extensive negotiation and project refinement, the council acting as the city's Redevelopment Agency approved an exclusive negotiation agreement (ENA) with Wilshire Ventures Corporation (WVC) for development of five parking lots consistent with the San Fernando Corridors Specific Plan. A separate agreement was negotiated with Gangi Development for City Parting Lot #3.[34] President of WVC Enrique Fainchtein was the principal developer of the parking lots project. A map showed six parking lots and their addresses on the central business district, including five-story buildings, 359 two- and three-bedroom condominiums, several live/work lofts, and onsite parking facilities accommodating residents, commercial, and previously existing parking spaces. Per the initial requirement of the RFP issued by the city, 20 percent of the total residential units were set aside for low- and moderate-income households at affordable rates. In general, such project sites included a ground-floor commercial and parking area and two to three upper floors reserved for residential condominiums. The ground floor was reserved for retail shops, restaurants, entertainment venues, galleries, and personal and business services. In addition, levels of subterranean parking spaces were allocated for residential use only, while guest parking spaces were provided in the second floor and mezzanine area. Previously existing onsite public parking on each project site was to be reintroduced as part of the project's onsite ground parking facilities.[35]

Battle for the City's Mixed-Use Parting Lots Project

The mixed-use parking lots development was considered by the city administrator the best project that would carry the future of the city. Without it, the city would lose an opportunity to infuse residential and commercial development into the city's downtown area while increasing the availability of affordable housing. The developer's plans exceeded other previous major city construction projects. The taxpayers' cost was minimal. Developer Fainchtein received letters of interest from prospective financial partners and from prospective commercial tenants such as AT&T, Fresh & Easy Neighborhood Market, Panda Express, and T-Mobile. Mr. Fainchtein had provided proof that he was working to secure financial partners necessary to complete the project. But rancorous small interest groups, including Sev and Martha Aszkenazy's grassroots supporters took control of the debate, making a supreme effort to block Enrique Fainchtein's first development contract in San Fernando.[36] They said that his project would have a negative impact on the city, and that the buildings were too tall in comparison to other buildings in the area. Sev Aszkenazy's architect argued that traffic congestion would cause serious problems. Agency Board Member Steve Veres and others questioned the developer's professional experience and financial standing, and the number of lawsuits levied against him. Veres enjoyed an overt friendship with Sev Aszkenazy.[37] Several tenants on the central business district were afraid of losing their businesses in the San Fernando Mall to the new commercial development. Others made tenuous arguments that housing tenants would occupy parking spaces reserved for commercial use. In light of the economic downturn, Martha Aszkenazy was concerned that if the condominiums did not sell then the city could be stuck with converted rental apartments. The latter argument was perhaps the most plausible.

Proponents of the project were thrilled at the Wilshire Ventures Corporation's (WVC) plan to redevelop the existing surface public parking with new shopping opportunities for city residents that promised to improve the city's economic base. The live-work lofts were to be marketed to young professionals who wanted to settle in San Fernando. Proponents also praised the architectural design of the buildings that looked to improve the overall appearance for the downtown business district. The architectural element and detail of the buildings were consistent with the oldest and most historical structures in the city.[38] Strong support for developer Enrique Fainchtein was voiced. He was required to pay millions of dollars in fees in lieu of parking for the city parking spaces that the developer was unable to provide. He was also obligated to replace the loss of parking spaces on surface lots with parking structures on the project areas and pay Quimby fees valued in hundreds of thousands of dollars. Quimby fees are used by local governments to develop new or improve existing recreational facilities for the community. The project also planned to use local union workers and local builders' supplies. The pedestrian-oriented projects were considered by many as projects that were consistent with the city's long-ranged planning efforts to connect the downtown to the city civic center and create new opportunities for residential and commercial development.

Opportunity Lost

At the March 3, 2008, Redevelopment Agency meeting, Agency Board Executive Director José Pulido recommended that the Agency board consider approval of a seven-month extension to the exclusive negotiation agreement with Wilshire Ventures Corporation (WVC) in order to complete the environment impact report (EIR) for the city parking lots project and negotiate a disposition and development agreement (DDA) for the redevelopment of the lots. It was the Agency board director's assessment that WVC had made significant progress under the EIR, warranting a time extension to complete the report. After a heated debate and threats of a recall, staff recommendation was denied on a 3 to 2 vote, ending the life of the San Fernando mixed-use parking lots project.

Expediency Triumphed

Agency Board Chair Nury Martínez caved in under pressure from the anti-project group, joining Agency board members Steve Veres and Maribel de la Torre to prevent the project from moving forward. Martínez believed that Enrique Fainchtein might not be able to put together a realistic financial package to complete the construction contract with the City after he lost his business partner, but Agency board members Julie Ruelas and Dr. José Hernández disagreed. They felt they had to do the right thing for the city and Enrique Fainchtein. They went ahead in support of the developer who had a splendid record of building major structures in Mexico City. They believed that WVC should have been allowed to demonstrate they could successfully complete a city-sponsored project which was intended to enhance the downtown and provide quality housing and businesses. WVC had almost spent $1 million of their own money just for the opportunity to present their project for approval. Also, WVC had paid all amounts due the city. Most obviously, Agency board member Nury Martínez voted against the proposed project because she feared the threat of recall by zealous project critics. During the meeting, some folks were mulling desperately in the back of the council chambers on how to win the third vote, sending text messages to the council threatening to recall any council member who continued to support the project. That was a serious threat; it was bullying. Surprisingly, Nury Martínez, who usually stood up for the city, bolted, and voted against staff's recommendation to extent WVC the time to complete the EIR. She had been, at heart, part of the progressive team of Julie Ruelas and Dr. José Hernández in the city council; however, this time expediency triumphed. She undoubtedly made a sound political move, underscoring again a truism of politics. On the other hand Professors Ruelas and Hernández had enough backbone to stand up on their own principles without pressure from anyone but their constituents and their consciences.

City Administrator Disturbed at the General Tone of the Debate

City Administrator José Pulido, an expert in redevelopment, was disappointed and troubled during the debates over the San Fernando mixed-use parking lots project as crass accusations were being directed at Enrique Fainchtein. José Pulido, a native of San Fernando, was pushing hard for approval of the parking lots proposal, which he believed was a city model of economic development for a sustainable future. He listened to critics' recommendations, continued to make attentive corrections that were not satisfying to them. He got tired of listening, and lashed out at them. He decried the role of vested interest in San Fernando economic development. First he took on Agency board member Steve Veres for misleading statements he had made in the local press about the city's economic development record. In a memo addressed to the Agency board's chair, Mr. Pulido had strong words for Mr. Veres. Pulido wrote:

> The accusations of Agency Board Member Steve Veres are serious. They are misleading. Our community has prospered and will continue to do so because the City Government has the trust of its citizens. Unfortunately, these

types of remarks quickly negate all of the achievements and progress that San Fernando has made over the last six years, while under the direction of the Agency Board/City Council.[39] ...There has been for years a number of special interest groups that have done everything within their power to undermine any development in the downtown. What some of these special interest groups, acting under the guise of having the "city's" interest at heart, don't realize is that their actions over the years have come at a great expense to the city's taxpayers in lost property and sales tax revenues that could have been used towards improving the quality of life for San Fernando residents and business—especially our public safety.... Interestingly enough, when the Redevelopment Agency provided those special interest groups with an opportunity to submit development proposals through the Agency Parking Lots Request for Proposals (REP) on September 16, 2004, none of them did.[40]

Very little of this is new in San Fernando. The city had always been targeted for control by individuals, developers, or political machines seeking to establish a base of operation either for business gain or for political adventure. Helpless informed citizens had voiced concern about this dilemma; however, unusual for an appointed official, José E. Pulido was the first city administrator to speak so boldly about this trend.

The Recall of 2009

The Politics of Personal Destruction

During a special municipal election on January 13, 2009, voters on a 2-1 margin recalled Councilman José Hernández and Mayor Julie Ruelas for the delay of the construction of the pool, with the excessive budget of the aquatic center, and with voting for a parking lot project that would have transferred five city-owned downtown parking lots for $10 each, a mendacious political ploy. The two were also charged with refusing all settlement offered in the San Fernando Station case until the city was forced to pay settlement and legal fees in excess of $2 million. Councilman José Hernández was accused of making racist remarks, biasing his decision making that led city costs in excess of $2 million.[41] The recall was not a citizen's uprising; rather, it was led by a recall group consisting of staff, relatives, friends, and business associates of Martha and Sev Aszkenazy, a developer with a sizable presence and influence in city hall. Mario Hernández, Martha Aszkenazy's brother-in-law, was a member of the recall campaign committee. Councilman Steve Veres, the ring leader, was chief organizer of the campaign to unseat the targeted council members.[42] The sinister forces were led by Adriana B Gómez, a top employee of Sev Aszkenazy's development company. She was the prime mover of the recall campaign.[43] Steve Veres, Martha and Sev Aszkenazy, and their top aide each contributed $500 to help finance the recall campaign committee. Adriana B. Gómez loaned the recall committee $1,000.[44] The recall zealots met in an office owned by the Aszkenazys.[45] The town weekly newspaper, *San Fernando Valley SUN* (*the SUN*), owned by the Aszkenazys, unleashed an onslaught of articles attacking the good names of Professors Julie Ruelas and Dr. José Hernández.[46] This was great power politics adapted to the present time. It was difficult to debate big lies over and over again. As a World War II Nazi propaganda minister used to say, push a lie long enough and people will believe it. According to a former recall organizer, the stories went so viral and fast that facts were tossed aside.[47]

Opponents of the recall denied the charges. They claimed that special interests were behind the recall. They said the recall was a naked grasp for two council positions. The swimming pool project, originally championed by Councilwoman Maribel de la Torre, was estimated at $9 million, but the price increase was due to the rise in costs of materials which was seen throughout the world, something for which no one could have prepared. The pool project had been approved unanimously. De la Torre had spearheaded the expensive aquatic center project, serving as chair of the council's Swimming Pool Advisory Committee. The parking lot land giveaway was nonsense. What city would give away their land and what residents would allow this to happen?

The lawsuit by Sev Aszkenazy against the residents of San Fernando was brought because the city council refused to grant him a liquor permit in an area saturated with establishments selling alcohol. He charged that he was denied the permit to sell alcoholic beverages because of religious bias, but the courts determined that these allegations were based on hearsay and dismissed these charges. Instead, the courts found that the city had failed to follow proper procedures in denying the permit and found in his favor solely on these grounds. The settlement amount increased only because the plaintiff prolonged the hearings as long as possible.

Finally, opponents of the recall pointed out another reckless disregard for the truth when the recall operatives accused Mayor Ruelas and Councilman Hernández of having refused all settlements offered by the plaintiff until the city was forced to pay settlements and legal fees in excess of $2 million. Bottom-line question: Where did the recall organizers find this information when all settlement negotiations were conducted behind closed-door sessions?

Neither the city nor Mayor Julie Ruelas and Councilman José Hernández lost in a court of law. The case settled. Before settling, three different court judges had agreed there was not enough evidence to substantiate anti-Semitism allegations as a motive for denying Aszkenazy's company permission to sell liquor. To this date, the high-end steakhouse restaurant has not been open for lack of a tenant to manage the family restaurant. The CUP is renewed annually in hopes someone may come along and provide a nice place to eat in San Fernando.

The Greatest Fraud

The 2009 recall of two outstanding community leaders was the greatest fraud ever in San Fernando. They held impressive public service resumes that political newcomers need years to match. The taxpayers' costly special election was held two months before the end of Hernández's four-year term when he had planned to retire. The city was hijacked by a combination of greed and self-indulgence. No government can remain stable for long when self-serving citizens act irrationally.

Consequences of the Recall

Recall leaders won a pyrrhic victory. A recall election is a useful tool for politicians' misconduct. But that was not the case in San Fernando. Recall organizers carried out a crafty stratagem recall not because of any corruption or incompetence, but because of a difference of opinion on issues. If public servants are recalled for political reasons, sooner or later it will happen again and again, triggering a vicious cycle of retribution. Sometimes leaders need to take unpopular positions, but as long as these conditions of retribution exist, no public official can effectively serve the community well. Furthermore, San Fernando recall organizers and sponsors' actions cut into the fabric of the Mexican American community by picking and tearing at the thread of its well-respected and acknowledged leadership, bringing chaos to a well-structured city government.

The Day San Fernando Changed

The Community Loses Its Sense of History

During the first working council meeting, Steve Veres was appointed mayor of San Fernando. He told the jovial audience, "The recall is about change and giving the community what they want."[48] In his first order of business, he replaced city commissioners previously appointed by Julie Ruelas and Hernández. However, the most controversial action during the meeting was the change of César Chávez Park to San Fernando Recreation Park. Both Councilwomen Maribel de la Torre and (newly elected) Brenda Esqueda were so adamant about changing the name of César Chávez that they led the name change without input from the public.[49] That was one of the first sleazy ploys of the new council, when the recall group had promised to keep the public informed about what was going on in city hall. The naming of the park by the previous council was one of the proudest moments for San Fernando residents, for they were honoring the champion of farm workers' rights and a great American humanitarian. Later, the section of First Street adjacent to the César Chávez Monument named after Robert F. Kennedy, Jr. in recognition of RFK's support for César Chávez was also removed from the street sign. They discontinued any support for the historical annual March for Justice in San Fernando and the César E. Chávez Award. Maribel de la Torre, Steve Veres, and Brenda Esqueda were not wedded to the farm workers' rights movement. Day workers from various countries in Latin America who were looking for work to make a better life for themselves and their families were threatened, harassed, and victimized by officers of the San Fernando Police Department.[50] Brenda Esqueda, who had replaced Dr. José Hernández on the council, announced her support of the draconian Arizona SB 1070 law which criminalized undocumented immigrants.[51] Some city employees felt threatened if they spoke out about conditions in the work environment. A resident upset at the current direction of the new council wrote, "Our community has a history of showing respect to our city workers, contractors and vendors, because we are all the children and grandchildren of the labor movement. It seems that our current council has largely disregarded that tradition."[52] How ironic the new council actions were when local labor leaders Mike Quevedo and Ralph Arriola, former head of the Latin American Civic Association (LACA), the Los Angeles County Federation of Labor, and Service Employees International Union Local 721, confusing bedfellows, supported a number of the recall organizers, sponsors, and elected officials who had never been friends of working men and women.

The attack on the Chicano community continued as the new council ended the Mayor's Menudo Cook-Off as being too ethnic. The duly elected representatives of the city with a 93 percent Latino population also lashed out at English-limited residents who spoke in Spanish as they addressed the council. An end was put to the Spanish-language translation of the Fourth of July fireworks narration. In many other ways, Mayor Steve Veres and Councilwomen Maribel de la Torre and Brenda Esqueda had been hostile towards the Mexican culture. In short, San Fernando lost its sense of history. It lost its sense of community. As the noted Chicano historian has written, "Without a sense of community and a sense of history as a community, people become vulnerable to the plans and whims of the dominant group which can not only displace them but control them in other ways as well."[53]

During a council meeting, a disaffected member of the recall committee vented her concerns as she addressed Mayor Pro Tem Brenda Esqueda: "Didn't you come to my house and complain to Leslie and me about how Adriana Gómez and Mario Hernández had lied …. Didn't you tell us you believed they had used the Recall and your family to pave the way for Mario's run for City Council? …. I sincerely hope you can come to your senses and realize that you are just being used in the same way they used you as a placeholder for Mario. … Please be aware that when this crew is through with you, they will discard you like any other used condom."[54]

It is impossible not to be disgusted at anyone who could have benefited so much from the recall election of 2009. For an example, the disaffected member of the recall committee in another occasion wrote, "I wonder if it's possible for The [*San Fernando Valley*] *Sun* to fairly or objectively, report on city government when the Aszkenazys, who own and publish it, are in a position to gain so much if they control our city council, too? Isn't it a bit too cozy for Sev and Martha Aszkenazy's brother-in-law, Mario Hernández, to sit on the very council that will [sic] be handling out city land and contacts for development in San Fernando?"[55] Mario Hernández replaced former Mayor Julie Ruelas in the council after the 2009 recall.

San Fernando Loses Its Professional Staff

Six employees quit from the small municipal's management team. These included the city engineer, finance director, an assistant director of parks and recreation, and City Administrator José Pulido, and his assistant administrator and city administration's executive secretary. The city administrator was seen as responsible for the council's crisis and poor staff morale, left town unscratched, pleased with the work he accomplished in San Fernando. He said, "I have nothing to be ashamed of. People will look back on this time and realize that it was a special time in San Fernando when things got done. … Yes, there were some issues, but that's a normal part of municipal life."[56] He moved immediately to a higher-paying job as city manager of Temple City, California. But on January 13, 2014, the Temple City Council voted unanimously in closed session to fire him just a month after giving him a $10,300 bonus for outstanding work. In a press release, the mayor reported that the city council needed stronger leadership to lead the city in the future.

The chief of police and community development director retired. The latter was an important player in the liquor permit dispute. Mayor Steve Veres and Councilwoman Nury Martínez decided not to run for reelection. Veres and Martínez left town also unscratched, as they were elected to higher public offices in the Los Angeles Community College Board and the Los Angeles City Council, respectively. In 2010, the San Fernando City Council was composed of Mayor Mario Hernández, Mayor Pro Tem Brenda Esqueda, and members Maribel de la Torre, Antonio López, and Sylvia Ballin. Sylvia's husband is a business tenant at Sev Aszkenazy's Library Plaza Shopping Center. Veteran Councilwoman Maribel de la Torre was now in power over an inexperienced council void of a professional staff. The new council began their work with a new city administrator hired with unknown experience, while adding additional responsibilities to the post, as supervisor of finance and park activities.

A Dysfunctional City Government

San Fernando is ailing. The malady may be a result of a dysfunctional city hall, a callous city council, and a makeshift city staff. The recall operatives' promise of transparency, openness, and of bringing the community together failed. The council majority of Mayor Mario Hernández, Mayor Pro Tem Brenda Esqueda, and Councilwoman Maribel de la Torre quickly seized control of the municipality, excluding the other two colleagues in major council decisions. One might say that they got a little power and went crazy with it. The three are in the center of scandals, upheavals, and controversies that include conflict of interest votes, extramarital affairs, and Brown Act violations. The problem first started when the council majority considered a plan to employ a private fire department without considering the legal ramifications and community participation. San Fernando contracts with the City of Los Angeles Fire Department for fire and emergency services. This angered the public and interested them in what the new council was up to. Then the city was hit by one public scandal after another which distracted the city leaders from attending to city businesses. A San Fernando police dispatcher was arrested for allegedly exposing himself to a store clerk at a strip mall. He was later terminated. A police officer was put on leave following allegations of falsifying a police report. A jail suicide was also under investigation and family members of the inmate have retained legal counsel. YouTube posting of traffic ticket fixing caused more headaches for the police department. The mayor pro tem and a San Fernando police sergeant were accused of having an ongoing personal relationship. She refused to disqualify herself from voting on police matters. The romantic relationship caused a family breakup as her former husband has gone to the media for public disclosure of the relationship.[57] But nothing had raised the ire of folks in this family-oriented town more than Mayor Mario Hernández's announcement during the November 21, 2011, council meeting that he had been having a sexual relationship with Councilwoman Maribel de la Torre with his wife present in the council that was self-inflicted, self-destructive. Martha Aszkenazy is the sister of the estranged wife of the mayor. His unusual confession shocked the hundreds of angry citizens jammed into the council chambers as national and global media caught the mayor's indiscretion. In addition, the mayor announced from his seat that he had lost his business and filed personal and corporate bankruptcy. Maribel de la Torre admitted her relationship with the mayor during the March 5, 2012, council meeting.

Politically Resonant

Mayor Mario Hernández publicly placed some of the blame for his financial crisis on Sev Aszkenazy, who was also his former landlord. He said, "It was a big, bad landlord that helped push me out there. It was political retaliation…"[58] He explained that the conflict with his brother-in-law began in early 2011 when he opposed the design of a streetscape Aszkenazy had proposed for one of his projects. After that, the landlord stopped giving him extensions on his rent, even though other business tenants had received such consideration. The mayor also explained how Sev Aszkenazy used his newspaper to his advantage to influence public perception. The mayor admitted that he owed more than $440,000 to a trust overseen by his sister-in-law.[59]

San Fernando Chief of Police Love Escapade

The predominately Latino, working-class city of 24,000 residents gained notoriety again with another spectacular real-life telenovela, or soap opera. On April 18, 2011, a lawsuit was filed on behalf of a former San Fernando police cadet for damages that included wrongful termination, emotional distress, and violation of civil rights. The lawsuit alleged that she was wrongfully terminated following an affair with Chief of Police (then Lieutenant) Anthony "Tony" Ruelas. The police cadet had an array of e-mails in her possession of love communications between the two. She also alleged that they had sexual intercourse in a city police car during the police officer's work hours.[60] In the meantime, the council retained his service, approved a vacation time, and made no attempt to discipline the top administrator. The council majority had complete support of the police chief, while the San Fernando Police Department was divided over the chief's woes. The lawsuit along with other lawsuits against the city is pending.

A Second Wrongful Termination Lawsuit

The first female officer to earn the rank of sergeant in the San Fernando Police Department filed a wrongful termination lawsuit against the city claiming discrimination based on her sexual orientation.[61] She also blew the whistle on a controversial cell death. She charged that documents were falsified to give the appearance that proper jail checks were conducted on the night watch where an inmate reportedly hanged himself with a bed sheet. The city cannot comment on the lesbian case because it's a personal matter. Only one side of the story has been presented. The suicide of the inmate that occurred on June 11, 2011, is under investigation by the Los Angeles County Sheriff's Department.

Residents come to every council meeting to vent their displeasure at the poor city management and the shameful leadership of the council majority. Residents have asked them for their voluntary resignation to avoid facing a recall. They boo, shout insults, and point fingers at Mario Hernández, Maribel de la Torre, and Brenda Esqueda as a show of contempt for their elected representatives. Police have been requested to restore order. A controversial Decorum Ordinance was passed on a 3 to 2 vote while people protested. The ordinance prohibits the public from addressing the council on issues that are not on the agenda. People are questioning the constitutionality of the ordinance.

San Fernando Recall # 2

Angry residents have seen enough of their city being laughed at on talk shows. A recall committee composed of community and business people have now more than the required valid signatures for the city to hold a special election to recall Mario Hernández, Maribel de la Torre, and Brenda Esqueda. The signatures were verified by the county, and a special recall election was scheduled for November 6, 2012, to coincide with the general election. Voters now decide whether to retain or remove them from public office.

Purpose of the 2012 Recall

Julian Ruelas, a member of the current recall committee and nephew of former mayor of San Fernando, Julie Ruelas, said about the purpose of the recall: "The goal of the [2012] recall committee is to clean City Hall from top to bottom, and that includes the San Fernando Police Department."[62] Mayor Mario Hernández told the *Daily News*, "The problem in San Fernando is simple. Sev Aszkenazy owns half the town and manipulates its local government."[63]

The Fog of Falsehoods Drifts Away

During a council meeting, Brenda Esqueda noted that she participated in the 2009 special recall election of former Mayor Julie Ruelas and Councilman Dr. José Hernández and many times did not question what recall leaders were saying. Now that she is the subject of a recall she recommended those involved in the current recall efforts to check the validity of what they're being told. She said, "I see a lot of wrong things that happened in the first recall happening again."[64] She apologized for the injustices of the 2009 recall.[65] Recall leaders Gilbert Berriozabal and Henry Romero also apologized.

Vindication

During the February 6, 2012, council meeting, a reporter approached former councilman and mayor, José Hernández, and asked him what he thought of the city's current residents' dilemma. He said, "This is what the community wanted, and this is what the community got. If I were in the Council, I could have been very helpful to deal with the situations that exist now. I think I would have been able to provide stability, and new direction for the city." He added, "After 16 years as a Council Member and Mayor of San Fernando, I had background information about the great things we have done ... I made many good decisions benefiting San Fernando and some poor decisions. I take responsibility for both decisions." When asked about his rejection by voters, Hernández replied, "What hurt me the most about the recall was my pride. And seeing what I see now, I think I have regained part of my pride back."[66]

And so this ends the story of self-government in San Fernando. One hopes that San Fernando politics will pivot around questions central to the lives of residents in the future.

Notes

1. Mexican American Political Association, San Fernando Valley Chapter, May 4, 2004.
2. Ibid.
3. These are Ruben Rodriguez's own words. See also Ruben Rodriguez's letter to Mayor de la Torre and council members on the mayor's tacky statements, August 2, 2004.
4. Assemblywoman Cindy Montañez, a strong supporter of open space, was a former councilwoman and mayor of San Fernando. She is sister to Mayor Maribel de la Torre.
5. For a detailed description of the City Corridors Specific Plan, the reader is referred to the City of San Fernando Maclay, Truman and San Fernando Road Corridors Specific Plan available at the office of Community Development Department. See also Minutes of City Council Meeting, July 17, 2006.

6. See Minutes of City Council Meeting, September 19, 2005.
7. See Minutes of City Council Meeting, August 20, 2007.
8. See Minutes of City Council Meeting, July 17, 2006.
9. Ibid.
10. See Minutes of City Council Meeting, April 24, 2006 and December 8, 2007.
11. Please refer to Roberto Lorederman, "Anti-Semitic Colors Liquor License Fight in San Fernando," *Jewish Journal of Greater Los Angeles,* April 18, 2008.
12. Please refer to Report on Existing Liquor Permits and City Regulations submitted by Community Development Director Paul A. Deibel to city council on April 17, 2006. See also *San Fernando Valley SUN* (the *SUN),* April 21, 2006.
13. See University of California, "2012 Research Impact, Real World Solutions," University of California, Riverside.
14. Quoted in the *SUN,* April 21, 2005.
15. State of California Los Angeles County Superior Court Case No. BS097994.
16. At a hearing held, City Administrator José Pulido testified that in the summer of 2004, in connection with a senior housing project, he heard Dr. José Hernández say a disparaging remark against Sev Aszkenazy's religion. The alleged remark was made nine months before the city's action at issue. The city administrator's statement proved costly to city's taxpayers. His motive for the statement was unclear.
17. Hernández had voted on many occasions in favor of the plaintiff's projects. His voting record of these projects can be found in the City Community Development Department.
18. "The Order of Business of each Council Meeting shall be as contained in the Agenda as prepared by the City Administrator." Procedural Manual, City Council of the City of San Fernando, as amended by Ordinance No. 1543 on July 23, 2003.
19. March 19, 2005, city council meeting.
20. Report of J. Michael Echevarria,, attorney for Councilman Dr. José Hernández and Mayor Julie Ruelas, December 3, 2007.
21. March 3, 2008 and September 15, 2008, city council meetings.
22. See Roberto Loiedermaan, "Anti-Semitic Charge Colors Liquor License Fight in City of San Fernando," *Jewish Journal of Greater Los Angeles*, April 18, 2008. See also March 3, 2008 and September 15, 2008, city council meetings.
23. Ibid.
24. Ibid.
25. September 15, 2008, city council meeting.
26. Ibid.
27. Signed by All Parties and originally filed on February 21, 2008, Los Angeles County Superior Court No. BS097994.
28. Ibid.
29. This was the position of City Attorney Michael Estrada as cited in the *Daily News*, March 13, 2008.
30. City Public Works Director Ron Ruiz assisted in this section. See Michael Knight, "Pool Project in a Hole," *San Fernando Valley SUN*, April 21, 2005.

31. U.S. Department of Commerce, U.S. 2010 census data.
32. Ibid.
33. For more detailed information, see the *Daily News*, September 8, 2010, and the *San Fernando Valley SUN*, August 5, 2010 and September 16, 2010.
34. A life cycle of the San Fernando mixed-use parking lots development is found in City Administration Memorandum to Redevelopment Agency Board Chair Julie Ruelas and Board Members from Agency Board Executive Director José Pulido, March 3, 2008.
35. This section was made possible by the assistance of City Planner Fred Ramírez. See also Draft of San Fernando Downtown Parking Lots Environmental Impact Report prepared for the city, February 20, 2008.
36. A summary of the project critics is found in *San Fernando Valley SUN* (the *SUN*), October 19, 2006. The newspaper is owned by Sev and Martha Aszkenazy.
37. *The Daily News*, November 28, 2005.
38. Draft of the San Fernando Downtown Parking Lots Environment Impact Report, op. cit.
39. Quoted in a memorandum of Redevelopment Agency Board Executive Director José Pulido sent to Agency Board Chair Julie Ruelas and Board Members December 7, 2007.
40. Ibid.
41. City of San Fernando Sample Ballot and Voter Information Pamphlet, Special Municipal Election, January 13, 2009.
42. This information is based on Steve Veres's e-mail correspondences with recall leaders. The information was also provided by Mayor of San Fernando Brenda Esqueda and former lead recall organizer in an interview with the present writer held on May 27, 2012. Other leaders of the recall of former Mayor Julie Ruelas and Councilman José Hernández were members Maribel de la Torre, Adriana Gómez, Mario Hernández, Veronica Casillas, Julie Cuellar, Henry Romero, and Gilbert Berriozabal. Recall sponsors included labor leader Mike Quevedo and his wife Barbara, former Latin American Civic Association Director Ralph Arriola, teachers Rodolfo S. Vásquez and María Elena Tostado, Ralph Pérez, Nick García, Josephine Najar, liquor market owner Mike Majers, Martha Aszkenazy's brother Frank Díaz, Simon and Shaun Wysbeek, Frank Soto, and Service Employees International Union Local 721. The recall sponsors were listed in the Sample Ballot of the January 13, 2009 Special Municipal Election.
43. This information was provided by former recall leader Henry Romero who said he observed her leadership role in the recall campaign committee while attending campaign meetings.
44. Councilwoman Maribel de la Torre and former lead recall organizer assisted in this section in an interview with the present writer on May 21, 2012.
45. Mayor Brenda Esqueda and former lead recall organizer assisted in this section in an interview with the present writer on May 27, 2012. The recall campaign committee listed the address of its office at 233 N. Maclay, City of San Fernando. The office is located in Sev Aszkenazy's Library Plaza Shopping Center.
46. See the following *SUN* editions as examples: February 21, 2008; March 13, 2008; April 3, 2008; April 10, 2008; July 24, 2008; and January 15, 2009.

47. This information was provided by Mayor Pro Tem Brenda Esqueda and former lead recall organizer in an interview with the present writer on May 27, 2012. She is the subjected of Recall # 2.

48. Minutes of city council meeting, January 26, 2009. A discussion of this meeting is also found in the *SUN*, January 29, 2009.

49. César Chávez Commemorative Committee Member Alex Reza e-mail correspondences with friends of the labor leader, January 28, 2009.

50. Sam Córdova, "Injustices, Inhumanity by San Fernando Police Department," *SUN*, June 4, 2009.

51. This statement was made by the president of the San Fernando Police Officers Association during the March 5, 2012, city council meeting.

52. Letter to the *SUN* editor, October 27, 2011, by Linda Campanella Juron.

53. Rodolfo F. Acuña, *Anything But Mexican,* op. cit.

54. This statement was made by Sharron Aisenman during the February 23, 2009, city council meeting. Sharron and her husband Leslie were actively involved in the recall of former Mayor of San Fernando Julie Ruelas and Councilman Dr. José Hernández.

55. Sharron Aisenmann Letter to *SUN* Editor Dianna Martínez, February 26, 2009.

56. Quoted in the *Daily News*, October 7, 2009.

57. For a story of the estranged husband, see *SUN*, April 19, 26, 2012.

58. This statement was made during the November 21, 2011, city council meeting. It was also quoted in the *Los Angeles Times,* January 27, 2012 and in the *SUN*, November 24, 2011.

59. Interview with Mayor Mario Hernández and the present writer on January 13, 2012. See also the *SUN*, November 24, 2012.

60. For an interlude of the sex scandals of the chief of police and others, see the *SUN*, February 17, 2011; April 7, 2011; May 24, 2011; and December 22, 2011. For a summary of events that led to the second recall, see the *SUN*, January 26, 2012.

61. See these accounts in the *Daily News*, December 11, 2011; and the *SUN*, February 9, 15, 23 and March 1, 2012.

62. This quote appeared in the *SUN*, March 1, 2012.

63. *Daily News,* December 11, 2011.

64. Brenda Equeda made this statement during the February 23, 2012, city council meeting. The statement also appeared in the *SUN*, February 23, 2012.

65. This statement was made by Brenda Equeda in an interview with the present writer, May 27, 2012.

66. This statement also appeared in the *SUN*, February 9, 2012.

CHAPTER 13

Summary and Conclusions

This book on the Limits of Social Change: The Case Study of a Mexican Community provides an understanding of the complex issues underlying the politics of social change and public policy as demographics evolve from White to Latino empowerment. The major theme of the study is social change which took some strange and interesting twists and turns. The importance of government action in the quest for community empowerment in a small California town is underscored; yet the book stressed that governance is a brutal business often mired in divisive and ugly politics. The study demonstrated how a political system may be near the breaking point. Nonetheless, it raises public awareness of the many achievements and flaws progressive Mexican Americans made to the evolution of power in California municipal government. They learned to govern the hard way. Boosting public policy required patience and a grooming process of good leadership that Latinos had not often been given the opportunity to exercise. Change was brought about because of the quality of leadership learned within the Chicano community, and to an extent because of the Valley economy which made progress possible. It also emphasized the quality of change that took place, not just the amount of change. But by 2009 it was their own success that put the Mexican American progressives out of business.

Nothing in the study has been invented. Documentation is found in the Notes at the end of each chapter. A great deal of the information was new, drawn from the author's community activism and government service, from interviews, minutes of government agencies, newspapers' accounts of issues, scholarly materials, and the like.

A Story Worth Hearing

Every community has a story to tell and every story is worthy of hearing. Mexican American civic participation is rarely taught in government or history sessions. In Arizona, for example, the highly successful Mexican American Studies program has been removed from high school academic programs. Why not let young people know about the sacrifices that others have made for them, hoping that they dedicate themselves to the positive ideals made by those who came before them? The Arizona program had offered courses in history, literature, art, and community study, courses that motivated students to stay in school. Furthermore, the organized life of Chicanos/Latinos in a small city has not been given enough attention by social scientists.

A rich cache of true stories was put together for the reader to witness a people's movement of self-governance. The stories represent a Chicano watershed movement in the city's history, and a huge step in their progressive political activity. As such, it was an American story of success. The book was divided into five parts. First, the story focused on the beginning of the San Fernando community, the earliest organized community in the San Fernando Valley surrounded by the historic San Fernando Mission. Despite the fact that Mexicans and Native Americans established the first social order in the Valley, they were relegated to second- and third-class citizenship when they became part of the United States. Mexicans toiled the soil, helped to build the railroad, and built the first Valley schoolhouse. They helped to build cars, participated in the construction of housing during the Valley housing boom, as well as in the industrialization of the region. There was a constant migration of Mexicans, Mexican Americans, and Latinos and their families into the Valley in response to the demands for labor in agriculture and in the growing industrial sectors. The latter helped to make progress possible for all Valley residents. Isolation ultimately allowed Mexicans to strengthen their culture and develop genuinely self-contained local institutions. They promoted their traditional norms which emphasized cooperation, self-sufficiency, and generosity which became major forces in advancing their lives. Unparalleled family values such as respect for work and religion, integrity, honesty, courage and discipline were essential ingredients that led them to attain leadership excellence in the defense of their country, and in their social, economic, and political life. Community, family, and friends were important features that best described San Fernando, and particularly Mexican Americans.

The second part of the book dealt with the search for an identity and with political power, and the persistent demand for full participation in the political process. Getting politically engaged really matters. Greater citizen participation has been shown to help bring communities better jobs, stronger economic growth, safer neighborhoods, higher performing schools, and affordable housing. Rapid growth of new Latino families in the city, returning World War II war veterans hungry for education and new job opportunities, the demand of the Valley for increased workers in agriculture and in the newer industries, and government poverty programs all created strains in the power paradigm of white conservatives that griped the city's Mexican American communities for too long. The rights of people to participate fully in their communities invariably had been resisted and delayed. But the walls of resistance finally fell as the activist leaders persisted to openly challenge the political monopoly of the old order.

The third part specifically focused on Chicano progressive activists' drive to empower their communities. It began as their struggle for community empowerment was reborn in the late 1960s and early 1970s.[1] First they reevaluated their political, economic, and educational position in Los Angeles and elsewhere in the country. They took to the streets, boycotted business, and brought schools and universities to a standstill in their demands for an inclusive society. The Chicano movement for civil rights, as it was called, was seen as a direct link between the protester and an incompatible political system that failed to fully embrace their rights for quality education, safer neighborhoods, affirmative action in admission to higher education and job opportunities, and freedom from poverty, police harassment, and discrimination. They also took their issues to the courts. It was proof, once more, that only by using peaceful demonstrations effectively can people rise up to their rightful place in history. Opportunities created by the Chicano civil rights victories brought forth a new generation of Chicano progressive loyalists, academicians, and students to challenge again the established order in San Fernando and elsewhere as changing demographics in the city gave them substantial representation, hastening a positive transformation of power.

The fourth part of the book, of the dynamics of Chicano decision making, showed how Chicanos indisputably used the political process to take charge of local government, making decisions that set new patterns of behavior for the rest of the community. It examined an extraordinary series of decisions that helped determine Chicano political life in San Fernando. Political power was the key to their success. Their community organizations served as a vehicle to engage participation in government and to make government more representative and efficient.

A Progressive Agenda

The Chicano political agenda was no different here than in other communities. Chicano elected officials wanted a city where children were safe, where young people could find healthy recreational activities, and could enroll in art and cultural programs. They removed identified gang members that posed a threat to children at Las

Palmas Park. After-school programs were important, too. They supported construction of first-class recreation facilities, a first-class library, a new highly academic high school, and a museum. Historical preservation was a major priority as well. They acted to uphold the principle that a community saturated with sales of alcoholic beverages was detrimental to the public's health and safety. The historical San Fernando Memorial Hospital was reopened and put to smart use by a local hospital as health care providers are serving the health needs of the region. These programs were fitting for a family-oriented city with numerous children in most households. Senior citizens were not neglected either. A beautifully designed recreational building and an affordable housing project were built especially for them. Subsidies for housing improvements and first-time home-buyer programs for younger residents were provided. A citywide trolley system was established, and assisted in locating the Los Angeles Commuter Rail Station on Hubbard and First Streets, giving San Fernando residents easy access to commuter rail transportation. They recruited major businesses such as the Rydell Automotive group, Sigue Corporation, Arroyo Builders Materials, Mac-Donald Restaurants, Starbucks Coffee, and more, which have produced significant tax revenue and jobs through their efforts. They assisted in improving the Swap Meet which saved 1,000 jobs and small-family businesses. They supported equal opportunity in city employment and negotiated with building contractors that worked in city projects to buy construction materials locally, and hire local union workers. A building workers' union agreed to sponsor an apprenticeship designed to recruit local unemployed men and women. Neighborhoods were kept clean and street boulevards were landscaped promptly and trees protected, receiving the National Tree Award. Patriotic and cultural festivals flourished; their heroes were recognized. In addition, they co-financed the annual San Fernando Relay for Life. There was a strong sense of community and people's trust in their government. The city was industrious and thriving, a reflection of their pro-business policies and care of the public purse. Actually, there was nothing particularly ethnic about this agenda.

In short, Chicana/o leaders were mindful of Thomas Hobbes's concept of power written many years ago which said: "All men [women] seek security, to live well and can only achieve this goal by commanding the power to control the environment in which they reside."[2] Hobbes was an English philosopher best known for his famous 1651 book *Leviathan* which led the discussion for much of subsequent Western political thought.

A Pioneer in Social Change Praised

Trailblazer Jess Margarito, a native son of San Fernando, holds a special place in local Chicano political history. He is noted for laying the groundwork for the empowerment of San Fernando Latino residents. He projected himself as a progressive with a sense of family importance, cultural respect, and a social conscience. He sowed the seed for securing social acceptance for a process that seemed irrevocable at using government for enriching people's life. Further, he charted the political course for other Mexican Americans elected to represent the Valley in the Los Angeles City Council, Los Angeles Unified School District and Los Angeles Community College District Boards, State Assembly and Senate, and U.S. Congress, including San Fernando City Council representatives who assumed his progressive mantle.[3] Jess Margarito has retired from politics, and currently manages a non-profit organization that assists immigrants with their legal papers.

Finally the fifth part, of the end of an era, provided some interesting observations of Chicano progressive political behavior. Their great gift to municipal government was to provide a model to affect change in response to the cultural and political revolt against authority that took place in the 1960s and early 1970s. It was evident from the foregoing study that Chicanos took advantage of every opportunity available to them, got educated and motivated people to political action. They got elected to public office and made decisions, setting a brilliant record of positive civic and cultural life in the city. They governed brazenly, pursuing ambitious economic, social, and cultural programs. They went from needling the White conservative establishment to becoming the establishment themselves. However, the most interesting finding of their actions was that while they were a political force for bringing social change, they were mightily touched by the change. In a sense, it was their success that drove them out of a job in San Fernando. They learned, however late, that there were limits to social change. While the City Council was all Latino, its influence in recent years was diminished by its diverse personalities and personal interests. They are not immune from the politics of power. The successful recall election of former Mayor Julie Ruelas and Councilman José Hernández in 2009 marked the end of the progressive era in the city, undermining its political structure. This political drama was led by two council members, an errant top administrator, a bizarre lawsuit, a controversial downtown development, a utopian aquatic center, and a self-serving "citizen" group seeking power aided by the town's weekly newspaper. The recall was not an attempt to hold the elected officials accountable for their failures, but to replace them with individuals with a personal agenda. The effect was predicated. The actions of recall sponsors led the city into chaos and poor government, which highlighted the dire consequences of the recall. At the root of San Fernando's dysfunctional politics lie some ideas about what went wrong. Perhaps, the most immediate, was the disappearance or weakening of community direct action organizations such as Raza Unida Party, San Fernando Community Improvement Council (CIC), Valley Organized in

Community Efforts (VOICE), Mexican American Political Association (MAPA), Latin American Civic Association (LACA), San Fernando Democratic Club, and Pueblo y Salud. That left San Fernando residents vulnerable to political control by unscrupulous private interests. These community organizations had the strength to resist the moneyed interests. Their leaders were no longer in the political spotlight. A few remain to inspire the youth, but they are old and tired, and there is no one of their caliber to replace them.

Another explanation for the disintegration, possibly most important, was that social change was always found in inequalities of neglected groups. In San Fernando, frustration declined, and more opportunities were available as Latinos gained greater political voice. Once the goal of self-governance was achieved, many retreated from group life. They entered the mainstream, downplayed their cultural roots, and sought personal gain. This idea parallels the findings of an earlier study by the present writer that concluded that groups often unite around a cause then crumble once their cause had been achieved.[4] Many Latino men and women are now found in all important city positions and many police officers, now multiethnic, looked like the people in the neighborhoods they patrol. Latinos, mostly Americans of Mexican heritage, constitute the predominately voting bloc in the city. There is no longer a need for self-determination and community empowerment.

City Hall's Latest Scandal

In the latest twist, the community continues to be embarrassed at the sorry state of their current representatives even involving a sexual scandal. On June 28, 2012, police were called to the home where Councilman Mario Hernández was staying. When the police arrived, they found his face and neck bruised. He had sustained other injuries which they photographed carefully following appropriate police procedures. Mr. Hernández had a physical altercation with his lover, Councilwoman Maribel de la Torre, alleging that the councilwoman charged into his bedroom in a rage, choked him, and told him she "could kill him." She allegedly punched him in the face, ransacked his bedroom, smashed some picture frames, and broke his laptop. He immediately submitted a police report concerning the confrontation to the San Fernando Police Department. Both parties claimed the other was the aggressor. She felt that she was defending herself, and complained that he first assaulted her. Both obtained restraining orders against each other. The fight started from an argument over a trip Hernández had planned to take without her. Later, he had second thoughts about filing charges against his girlfriend. He asked the San Fernando interim chief of police to remove the police report. The police chief refused. In California, once a report of battery or domestic violence is filed, it cannot be retracted until it has been investigated by the county district attorney. Subsequently, the interim chief of police was abruptly released from his job. However, after reviewing the report, the Los Angeles County district attorney decided to proceed with the case.

On July 10, 2012, Councilman Mario Hernández tendered a letter of resignation from the San Fernando City Council effective July 6, 2012, because of the "inconvenience caused by his personal life and have continued to cause embarrassment to the city."[5] He hoped his departure would heal the city. Their love story first became the subject of talk shows when then Mayor Mario Hernández announced his affair with De la Torre while his wife was sitting in the front row at a council meeting in 2011. After he resigned from his office, he asked the district attorney to drop the charges against his ex-lover. But the district attorney decided that there was enough evidence to order the case to trial. On August 21, 2012, Maribel de la Torre was arraigned in the Los Angeles County Court House in San Fernando on two misdemeanor counts of battery and vandalism. She pled not guilty. Mario Hernández stood by his woman as he said he would not testify against her. On December 12, 2012, battery and vandalism charges in the domestic violence case were dropped against her because the victim, former councilman and mayor Mario Hernández failed to appear for court.

A Familiar Ending

On August 6, 2012, the people's business took a back seat again as council members bickered and snipped at each other during the council meeting. Private citizen Mario Hernández, who sat in the audience, extended his support to the embattled Mayor Brenda Esqueda and Councilwoman Maribel de la Torre. Others in the audience joined in the free-for-all discussion. Councilwoman Maribel de la Torre described the council meeting as a "circus" and "chaotic." Responding to de la Torre's remarks, a woman in the audience shouted that Sev Aszkenazy, a developer and co-owner of the local weekly newspaper, was the "cause of the entire chaos in the City."[6] Mayor Brenda Esqueda used her time to accuse Recall Committee Julian Ruelas and [Sev] Aszkenazy and others for "plotting their next move," something she called "scary."[7] She also said that Sev Aszkenazy kept businesses from coming into the city, a recurring theme of former friends of Aszkenazy who were at one time his allies, and other critics. But the mayor added, "Those days of one individual trying to control development in the City are over."[8] There was no way to prove this story, but it had the ring of truth. Many city residents walked out of the room disgusted at the worsening political climate of their community. The problem was solved, however, when Mayor Brenda Esqueda and members Maribel de la Torres and Mario Hernández were recalled from office during the November 6, 2012, special election. Mario Hernández had resigned from the council in July, but his name was still on the ballot.

Looking Ahead

Evidently, this study has shown that group struggle is never ending, a stark reminder that politics of interests usually go that way. City officials are often overwhelmed by the implacable pressure of a handful of citizens who are impossible to please. The city is struggling to survive amid a lingering recession, a disastrous leadership, and an array of lawsuits. Balancing the budget will require discipline and independence. There exists fatigue among the electorate, but if they are going to turn things around, they need to elect a smart and independent council loyal to the community and not to private interest. What the city needs is a few good mavericks who will put the city first. General-law cities do not have a charter to guide them in self-rule, but the city council can adopt rules and ordinances that regulate their activities. For example, the San Fernando City Council needs to pass a nonintrusive rule with a penalty clause that prohibits individual council members from giving orders or instructing staff to violate their professional standards. This is endemic in San Fernando government. The rule should also prohibit individual council members from asking staff for special personal favors such as waiving traffic violations, water bill payments, and domestic violations reports. The latter practice compromises the individual council member to the whims of the administration. Council members still would have the prerogative to seek information, advice, or suggestions from city officials.

A recent and disturbing trend is the rise of the city administrator as a political novice in city government. Previous councils have given the top administrator too much power and little public accountability. To curve this power, the police chief and other department heads, including the city clerk, should report directly to the council instead of the city administrator. They should no longer be beholden to the city administration. The city attorney should continue to work under the direction of the city council. The new city administrator should have an excellent track record of professionalism.

Ending text messages during council meeting debates is highly recommended. They undermine the people's right to know who is actually involved in the debate, and who is really making decisions. The controversial Decorum Ordinance, which prohibits public discussion of issues that are not on the council agenda, must be rescinded. People should not be excluded from venting their concerns in front of their council. Also, city commissioners must be free from any council member partisan influence.

They are an important and integral part of city government. They have the skill to convene, facilitate, and initiate ideas for cooperative planning and problem solving, irrespective of their political orientation. Council members should not be paid for serving as liaison to these commissions.

Thus, the deep roots of Mexican Americans in San Fernando have now been told. It's very likely that San Fernando will fast develop further away from their progressive agenda as a new coalition of Latino liberals, White conservatives, and city merchants, strange bedfellows will take over city government. Perhaps, they will no longer accept the social conscience behind their agenda. Nevertheless, the future of good government in San Fernando is in their hands. Council members have important jobs to do. They are supposed to improve the residents' quality of life by allocating city services, attracting good employees and businesses, and keeping neighborhoods safe. Still, there are many good families in town. There are third- and fourth-generation residents who may provide the basis for a strong, responsible government. They should not allow people from out of town to dictate their future and their children's future. But they must step up and lead. Reflecting the best interests of citizens is what San Fernando needs most in political leaders.

Notes

1. The Chicano Movement for Civil Rights of the late 1960s and early 1970s was a continuation of the Chicano Mutualism Movement of a previous Mexican American generation. See José Amaro Hernández, *Mutual Aid for Survival*, op. cit.
2. Quoted in Andrew Hacker, *Political Thought*, 204, op. cit. An English version of Thomas Hobbes, *Leviathan Parts I & II*, is by The Library of Liberal Arts, Oskar Priest, General Editor, New York: The Bobbs-Merrill Company, Inc., 1958.
3. The elective officials are Los Angeles City Councilman Richard Alarcón, State Assemblyman Felipe Fuentes, State Senator Alex Padilla, former State Assemblywoman Cindy Montañez, and U.S. Representative Tony Cárdenas.
4. See José Amaro Hernández, *Mutual Air for Survival*, op. cit.
5. The latest city hall saga appeared in local newspapers and major television networks. See, for example, *the Los Angeles Times*, July 8, 15, 2012; and *the San Fernando Valley SUN*, July 12, 19, 26, 2012, August 9, 23, 2012; and the *LA Weekly Newspaper*, October 11, 2012.
6. Quoted in the *San Fernando Valley SUN*, August 9, 2012.
7. Ibid.
8. Ibid.

SELECTED BIBLIOGRAPHY

Acuña, Rodolfo F. *Corridors of Migration: The Odyssey of Mexican Laborers, 1600-1933.* Tucson: University of Arizona Press, 2007.

-------. *The Making of Chicana/o Studies: In the Trenches of Academe.* New Brunswick: Rutgers University Press, 2011.

-------. *Anything But Mexican: Chicanos in Contemporary Los Angeles.* New York: Verso Press, 1996.

-------. *Sonoran Strongman.* Tucson: University of Arizona Press, 1974.

Adrian, Charles R. *A History of American City Government: The Emergence of the Metropolis, 1920-1945.* New York: Lanham Publishing Company, 1987.

Alinsky, Saul. *Reveille for Radicals.* New York: Vintage, 1969.

Alstyne, Richard W. *The Rising American Empire.* New York: Oxford University Press, 1960.

Ashby, Steven L. *Political Science, the Discipline and Its Dimensions: An Introduction.* New York: Charles Scribner's Son, 1970.

Barger, W. K., and Ernesto M. Reza. *The Farm Labor Movement in the Midwest: Social Change and Adaptation Among Migrant Farm Workers.* Austin: University of Texas Press, 1994.

Beltrán-del Olmo, Magdalena, and Frank Sotomayor, eds. *Frank del Olmo: His Commentaries on Columns from the* Los Angeles Times. Los Angeles: Los Angeles Times Books, 2004.

Benavidez, Roy, and Oscar Griffin. *The Three Wars of Roy Benavidez*. San Antonio: Corona Publishing Company, 1986.

Boskin, Joseph. *Urban Racial Violence in the Twentieth Century*. Beverly Hills: Glencoe Press, 1969.

Burt, Kenneth C. *The Search for a Civic Voice: California Latino Politics*. Claremont: Regina Books, 2007.

Chomsky, Aviva. *They Take Our Jobs*. Boston: Beacon Press, 2007.

de Tocqueville, Alexis. *Democracy in America*. New York: Alfred A. Knopf, 1947.

Díaz, David R. *Barrio Urbanism: Chicanos, Planning, and American Cities*. New York: Routlege Publisher, 2005.

Dole, Robert. *One Soldier's Story*. New York: Harper Collins Publisher, 2006.

Dupuy, Trevor N., et al. *Hitler Last Gamble: Battle of the Bulge, December 1944 – January 1945*. New York: Harper Collins Publisher, 1994.

Green, Philip, and Sanford Levinson, eds. *Power and Community Dissenting Essays in Political Science*. New York: Vintage, 1970.

Hacker, Andrew. *Political Theory: Philosophy, Ideology, Science*. New York: The Macmillan Company, 1961

Hernández, José Amaro. *Mutual Aid for Survival: The Case of the Mexican American*. Malabar: Robert E. Krieger Publishing Company, 1983.

Hunter, Floyed. *Community Power Structure*. Chapel Hill: University of North Carolina Press, 1953.

Johnson, Lyndon B. *My Hope for America*. New York: Random House, 1964.

Kaplan, Marshal, and Peggy L. Cuciti. *The Great Society and Its Legacy: Twenty Years of U.S. Social Policy*. Chapel Hill: University of North Carolina Press, 1986.

Márquez, Benjamín. *The Evolution of a Mexican American Political Organization LULAC*. Austin: University of Texas Press, 1993.

McWilliams, Carey. *North from Mexico: The Spanish-Speaking of the United States*. New York: Greenwood Press, 1968.

Meneheen, Beverly. *Richard Valens: The First Latino Rocker*. Tempe: Bilingual Press, 1987.

Meyer, Michael C., and William L. Sherman. *The Course of Mexican History*. New York: Oxford University Press, 1995.

Morín, Raúl. *Among the Valiant: Mexican Americans in World War II and Korea*. Los Angeles: Valiant Press, 2002.

Price, Glen W. *Origin of the War with Mexico*. Austin: University of Texas Press, 1967.

Romo, David Dorado. *Ringside Seat to a Revolution: An Underground Cultural History of El Paso and Juarez, 1893-1923*. El Paso: Cinco Puntos Press, 2005.

Talbitzer, Bill. *The Laborers in the West: A History of the Laborers Union of North America*, 2nd ed. Sacramento Region, Liuna: AFL-CIO Publishers, 1994.

Tienda, Martha, and Faith Mitchell, eds. *Hispanics and the Future of America*. Washington, DC: National Academies Press, 1990.

Zander, Alvin. *Effective Social Action by Community Groups*. San Francisco: Jossey-Bass Publications, 1990.

Articles in Professional Journals

Babchuk, Nicholas. "The Role of the Researcher as Participant Observer and Participants-Observer in the Field Situation." *Human Organization*, XXI (1962), 225.

Burgess, Ernest. "The Growth of the American City: An Introduction to a Research Project." *American Sociological Society*, 18 (1924), 88-97.

Cartwright, Dorwin. "Achieving Change in People." *Human Relations*, 4 (1951), 381-394.

Form, Williams H., and Joaan Rytina. "Ideological Beliefs in the Distribution of Power in the United States." *American Sociological Review*, XXXIV (February 1969), 19-31.

Harris, Chauncey D., and Edward L. Ullman. "The Nature of Cities." *The Annals of the American Academy of Political and Social Sciences*, 242 (1945), 7-17.

Vidich, Arthur J. "Participant Observation and the Collection and Interpretation of Data." *American Journal of Sociology*, LX (1955), 354-360.

Williams, Oliver P., and Charles R. Adrian. "The Isolation of Local Politics under the Nonpartisan Ballot." *American Political Science Review*, 53 (December 1959), 1052-2062.

Other Journals

Fox, Jacqueline. "Balance Act." *San Fernando Valley Business Journal* (December 8, 2003).

Kramer, Pat. "Original Mission City Strive to Spruce Up its Image." *San Fernando Valley Business Journal* (May 18, 1998).

Loiederman, Roberto. "Anti-Semitism Charge Colors Liquor License Fight in City of San Fernando." *Jewish Journal of Greater Los Angeles* (April 18, 2008).

Periodicals

Extensive use was made of news by the *Daily News* of Los Angeles, *Glendale News-Press, La Opinion, L A Weekly Newspaper, Los Angeles Times, Newsweek, San Diego Union-Tribune, San Antonio Light, San Fernando Valley SUN, Valley News and Green Sheet, Sundial* of California State University, Northridge, and *Washington Post.*

Statutes, Reports, and Publications of Government Agencies

California General Law Cities, Chart: General Law Cities v. Charter Cities Code Sections 36501 and 53725.

Black and Gold Year Book published by the Associate Students and San Fernando High School, San Fernando, California, 1950.

California General Law Cities Code 54950-54962.

Cato Institute Study on Immigration, *Newsweek*, August 23, 2009.

City of San Fernando City Clerk Archives.

City of San Fernando Maclay, Truman, and San Fernando Road Corridor Specific Plan.

City of San Fernando Ordinances No. 1428 and No. 1543.

General Telephone and Electric of California (GTE). Report: How Community Leaders View Priority Community Needs, Spring of 1990.

Johnson, Hans P. "Illegal Immigration: At Issue." San Francisco: Public Policy Institute of California, April 2006.

Northeast Valley Health Corporation Final Conference Report on Objectives and Conclusions, March 4, 1991

San Fernando Museum of Art and History.

Surgeon General's Workshop on Drunk Driving, Background Papers. U. S Department of Health and Human Services. Washington, DC, December 14-16, 1988.

Title VII, U.S. Civil Right Act of 1994.

University of California, Riverside. "2012 Research Impact, Real World Solutions," 2012.

U.S. Department of Commerce, Bureau of the Census. U.S. Census of Population, General Population Characteristics Data.

Court Decisions

Cano, et al. v. Davis, Case No CV 01-08477 MMM-RCX., 2010.

Jose Aranda,, et al. v. J. B. Van Sickle, et al., 1994.

San Fernando Station, LLC. v. City of San Fernando, et al., Los Angeles Superior Court Case No. BS097994.

Other Sources

Ambrose, Stephen. "Band of Brothers." HBO.

Guy History Website, World War II, "The Invasion of Normandy," 1994.

Lemon, Thomas F. "American Experience: The Battle of the Bulge." PPBS Documentary.

"Saving Private Ryan," a 1998 film directed by Steven Spielberg and staring Tom Hanks.

VHS videocassettes. Episode 1: Quest for a Homeland, Episode 2: The Struggle in the Fields, Episode 3: Taking Back the Schools, and Episode 4: Fighting for Political Power, produced by the National Latino Communication Center and Galan Productions, Inc. in association with KCET-Los Angeles, 1966.

ABOUT THE AUTHOR

Professor José Amaro Hernández was born September 11, 1930, in Eagle Pass, Texas, a town bordering Mexico. His youth was formed by the Depression and by racism, which he experienced while growing up in Texas. On occasions, he dropped out of high school, but finally graduated from high school and enlisted in the U.S. Air Force in 1950 during the Korean War for a four-year term. He held the rank of Tech Sergeant, earning several unit wartime decorations with three battle stars.

He is married to Carol O'Brien from Cincinnati, Ohio, where he once taught high school and also taught at Miami University of Oxford, Ohio. They have two daughters, Moira, a physician and Annie, a veterinarian, and three grandchildren.

Professor Hernández received a bachelor of arts degree in economics from St. Mary's University, San Antonio, Texas, a Catholic institution which mixed faith with the promotion of social justice; a master of arts degree in economics from the Ohio State University; and a Ph.D. in political science from the University of California, Riverside. He is a founding member and professor of Chicano Studies, California State University, Northridge, considered the largest and finest such department in the nation. Professor Hernández published several articles on citizen participation; however, his major publication, *Mutual Aid for Survival: The Case of the Mexican American* was published by Krieger Publishers in 1983. The book attaches great importance to the value of associational life. He retired in 1995 from California State University, Northridge, but continued to teach part time as Professor Emeritus in the department to keep in touch with students. Before retirement, he served as coordinator of the urban studies and planning program at California State University, Northridge. Additionally, he served as city planning commissioner for two years, and councilman and mayor of San Fernando for 16 years. He is grateful to his late Mother and Dad, wonderful parents, who taught him at an early age to be of service to others. Their concern for others has always stayed with him.

INDEX

A

Acevedo, James, 137

Acuña, Dan
 on alcohol issues, 106, 108
 city council discord (1990s), 119
 city council election of, 72
 City Recreation and Community Service
  Department controversy
  (1990), 75–76, 81–85
 as mayor, 88

Acuña, Rodolfo F. "Rudy"
 Anything But Mexican, xvi, 54
 César E. Chávez Social Justice Award
  recipient, 95
 community activism by, 41, 42
 founding of Chicano Studies
  Department at California
  State University, Northridge,
  35–37

Adrian, Charles R., 58

affirmative action issues
 City Recreation and Community Service
  Department controversy
  (1990), 77
 equal opportunity in workplace and,
  111–115
 Proposition 209, 122–123

agenda procedures, 102–103

agriculture
 "a la pisca," 6
 "Braceros," 4
 grape boycott, 34, 35, 41
 immigrant farm labor and Mexican
  American citizen
  participation, 5–7
 "smudgers," 5

Alarcón, Richard, 70

Alatorre, Richard, 70

Alatorre, Soledad, 95

Alba, Anthony, 151–152

alcohol issues, in San Fernando, 103–110,
  168–171

Pueblo Construction Company, 130–131,
        137–138, 148
Pueblo & Salud, Inc., xviii, 82, 93, 103,
        107–109
Pulido, José, 149, 156, 157, 158, 161, 171,
        175, 176–177, 181
"push-pull" factors, of immigration, 2

Q
Quevedo, Mike, 180
Quimby Act Fund, 92

R
Ramirez, Guadalupe, 46–47
Ramirez, José, 54–55, 95
Ramirez, Norma, 95
Ramos, Richard, 131–132, 136, 139, 142,
        143, 147, 156
Rascón, Sergio, 125
La Raza Unida Party
        Arriola and, 57
        City Recreation and Community Service
                Department controversy
                (1990), 81–82
        emergence of, 53–54
        inception of, xviii
        José Aranda, et al. v. Van Sicle, et al., 61
        Los Angeles Police and 1976 election,
                54–55
redistricting, politics of, 150
"redlined districts," 23–24
Reseda High School, 41
Reyes, Sarah, 150
Reza, Alex, 95
Richards, Watson, Drefuss and Gershon, 77,
        124–125
Richardson, Roy, 66, 72, 75, 77
Richman, Monroe, 46
Rivetti, Dominick, 152
Robledo, Silverio, 124–127, 130, 136, 138–
        139, 142–143, 147
Rodríguez, Ruben, 68, 82–85, 94, 105, 165

Roosevelt High School, 35
Rose, Carol, 95
Rose, Ed, 95
Rosenberg, Irwin, 105
Ruelas, Anthony "Tony," 183
Ruelas, Julian, 185, 195
Ruelas, Julie, 95, 156, 159, 166, 168–172,
        176–179, 181, 184–185, 193
Ruiz, Everto, 95
Ruiz, Raul, 38, 39
Ruiz, Ron, 96
Rush, Father Thomas, 70
Rutan and Tucker, 76–78

S
St. Ferdinand Church, xvii
Salazar, Ruben, 38–39
Sanchez, Corrine, 68
Sandoval, Rafael, 41
San Fernando (case study)
        alcohol issues, 103–110, 168–171
        city council challenges (late 1990s, early
                2000s), 147–164
        city council challenges (mid 2000s),
                165–188
        city council controversy (2012), 194–196
        city council development conflicts
                (1999), 135–145
        city council discord (1990s), 119–134
        City Recreation and Community Service
                Department controversy
                (1990), 75–86
        community activism, in 1960s and
                1970s, 33–49
        conclusions, 189–194
        early Mexican American citizen
                participation, 1–19
        economy and job opportunities, post-
                World War II, 21–32
        employment and affirmative action
                issues, 111–115
        future of city, 196–197